NARRATING HISTORY,
DEVELOPING DOCTRINE

American Academy of Religion Academy Series

edited by
Susan Thistlethwaite

Number 82
NARRATING HISTORY,
DEVELOPING DOCTRINE

by
Bradford E. Hinze

Bradford E. Hinze

NARRATING HISTORY, DEVELOPING DOCTRINE

FRIEDRICH SCHLEIERMACHER AND JOHANN SEBASTIAN DREY

Scholars Press
Atlanta, Georgia

NARRATING HISTORY, DEVELOPING DOCTRINE

by
Bradford E. Hinze

Library of Congress Cataloging in Publication Data
Hinze, Bradford E., 1954–
Narrating history, developing doctrine: Friedrich Schleiermacher and Johann Sebastian Drey/ Bradford E. Hinze.
p. cm. — (American Academy of Religion academy series; no. 82)
Includes bibliographical references and indexes.
ISBN 1–55540–874–5 (cloth: alk. paper)
ISBN 1–55540–875–3 (pbk.: alk. paper)
1. History (Theology)—History of doctrines—19th century.
2. Dogma, Development of—History of doctrines—19th century.
3. Schleiermacher, Friedrich, 1768–1834—Contributions in theology of history. 4. Schleiermacher, Friedrich, 1768–1834—Contributions in concept of development of doctrine. 5. Drey, Johann Sebastian von, 1777–1853—Contributions in theology of history. 6. Drey, Johann Sebastian von, 1777–1853—Contributions in concept of development of doctrine. I. Title. II. Series.
BR115.H5H526 1993
230'.092'2—dc20 93–1417
CIP

Printed in the United States of America
on acid-free paper

TABLE OF CONTENTS

ACKNOWLEDGEMENTS

Many people helped me at various stages of this project. I want to acknowledge them with deep gratitude. I have learned a great deal from my dissertation director, Brian Gerrish, both from his suggestions on this project, and from his own written work, which provides a model of historical theology in service to contemporary theology. I am indebted to Bernard McGinn, Paul Ricoeur, and David Tracy for inspiring my interest in biblical and theological narratives and their hermeneutical implications. Anne Carr, Wayne Fehr, John Thiel, K. Joachim Larché, Katherine Thome, and Anthony Chvala-Smith offered helpful suggestions and generous assistance. I am grateful to Dr. Abraham Kustermann for the opportunity, before making my final revisions, to participate in a Symposium on the theology of Johann Sebastian Drey held in March of 1992 at the Academy of the Diocese of Rottenburg-Stuttgart. Thanks to my colleagues in the Department of Theology at Marquette University for their support during the preparation of this manuscript. Finally, I want to thank Christine for her support and editorial suggestions, and Paul and Karl for enlarging my vision of life and education. I dedicate this work to the memory of my father, Alvin Richard Hinze, who died in 1983, and to my mother Virginia Waitekunas Hinze.

INTRODUCTION

Friedrich Schleiermacher (1768-1834) and Johann Sebastian Drey (1777-1853) are central figures on the threshold of a new era in theology, one the so-called father of modern Protestant theology, and the other the founder of the Catholic faculty at The University of Tübingen and the harbinger of significant changes in Catholic thought. Placed side by side, it becomes evident that, even though they come from different backgrounds and theological traditions, Drey and Schleiermacher share a similar worldview and are in conscious dialogue with the same intellectual currents. The issues they grapple with are not simply set by the confessional polemics of the Reformation and post-Reformation periods; rather, it is modernity which has made a claim on their common attention. Catholic and Protestant theologies converge during this period in new ways as theologians attempt to offer an apologetics for the Christian faith in response to prevailing critical currents of thought. Theirs is a common world of thought and concern.

A concern for apologetics is not all that Drey and Schleiermacher share. Equally fundamental is their kindred understanding of history. They have compatible philosophies of history, that is, congenial in how they understand the nature of historical movement and reach judgements about historical change. More importantly and without denying their genuine differences, they concur in significant specific ways about the theological meaning of history and its dynamic movement.

Schleiermacher's and Drey's understandings of history, in fact, influence everything about their theology. In particular, their construals of history inspire and govern their pioneering theories of doctrinal development and their articulation of the theologian's tasks in this process of development. Besides generating ways to understand doctrinal development, their configurations of history justify or legitimate certain understandings of doctrinal continuity, criticism, and change in the face of both intransigent and hypercritical persons, positions, and intellectual traditions.

The specific thesis of this investigation is that Schleiermacher and Drey share a configuration of history, which, despite instructive differences, generates a historical understanding of revelation and provides both thinkers with a theological justification for the criticism, reform, and development of doctrines.

All theories of doctrinal development, it can be argued, whether the older logical theories, the variety of organic theories, or newer models based on scientific paradigm shifts or dependent on recent theories of interpretation, operate with implicit or explicit theologies of history that have a significant impact on how development is perceived. This has seldom been treated in discussions of doctrinal change,[1] which tend to focus on criteriological issues regarding the sources, procedures, and explanations for genuine doctrinal development.[2]

---

[1]See, e.g., Martin Werner, *The Formation of Christian Dogma: An Historical Study of Its Problem*, trans. S.G.F. Brandon (London: Adams & Charles Black, 1957); B. A. Gerrish, "Schleiermacher and the Reformation: A Question of Doctrinal Development," *The Old Protestantism and the New* (Chicago: The University of Chicago Press, 1982); Nicholas Lash, *Change in Focus: A Study of Doctrinal Change and Discontinuity* (London: Sheed and Ward, 1973); John O'Malley, "Reform, Historical Consciousness and Vatican II's Aggiornamento," *Theological Studies* 32 (1971): 573-601; idem., "Developments, Reforms, and Two Great Reformations: Toward a Historical Assessment of Vatican II," *Theological Studies* 44 (1983): 373-406. Edward Farley criticizes the axiomatic role of salvation history models in traditional views of doctrinal authority, *Ecclesial Reflection: An Anatomy of Theological Method* (Philadelphia: Fortress Press, 1982).

[2]One only has to look at several of the major studies of theories of doctrinal development to see that this is a neglected area of research: Owen Chadwick, *From Bossuet to Newman: The Idea of Doctrinal Development* (Cambridge: University Press, 1957); Jaroslav Pelikan, *Development of*

Theologies of history, of course, influence much more than how doctrinal change is understood. It has more often been emphasized that one's vision of history and construal of the relationship between the spiritual and the temporal determine how one interprets the moral and social responsibilities of the Christian and the Church in the world. Schleiermacher's and Drey's works have been examined from this perspective.[3] Schleiermacher himself writes of the close interrelationship between a philosophy of history and ethics.[4] In addition, it has often been shown that substantive issues in systematic theology are affected by how history is understood, including how the relationships between nature and history, creation and redemption, redemption and liberation, Church and world are conceived. These ethical and substantive dogmatic issues are germane to this study insofar as they shed light on Schleiermacher's and Drey's theological construals of history and on their understandings of revelation and doctrinal development.

When the relation between a theologian's understanding of revelation and doctrinal change and his or her views of history has been explored, it has been common to speak about the shift from

---

Christian Doctrine: Some Historical Prolegomena (New Haven: Yale University Press, 1969), and *Historical Theology: Continuity and Change in Christian Doctrine* (London: Hutchinson & Co., Ltd., 1970); Jan Hendrik Walgrave, *Unfolding Revelation: The Nature of Doctrinal Development* (Philadelphia: The Westminster Press, 1972).

[3]Thus an adequate treatment of Schleiermacher's Christian ethics will include a discussion of his theology of history; see Hans-Joachim Birkner, *Schleiermachers christliche Sittenlehre* (Berlin: Verlag Alfred Töpelmann, 1964), 38-39; on Drey, see Josef Rief, *Reich Gottes und Gesellschaft nach Johann Sebastian Drey und Johann Baptist Hirscher* (Paderborn: Ferdinand Schöningh, 1965); on the general question, see James M. Gustafson, "The Relevance of Historical Understanding," in *Theology and Christian Ethics* (Philadelphia: United Church Press, 1977).

[4]In *Die christliche Sitte* Schleiermacher states: "Philosophical ethics has to do precisely with the philosophy of history, as it is clear that a system of life rules for the individual cannot be constructed from the pure idea of reason without requiring that a common life without contradiction develops from that" (28-29).

a pre-modern to a modern approach to history as a transition from a classicist vision of reality to "historical consciousness." But this construal can gloss over the variety of ways historical development is configured and its meaning assessed. Recent research has shed important new light on the role of the imagination, metaphors, and narrative structures in historiography and in philosophies of history. The formation of a historical plot--setting forth the interaction of events, persons, communities, institutions, and their meaning--is not simply the task of ordering matters sequentially; rather it is an imaginative act of construction.[5] It has even been suggested that historians and philosophers of history employ diverse plots similar to the tragic, epic, comic, and ironic plots of classic drama.[6] Wittingly or not, historians are not merely presenting history "*wie es eigentliche gewesen ist*," but are constructing plots which interpret historical experience.

This research into the role of the imagination, metaphors, and plots in the writing of history and in philosophies of history has immense relevance for interpreting the diverse ways the narrative character of Christianity is presented in the Scriptures as well as in diverse theologies of history. On the basis of this new research, it is no longer sufficient to examine Schleiermacher's and Drey's interpretations of history as representatives of "the emergence of historical consciousness" in terms of formal and abstract philosophical principles about the nature of progress and decline or about the epistemological foundations for making historical judgments. Rather, one must examine the concrete imaginative

---

[5]Paul Ricoeur speaks of this as the imaginative act of "emplotment," (French: *intrigue*), which is his rendering of Aristotle's word *muthos*. See *Time and Narrative*, Vol. 1., trans. K. McLaughlin and D. Pellauer (Chicago: The University of Chicago Press, 1984), 31 and 237, n. 4.

[6]Haydn White, *Metahistory: The Historical Imagination in Nineteenth Century Europe* (Baltimore: Johns Hopkins University, 1973) and *Tropics of Discourse: Essays in Cultural Criticism* (Baltimore: Johns Hopkins University, 1978).

ways they plot history and thereby attribute meaning to historical experience.

Accordingly, the central task of this study is to investigate the primary theological texts of Schleiermacher and Drey in order to determine how they plot history and to show the significance of these historical configurations for their respective understandings of doctrinal continuity and change.[7] The first chapter will examine how Schleiermacher and Drey utilize key ideas--the kingdom of God, organic life, and the process of education--to construct the plot for their theologies of history.[8] Each of these ideas function in their theologies as metaphors, models, and narrative patterns.[9] They function as root metaphors insofar as they serve as linguistic figures that describe and express reality and thereby supply a structure and orientation in their written works. As metaphors they also at times yield semantic innovations, resulting in new insights and knowledge. These metaphors are so fundamental in their work that they function as models insofar as they offer a sustained and systematic framework for understanding certain terms and relations.

---

[7]This study offers a comprehensive analysis and comparison of Schleiermacher's and Drey's configuration of history and its significance for their theologies. Although mention will be made of (1) a few key influences on their theologies, (2) the intellectual milieu in which their works emerged, and (3) several alterations in their theological judgments, this study is not intended as a systematic analysis of the genesis and changes in their respective positions.

[8]As we will see, these different metaphors are imbued with theological significance for them, but they also simultaneously have an impact on how they understand certain epistemological issues related to matters concerning doctrinal development. I will speak of their visions of history as theologies of history rather than philosophies of history, because of the decisive character of their theological claims about history.

[9]On metaphors and models, see Paul Ricoeur, *The Rule of Metaphor: An Interdisciplinary Study* (Toronto: University of Toronto Press, 1977); Sallie McFague, *Metaphorical Theology* (Philadelphia: Fortress Press, 1982); Mary Gerhardt and Allan Russel, *Metaphorical Process: The Creation of Scientific and Religious Understanding* (Fort Worth: Texas Christian University Press, 1984).

These metaphors and models of the kingdom of God, life, and pedagogy provide the semantic context for Schleiermacher's and Drey's reflections on the historical identity of Christianity and the means for interpreting it. However, these ideas work not only as metaphors and models in their theologies, disclosing a diversity of meanings that are often interrelated; they also generate narrative patterns for configuring and interpreting historical identity and change in Christianity. Each of these ideas provides a narrative structure in their respective theologies which deserve scrutiny individually and together.[10]

I wish to suggest that the use of the language of the kingdom of God by these thinkers warrants calling their vision of history "sacramental." While neither Schleiermacher nor Drey use the term in this way, its use is not meant as a ploy to smuggle in some external agenda, nor does the interpretation offered here depend on its inclusion. I do believe the term's fundamental meaning as a concrete medium of God's grace and salvation warrants its usage. The term sacramental has incarnational and ecclesial overtones that are both profoundly classical and romantic.

A sacramental vision of history is one of three dominant narrative plots, one of three types of theologies of history that can be discerned in the history of theology. Besides a sacramental theology of history, there is an apocalyptic model and a model of manifest destiny. These three theologies of history can be found throughout the history of Christianity. Only in our own day are they being more clearly distinguished in literary form and theological substance, as well as in terms of their diverse theological, social, and political effects.

---

[10]This study investigates the narrative strategies found in Schleiermacher's and Drey's theologies without evaluating them in terms of recent research on biblical narrative and the uses of narrative in the history of theology. See Hans Frei, *The Eclipse of Biblical Narrative* (New Haven: Yale University Press, 1974); Terrence W. Tilley, *Story Theology*, Theology and Life Series, vol. 12 (Wilmington, Delaware: Michael Glazier, 1985); *Why Narrative? Readings in Narrative Theology*, eds. S. Hauerwas and L. G. Jones (Grand Rapids: Wm B. Eerdmans Publishing Co., 1989).

Schleiermacher and Drey offer us a theology of history which bears resemblances to a loosely-defined tradition which includes the author of Luke-Acts, Augustine, Thomas Aquinas, and John Calvin. This dominant tradition of interpreting history can be called sacramental because it emphasizes the mediating role of the Church in history. This emphasis on ecclesial mediation builds on certain fundamental convictions about the role of physical, linguistic, personal, and ecclesial mediation in the experience of God and the life of faith. In this tradition there is no immediate experience of God that issues forth in an indubitable knowledge of God.[11] Rather God's presence is sacramentally mediated through creation and through the historical experience of the community of Israel. Christ is for those who believe the definitive sacrament of God, the indispensable medium of salvation. Yet with the death of Christ, direct access to the physical medium of Jesus Christ for this saving relationship with God come to an end. After the death and resurrection, the Spirit-filled Church becomes the primary sacrament of Christ in history, the body of Christ, the earthly extension of the risen Lord.[12] This sacramental understanding of history emphasizes the definitive revelation in Jesus Christ. At the same time, it stresses the centrality of the *ecclesial* mediation of Christ's redemption. In its classic form, found in Luke-Acts and Augustine, this vision of history understands time from Christ to the end of the world as the time of the Church. This time is understood as homogeneous, because while history can appear

---

[11]Franz Schupp correctly argues that the romantic affirmation of historical mediation challenges a dominant criticism of figures like Drey (and Schleiermacher I would add) for emphasizing the immediacy of experience. "Die Geschichtsauffassung am Beginn der Tübinger Schule und in der Gegenwärtigen Theologie." *Zeitschrift für katholische Theologie* 91 (1969): 150-155. Recent figures like Bernard Lonergan speak of "mediated immediacy"; *Method in Theology* (New York: Harper, 1972), 77, 273, 340.

[12]It has been argued that certain figures within this tradition exhibit a salvation history model, but what this means and whether this is valid has been a contested issue. See Bradford E. Hinze, "The End of Salvation History," *Horizons* 18 (1991):227-45.

better or worse for individuals and groups, mundane historical experiences have no significant effect on the economy of salvation and the Church's mediation of salvation.

Schleiermacher and Drey share with that tradition, on the one hand, a rejection of an apocalyptic theology of history.[13] The apocalyptic tradition has its historical roots in the Jewish inter-testamental period, where the genre of the apocalypse may be discerned in Enoch literature, the Sibylline Oracles, the books of Daniel, Ezra, and Baruch.[14] These texts have an impact on the earliest strata of the New Testament traditions. Certain metaphors, symbols, and narrative constructions of the apocalypse genre are passed on through forms of apocalyptic eschatology. This model of history is transmitted in the history of Christianity through diverse apocalyptic and millenarian figures and movements. What distinguishes this model is its triadic plot of crisis, judgement, and vindication. At times it manifests a deterministic and dualistic view of history and includes an expectation of an imminent end.

On the other hand, Drey and Schleiermacher share with the sacramental tradition a critique of the manifest-destiny or evident-providence view of history associated initially with Eusebius and his heirs. This third model finds God's control over history evident in the uniting of the providential destinies of the Christian religion and the Roman empire.[15] While this view has sometimes been

---

[13]For the origins and history of apocalypticism, see John J. Collins, *The Apocalyptic Imagination: An Introduction to the Jewish Christian Matrix of Christianity* (New York: Crossroad, 1984); Klaus Koch, *The Rediscovery of Apocalyptic*, trans. M. Kohl (London: SCM Press LTD, 1972); Bernard McGinn, "Early Apocalypticism: The Ongoing Debate," in J. Wittreich and C.A. Patrides, *The Apocalypse in Enlgish Renaissance Thought and Literature* (Manchester, England: Manchester University Press, 1984), 2-39 and Bernard McGinn, *The Calabrian Abbot: Joachim of Fiore in the History of Western Thought* (New York: Macmillan Publishing Company, 1985).

[14]See John Collins, "Introduction: Towards the Morphology of a Genre," *Apocalpyse: The Morphology of a Genre. Semeia* 14 (1979): 9.

[15]See McGinn, *The Calabrian Abbot*, 51-73, and Glenn F. Chesnut, *The First Christian Historians* (Paris: Editions Beauchesne, 1977).

confused with the sacramental model, since both traditions have worked together during periods of the Christian Church, Augustine's rejection of the Eusebian vision of history stands as a definitive articulation of their distinctiveness. The reception of the work of these two figures generated separate yet interrelated traditions.

Certainly the apocalyptic and the manifest-destiny models speak of the mediation of God in history through the Church. However, their understandings of ecclesial mediation of God's salvation in history differ from that of the sacramental model. In the apocalyptic model there is an immediate manifestation of God or of God's plan through the apocalyptic vision, while in the manifest-destiny model God's plan is immediately clear in the close alliance of Church and empire. The apocalyptic viewpoint calls into question the purity and possibility of ecclesial mediation, whereas the manifest-destiny model can support a triumphalistic understanding of the Church's role of mediation in union with the empire or state, a union that has been practically realized. The sacramental model of history acknowledges the necessary mediation of the Church, but also recognizes the Church's ambiguous character, due to finitude, sin, and the veiled presence of God in the Church.

Two critical points distinguish Drey and Schleiermacher from earlier proponents of a sacramental theology of history: they do not operate with a homogeneous view of time since Christ, nor with an understanding of truth as unchanging. For Schleiermacher and Drey the sacramental view of history is wedded to a distinctive organic view of temporality, and consequently, a historicized understanding of truth. Organic models of history employ root metaphors taken from organic processes in order to understand historical experience.

Previous research on linear and cyclical views of history helps clarify the significance of an organic interpretation of history. Scholars have in the past clearly distinguished a Hebraic linear conception of history from Greek and Oriental cyclical views. This simple contrast has been rightly criticized for not adequately presenting the manifold and rich time consciousness disclosed within the literatures of these diverse cultures.[16] Nevertheless, we find that in Christian theology, primarily through the sacramental tradition of Augustine, a linear view of history has been developed. The classic form of a sacramental linear view of history focussed on the definitive revelation of Christ in history and the mediation of the Church until the end of time. Within history there is no clear sign of progress (associated with the manifest destiny model) or decline (recognized by the apocalyptic vision). There may be a better or a worse within this linear view of history, but such differences have no significance for the ultimate design of history, which is concerned with the movement from the finite to the infinite, from the temporal to the eternal, that is, with a vertical movement. Within time we are to transcend time to reach eternity through the sacrament of the Church. The significance of personal, social, and political crises rests primarily in drawing us into the cosmic Christian drama, by drawing us out of this history into eternity. History from Christ to the end of the world is essentially homogeneous.

Schleiermacher's and Drey's organic view of history and development seriously challenges this classicist vision. Their understanding of the kingdom of God in terms of an organic dialectic allows them to affirm the centrality of the Church in history, while rejecting the homogeneous character of time from Christ to the end. World history is not merely the occasion for the encounter with God through the Church. The Church is intimately connected with the world. For Drey and Schleiermacher, earthly progression and decline are connected with the narrative of the kingdom, not divided as this-worldly and other-worldly.

It is important to recognize that organic views differ, sometimes sharply. Some emphasize the continuity of growth from the seed or the origins of life, while others recognize elements of disease or

---

[16]E.g., Paul Ricoeur, "The History of Religions and the Phenomenology of Time Consciousness," *The History of Religions: Retrospect and Prospect*, ed. J. Kitagawa (New York: Macmillan Publishing Company, 1985).

decay as a threat to organic vitality and survival.[17] Organic visions have been viewed on the one hand as the source of an evolutionary and progressive view of history.[18] On the other hand, organic views of history and society have also served to justify retrospective and conservative worldviews.[19] As we will discover, Schleiermacher's and Drey's views differ one from the other, and both diverge from John Cardinal Newman's well-known organic conception of history.[20]

For Schleiermacher and Drey, God's plan in history is not simply a matter of the organic unfolding of religions in the world and the progressive education of the human race as continuous growth, promise, and task. The continuity of this living faith is always threatened by the possibilities of a diseased ecclesial organism, senile theological traditions, the heterodox forms of piety

---

[17]It is important, following Troeltsch, to distinguish between the concept of development of the organological school and that of the dialectical school, (that is, the Hegelian school) even though in reality they are often fused. See Ernst Troeltsch, *Der Historismus und seine Probleme*, *Gesammelte Schriften*, Vol. 3 (Tübingen: J.C.B. Mohr [Paul Siebeck], 1961).

[18]See the criticisms offered by Jürgen Moltmann, *A Theology of Hope* (New York: Harper & Row, 1976), 69-76, and Johann Baptist Metz, *Faith in History and Society* (New York: Seabury Press, 1980), 3-13.

[19]See Paul Gottfried, *Conservative Millenialism* (New York: Fordham University Press, 1979); Alvin W. Gouldner, "Romanticism and Classicism: Deep Structures in Social Science," *For Sociology: Renewal and Critique in Sociology Today* (New York: Basic Books, 1973), 323-366.

[20]A comparative analysis of the positions of Newman, Drey, and Schleiermacher cannot be attempted here. Nevertheless, Newman's organic model as it is articulated in the *Essay on the Development of Doctrine* appears different from that of Drey and Schleiermacher in several important respects: Newman's model seems more closely linked with a classical (patristic, neoplatonic) understanding of history and doctrines than that of either German theologian; Newman's *Essay* was devoted to a retrospective defense rather than a retrospective and prospective examination of doctrinal change; and furthermore, Newman in this work is not interested in issues of theological revisions and ecclesial reform.

and Christian living.[21] While affirming belief in hidden providence and in the unity of human freedom and providential necessity, they recognize the impact of disorder in history, as well as radical shifts and revolutions in cultures, traditions, and languages.[22]

After presenting Schleiermacher's and Drey's theologies of history in Chapter I, we will explore in three chapters how their views of history influence their understandings of doctrinal development. Chapter II addresses the pivotal distinction these authors employ between inner and outer influences on the organic life of historical communities. In their analyses, this inner and outer structure of the historical process of communities is found evident in the Christian narrative and serves as the axis of development. We close this chapter by examining Schleiermacher's and Drey's articulations of the nature of orthodoxy, heresy, and hyperorthodoxy in relation to this inner and outer schema.

---

[21]This facet of their work does little to offset criticisms leveled against a sacramental model of history--with its belief in providence and its division of history into inner and outer history--by theologians influenced by Marx. Political theologians have targeted nineteenth century theologians influenced by German idealism and romanticism as the most recent embodiment and culmination of the sacramental worldview. They are accused of assimilating a liberal, bourgeois view of progress, avoiding the problems attested to by suffering, crises, and tragedy in history, and ignoring the influence of the material conditions on the movement of history. It is said that these liberal thinkers too quickly dissolve the discontinuities and non-identities in history into identity, too quickly find progress in the whole at the expense of the part. The tensions between the infinite and the finite, spirit and nature, freedom and necessity are too easily united through piety, through the imagination, through intuition. We shall find, however, that Schleiermacher and Drey are attuned to negative experiences and the dialectical character of history, even though they have their limitations when compared with the apocalyptic or materialist categories of recent political and liberationist theologies.

[22]Francis Schüssler Fiorenza and Nicholas Lash argue that 19th century thinkers are unable to deal adequately with the problems of historical discontinuity and historicism. See Fiorenza, *Papers of the Nineteenth Century Theology Working Group* (Berkeley, 1985), Part II, p. 10; idem., *Foundational Theology* (New York: Crossroad Publishing Co., 1984), 155-192; and Lash, *Change in Focus*, viii-viv.

Chapter III examines the contributions of theology and theologians to the process of dogmatic criticism and development. For Schleiermacher and Drey, theology is neither catechesis nor preaching. Theirs is not simply a narrative theology--a redescription of the primary language of the Bible, liturgy, and creeds--even though the Christian narrative does provide a web of beliefs that permeates their theologies. Instead, theologians contribute to doctrinal reform and development by fulfilling their interpretative, critical, and systematic tasks, but most importantly by being organic leaders within the Christian community. The theological enterprise must be faithful to the Christian narrative, critical of aberrations in Christian thought and practice, and creative in exploring the Christian experience of ecclesial faith.

Although Schleiermacher and Drey are not content with repeating the Christian narrative, this does not mean that they seek to find secure foundations for faith through some type of proof. John Cardinal Newman offered in his *Essay on Development* numerous notes for development. Neither Schleiermacher nor Drey isolated such specific criteria for doctrinal development. Yet we do find mentioned throughout their work criteria for judging valid doctrine. Chapter IV examines these specific criteria and seeks to argue that their theologies of history provide the background beliefs which justify and legitimate the diverse criteria they employ.

The final chapter asks: Which doctrines did Schleiermacher and Drey believe were in need of criticism, reform, and development? This chapter cannot be exhaustive, but it will touch upon important points where Schleiermacher and Drey creatively contributed to doctrinal development, while seeking to be faithful to the essence of Christianity.

Drey's and Schleiermacher's contributions to our understanding of history and doctrine are worthy of further historical and theological investigation, not only because they ushered in a new epoch in Catholic and Protestant theology, but also because they stand as lively theological resources for contemporary theology. By examining their theologies, we confront head-on a theological paradigm whose history of effects still continues, and by examining the reception of their theologies, we confront our own age, both what it shares with that earlier period and what we believe to be distinctive about our own.

A word about previous research is in order. While Schleiermacher's work shows no evidence that he knew Drey's writings, it has long been recognized that Drey had read and was influenced by Schleiermacher's *Über die Religion: Reden an die Gebildeten unter ihren Verächtern* (1799, 3rd edition, 1821), *Kurze Darstellung des theologischen Studiums* (1811, 2nd edition 1830) and *Der christliche Glaube* (1821-22, 2nd edition 1830-31).[23] There is sufficient evidence to assume that Drey worked with the first editions of these works, and while he may have read later revised editions, they did not alter his judgement of Schleiermacher's position.[24]

This study builds on the research done on Schleiermacher's and Drey's theologies by earlier generations of scholars. Owen Chadwick has written the classic history of the idea of doctrinal development. In it he acknowledged that Drey showed the mark of being a Schleiermacherian--this was not meant as a compliment. Here we will test that judgment and its valuation and will question the pride of place Newman receives in Chadwick's work as the progenitor of an adequate organic theory of development.[25] Jan Walgrave's typology of doctrinal theories also raises troubling questions. He places Schleiermacher in his so-called "transformationist" type, while Drey is in the "theological" type

---

[23]See, e.g., Josef Geiselmann, "Die Glaubenswissenschaft der Katholischen Tübinger Schule in ihre Grundlegung durch Johann Sebastian v. Drey," *Theologische Quartalschrift* 111 (1930): 49-117, especially pp. 95-96; Franz Schupp, *Die Evidenz der Geschichte: Theologie als Wissenschaft bei J. S. Drey* (Innsbruck: University of Innsbruck press, 1970), 18-20.

[24]There is no indication that Drey ever attempted to communicate in writing with Schleiermacher, nor did he pursue a meeting with Schleiermacher when the Berlin theologian visited Tübingen on September 28-29, 1830.

[25]Owen Chadwick, *From Bossuet to Newman*.

along with Newman.[26] The implication is that Schleiermacher is a doctrinal relativist and Drey is not. I will seek to show that this line of demarcation is far too sharp, even if in the end important differences between these two thinkers remain.

Ernst Troeltsch inspired a generation of research on Schleiermacher's view of history. Hermann Süskind, Hermann Mulert, Georg Wehrung, and Hanna Jursch remain indispensable and provide helpful analyses of diverse facets of Schleiermacher's understanding of history.[27] Hans Georg Gadamer's analysis and criticism of Schleiermacher's hermeneutic principles has not been adequately evaluated either in light of Schleiermacher's understanding of history as articulated in his *Geschichte der christlichen Kirche*, or in relation to the *Kurze Darstellung*, both in terms of what it says about history and what it says about historical theology.[28] I will consider the issues raised by Gadamer's work in Chapter II. Discussions about the implications of Schleiermacher's vision of history for his understanding of doctrinal development have too often remained trapped in the domain of formal principles of philosophies of history, or embroiled in debates about criteriological issues. I seek to remain close to the substantive

---

[26]Jan Hendrick Walgrave, *Unfolding Revelation.*

[27]Hermann Süskind, *Der Einfluß Schellings auf die Entwicklung von Schleiermachers System* (Tübingen Dissertation, 1909); idem., *Christentum und Geschichte bei Schleiermacher* (Tübingen: J.C.B. Mohr [Paul Siebeck], 1911); Hermann Mulert, *Schleiermachers geschichtsphilosophische Ansichten in ihrer Bedeutung für seine Theologie* (Gießen: Alfred Töpelmann, 1907); Georg Wehrung, *Der geschichtsphilosophische Standpunkt Schleiermachers zur Zeit seiner Freundschaft mit den Romantikern* (Strassburg: C. Müh & Cie, 1907); Hanna Jursch, *Schleiermacher als Kirchenhistoriker*, Buch I, *Die Problemlage und die geschichtstheoretischen Grundlagen der Schleiermacherschen Kirchengeschichte* (Jena Verlag der Frommannschen Buchhandlung [Walter Biedermann], 1933). Also helpful is the analysis by Wilhelm Gräb, *Humanität und Christentumsgeschichte. Eine Untersuchung zum Geschichtsbegriff im Spätwerk Schleiermachers* (Göttingen: Vandenhoeck & Ruprecht, 1980).

[28]Hans Georg Gadamer, *Truth and Method* (New York: Crossroad, 1991).

theological claims which undergird his views of history and criteriology.

As for research into the work of Johann Sebastian Drey, one must begin with Josef Geiselmann, who single-handedly staked out the domain of the early Catholic Tübingen school. His works of 1930 and 1942 remain ground-breaking and essential for further research. Building on his research, others, most notably Franz Schupp and Wayne Fehr, have sought to clarify the nature of Drey's enterprise, its scientific and historical character.[29] In each case there has been a recognition that Drey was influenced early by Schleiermacher's *Über die Religion* and *Kurze Darstellung*, and that he had read the *Glaubenslehre*. However, Geiselmann, Schupp, and Fehr conclude that the most lasting influence on Drey with respect to the central questions of the nature of theology and history can be found in the work of Friedrich Schelling. Once again, Walgrave's strategy is discerned: Schleiermacher is a relativist, but Drey is not because he makes certain theological and philosophical claims about the objective character of Christian revelation. These claims are said to have their origin in Schelling's philosophy. To assess this line of interpretation, we will need to reexamine in due course Schleiermacher's and Drey's positions in relation to Schelling's philosophy.

There have been very few comparative essays on Schleiermacher and Drey. Robert Stalder's work on Schleiermacher's understanding of apologetics includes a chapter on "the anonymous dialogue" the

---

[29]Franz Schupp, *Die Evidenz der Geschichte*; Wayne Fehr, *The Birth of the Catholic Tübingen School: The Dogmatics of Johann Sebastian Drey* (Chico, CA: Scholars Press, 1981). Since my original research was completed, two important works on Drey have appeared: Abraham P. Kustermann, *Die Apologetik Johann Sebastian Dreys (1777-1853)* (Tübingen: J.C.B. Mohr [Paul Siebeck], 1988); and Eberhard Tiefensee, *Die Religiöse Anlage und ihre Entwicklung. Der religionsphilosophische Ansatz Johann Sebastian Dreys (1777-1853)*, Erfurter Theologische Studien, Band 56 (Leipzig: St. Benno-Verlag, 1988).

Catholic Tübingen theologians had with Schleiermacher's work.[30] His study provides a helpful introduction to some of the issues I will examine here in more detail. Nico Schreurs examines a number of similarities in his essay, "J. S. Drey en F. Schleiermacher aan het Begin van de Fundamentele Theologie. Oorsprongen en Ontwikkelinge."[31] John Thiel has provided some of the most careful and thought-provoking comparisons of Schleiermacher's and Drey's understanding of doctrinal development and the nature of the theological task.[32]

The amazing omission in this comparative work is that no one has pointed out the centrality of the kingdom of God for both theologians. Albrecht Ritschl and Marlin E. Miller explored the importance of the kingdom of God in Schleiermacher's work and nearly every interpreter of Drey comments on the theme in his theology.[33] Yet no one has compared their interpretations of the

---

[30]Robert Stalder, *Grundlinien der Theologie Schleiermachers I. Zur Fundamentaltheologie* (Weisbaden: Franz Steiner Verlag GMBH, 1969), 82-127.

[31]Nico Schreurs, "J. S. Drey en F. Schleiermacher aan het Begin Van de Fundamentele Theologie. Oorsprongen en Ontwikkelinge." *Bijdragen, Tijdschrift voor filosofie en theologie* 43 (1982): 251-288. Recently Schruers has returned to this subject in "Johann Sebastian Drey und Friedrich Schleiermacher. Ein Forschungsbericht," (Unpublished).

[32]John Thiel, "Orthodoxy and Heterodoxy in Schleiermacher's Theological Encyclopedia: Doctrinal Development and Theological Creativity," *Heythrop Journal* 25 (1984): 142-157; idem., "J. S. Drey on Doctrinal Development: The Context of Theological Encyclopedia," *Heythrop Journal* 27 (1986): 142-157; idem., "Theological Responsibility: Beyond the Classical Paradigm," *Theological Studies* 47 (1986): 573-598; now see Thiel's book, *Imagination and Authority. Theological Authorship in the Modern Tradition* (Minneapolis: Fortress Press, 1991).

[33]Albrecht Ritschl, *A Critical History of the Christian Doctrine of Justification and Reconciliation*, Vol. 1, trans. J. S. Black (Edinburgh: Edmonston and Douglas, 1972), 440-511, and *The Christian Doctrine of Justification and Reconciliation*, Vol 3, trans. H. R. Mackintosh and A. B. Macaulay (Clifton, New Jersey: Reference Books Publishers, Inc., 1966), 8-14. Marlin E. Miller, *Der Übergang: Schleiermachers Theologie des Reiches Gottes im Zusammenhang seines Gesamtdenkens* (Gerd Mohn: Gütersloher

kingdom of God. Herein lies the central category of their theologies of history and a *leitmotif* for their respective dogmatic enterprises. The possible reason for this oversight is that too often Schleiermacher interpreters with dubious legitimacy have sought to deduce all issues from the introduction to the *Glaubenslehre* and the second speech of *Über die Religion*, instead of recognizing the dynamic and active function the metaphor of the kingdom of God has for his work. It must be clearly understood that Drey's first published treatment of the idea of the kingdom of God was developed independently of Schleiermacher's.[34] That Drey scrutinized Schleiermacher's interpretation of this motif as he read the first edition of the *Glaubenslehre* seem plausible. But, regardless of whether Drey's later use of this theme was in conscious engagement with Schleiermacher's formulation, their use of the kingdom of God stands as a fruitful avenue of comparison.

In contrast to previous research, then, this study examines Drey's and Schleiermacher's respective theologies of history as a fitting point of entry into their understanding of revelation and doctrinal development. Furthermore, I wish to explore how their interpretations of history play a decisive part in their understanding

---

Verlagshaus, 1970). In *The Dogmatics of Drey*, Fehr provides a clear analysis of Drey's treatment of the kingdom of God; also see Max Seckler, "Reich Gottes als Thema des Denkens: Ein philosophisches und theologisches Modell." In *Im Gespräch: der Mensch*, ed. H. Gauly et al. (Düsseldorf: Patmos Verlag, 1981), 53-62.

[34]The idea of the kingdom of God is mentioned in Drey's 1812-1813 notes, "Ideen zur Geschichte des katholischen Dogmensystems" (261, 263-264); his first published usage was in 1819: (1) in his review of the first volume of Marianus Dobmayer's *Theologia Dogmatica* in *Theologische Quartalschrift* 1(1819):416-440; (2) in his essay "Vom Geist und Wesen des Katholizismus," 210, 223, and (3) in *Kurze Einleitung in das Studium der Theologie*, e.g., §§ 27, 32. Schleiermacher mentions the kingdom of God in his 1803 book, *Grundlinien einer Kritik der bisherigen Sittenlehre*, in *Sämmtliche Werke*, III, vol. 1, p. 235. He occasionally preached on this theme before 1821 (see Miller, *Der Übergang*, 190-191) and he lectured for the first time of five times on the life of Jesus, giving special attention to Jesus' teachings on the kingdom of God, beginning in 1819-20.

of the proper criteria for authentic doctrinal development. The final step will be to assess the doctrinal issues of their day which these two authors considered in need of criticism, reform, and development.

CHAPTER I

NARRATING HISTORY IN FAITH

The theological interpretations of history developed by Schleiermacher and Drey build on certain convictions about the positivity of Christianity and utilize three dominant metaphors: the kingdom of God, organic life, and education. These root metaphors concretely display the specific divine positivity of Christianity. Each of these motifs can and should be understood independently, but it is their cumulative and interactive character that yields the plot for Schleiermacher's and Drey's theologies of history and generate basic categories and concepts that determine the way history is understood.

The Positivity of Christianity

Christianity as a positive religion is central to Schleiermacher's and Drey's theological interpretation of history. It is important to recognize, however, that the term "positive" has three meanings--(1) positive religions as distinct from natural religion; (2) positive theology in contrast to scholastic theology; and (3) positive theology as a practically and socially oriented science. Not all meanings are intended whenever Schleiermacher and Drey use the term.[1] Both employ the first and third distinction, but Schleiermacher does not use the second, while Drey does.

The first meaning of the term positive is central for their interpretations of the historical nature of Christianity. By way of contrast with natural religion, Christianity for Schleiermacher and Drey is a positive religion because it is historically rooted in the given reality or fact of Jesus. Accordingly, there is a rich specificity and historical concreteness attributed to the meaning of Christianity which unfolds and develops in time. The concrete specificity of Christianity is divinely "posited"; it has its source in God and develops from this point of origin.

The contrast between natural religion and positive religions proved crucial for rationalists and deists during the period. The writings of the young Lessing provide a clear example. Lessing argued that positive religion was merely a politically useful modification of natural religion, analogous to positive law which is the contingent application of natural law. The substance of positive religion, Lessing contended in 1760, is "equally true and equally false," because it served the "unity of public religion" but also "weakened and distorted the essentials."[2] Natural religion is the religion of reason, the essential core of religion as rational and moral. Positive religion is that which is institutional, public, traditional, and (for certain of the Enlightenment figures) pre-critical. Accordingly, certain deist and rationalist thinkers, when they discussed the determinant concept of positive religion in comparison to natural religion and natural theology, employed the

---

[1]For the diverse meanings of positive, see Wolfhart Pannenberg, *Theology and the Philosophy of Science* (Philadelphia: The Westminster Press, 1976), 242-250; Francis Schüssler Fiorenza, *Foundational Theology* (New York: The Crossroad Publishing Co., 1984), 251-264.

[2]*Lessing's Theological Writings*, trans. H. Chadwick (Stanford: Stanford University Press, 1956), 105.

terms "positive religion" and "positive theology" in a derogatory way, as having to do with a *cultus arbitrarius*.[3]

This gap between positive religion and natural religion becomes the basis for Lessing's "ugly ditch" between historical facts and religious truth. The facticity of Christianity does not guarantee the validity of Christianity. Historical events may be the occasion, but not the ground, for the inner rational truth of religion. There is only one religious truth, although it may be apprehended either through implicit belief based on authority, or through rational thought. Rational religion, for Lessing, is only inadequately represented in the fragmentary presentations of the variety of positive historical religions. Rational religion is not the original religion, but rather ideal religion. Rational religion as the ideal emerges as the positive religions of the world develop; each is a necessary stage in the development of moral and religious consciousness. Positive religions provide the education of the human race not as the touchstone which verifies religious truth, but as the condition for it.[4]

In opposition to the view propounded by Lessing, Schleiermacher argued in *Über die Religion* that natural religion was an abstraction from the concrete specificity of positive religions. As he puts it, "[t]he essence of natural religion consists in the strict sense

---

[3]Bretschneider reports that J. A. Ernesti "called revealed teaching positive because in it God had complemented natural religion with a *cultum arbitrarium*," quoted in Pannenberg, *Theology and the Philosophy of Science*, 246. Against Tindal and other Deists, Ernesti said these arbitrary things were put on earth for our own good and were not unworthy of divine perfection. The positivity of Christianity in this sense is crucial and problematic in Kant's and Hegel's understanding of Christianity.

[4]See Charles H. Talbert's introduction to *Reimarus: Fragments* (London: SCM Press LTD, 1971); Henry E. Allison, *Lessing and the Enlightenment* (Ann Arbor: University of Michigan Press, 1966); and Gordan E. Michalson, *Lessing's Ugly Ditch* (University Park: Pennsylvania State University Press, 1985).

in the negation of all that is positive and characteristic of religion."[5] The positive character of religions may appear merely arbitrary and therefore superfluous, but in fact "resistance to the positive and arbitrary is resistance to the definite and real."[6] This determinacy is necessary in order to find the Highest Being. "To be satisfied with a mere general idea of religion," Schleiermacher suggests to the cultured despisers of religion, "would not be worthy of you," because it is unworthy of religion.[7]

In Schleiermacher's dogmatic theology, *Der christliche Glaube*, known as the *Glaubenslehre*, Schleiermacher employs the same contrast between positive religions and natural religion. Positive religion signifies "the individual content of all the moments of the religious life within one religious communion, insofar as this content depends on the original fact from which the communion itself, as a coherent historical phenomenon originated."[8] Natural religion, in contrast,

> never appears as the basis of a religious communion, but is simply what can be abstracted uniformly from the doctrines of all religious communions of the highest grade, as being present in all but differently determined in each. Such a natural religion would mark out the common elements in all religious affections which are found in the ecclesiatical communions.[9]

---

[5]*On Religion: Speeches to its Cultured Despisers*, trans. John Oman, intro. Rudolf Otto (San Francisco: Harper & Row, 1958), 233.

[6]*On Religion*, 234.

[7]*On Religion*, 213.

[8]*Der christliche Glaube* 7th ed. (Berlin: Walter de Gruyter, 1960), translations taken from *The Christian Faith* (Philadelphia: Fortress Press, 1976) unless specified, § 10, p. 49; see also *On Religion*, 234.

[9]*Christian Faith*, § 10, p. 49.

Drey similarly contrasts positive religions with natural religion when he discusses the nature of apologetic and polemic theology.[10] Drey insists that this distinction, or apparent opposition, is crucial for the beginning student of theology to understand. One must understand the accidental elements of religion in their necessity for religion and for the Church. The source and givenness of the positive character of religion must be grasped, so that it can be understood as that which is necessary for humanity and its relationship to God.[11] "So many positive forms of religion stand in opposition to the Christian religion in its manifestation. . . ."[12] Positive religions are contrasted with one another not only at the phenomenal level in history (at the level of facts), but also at the level of ideas.[13]

For both thinkers, positive religions are concrete, historically rooted, and historically developing religions. Christianity, accordingly, is one among many positive religions, which include nature religions (unspecified) and the historical religions of Islam and Judaism.

Christianity is positive for Drey not only because of its historical determinacy, rootedness, and character, but also and most importantly because of its divine origin. In Christianity there is a divine origin for both the fact of Jesus and the master idea of his message. Thus we read:

> These religious ideas, thus Christianity, are of an entirely positive kind. They not only presuppose a determinate previous development and change of the religious situation, indicate a determinate condition of humanity in a religious sense, and develop

---

[10]*Kurze Einleitung in das Studium der Theologie mit Rücksicht auf den wissenschaftlichen Standpunkt und das katholische System*, ed. and intro. Franz Schupp (Darmstadt: Wissenschaftliche Buchgesellschaft, 1971; reprint of original Tübingen edition, 1819), §§ 237-238, 315-316.

[11]*Kurze Einleitung*, § 315.

[12]*Kurze Einleitung*, § 238.

[13]*Kurze Einleitung*, § 237.

> entirely new determinate views of the relationship of man to God, to his destiny, and also to the future, so that they are already in every regard joined to something historical as its foundation; they are positive in a still narrower sense, because the source of these ideas is presented as the result of a special event, as the result of an immediate intervention of God in the religious course of development. The source and emergence of these ideas are joined to a determinate man, who delivered them not for his own sake, but for a purely higher communication. . . ."[14]

Drey's statements about the divine positivity of Christianity convey his strong conviction that God has a determinate plan for history that has been emerging from the creation of the world.[15] This plan is spoken of as "the drama of providence"[16] and "the economy."[17]

---

[14]*Kurze Einleitung*, § 34; see also §§ 231, 232; and *Die Apologetik als wissenschaftliche Nachweisung Göttlichkeit des Christenthums in seiner Ersheinung*, 3 vols. (Frankfurt: Minerva, 1967; reprint from original Mainz edition, 1838), 1:1-3.

[15]Drey speaks of God's plan of revelation, of education, of redemption; the plan of Christ, and the plan and will of providence, which is identified with the kingdom of God. See, for example, "Ideen zur Geschichte des katholischen Dogmensystems," in *Geist des Christentums und das Katholizismus. Ausgewälte Schriften katholischer Theologie in Zeitalter des deutschen Idealismus und der Romantik*, ed. Josef Rupert Geiselmann, vol. 5 in series "Deutsche Klassiker der katholischen Theologie aus neuer Zeit," ed. H. Getzeny (Mainz: Matthias Grünwald, 1940), 243; "Vom Geist und Wesen des Katholizismus," in Ibid., 195; *Apologetik*, 1:174, 177, 339-344; 2:283.

[16]*Kurze Einleitung*, § 114. Also see *Apologetik* 2:67 and Drey's dogmatic lectures in Josef Geiselmann, *Die Katholische Tübinger Schule* (Frieburg: Herder, 1964), 213. Drey's usage is indebted to F. W. J. Schelling; see *System des Transzendentalen Idealismus*, *Sämtliche Werke* (Stuttgart and Augsburg, 1856-61), 3:602; also see Eberhard Tiefensee, *Die religiöse Anlage und ihre Entwicklung*, esp., 190.

[17]*Apologetik*, 2:283, Drey's dogmatic lectures, op. cit., 217. The economy is identified in both passages with the kingdom of God.

Is Christianity a divinely posited religion for Schleiermacher as it is for Drey? Although Schleiermacher does not use Drey's phrase, "the divine positivity of Christianity," nor does he speak of revelation as "an immediate intervention of God in the course of development," he does argue that positive religions in general and Christianity in particular have their source in God. In *Über die Religion*, Schleiermacher insists that pious recognition of the Infinite and the Eternal must be mediated through either nature, humanity, or history. "The consciousness of the pious is the immediate consciousness of the universal existence of all finite things, in and through the Infinite, and of all temporal things in and through the Eternal."[18] Religion in general "is an affection, a revelation of the Infinite in the finite, God being seen in it and it in God." This recognition of God in the finite has its clearest expression in history. "History is not of value for religion because it hastens or controls in any way the progress of humanity, but because it is the greatest and most general revelation of the deepest and holiest. In this sense, however, religion begins and ends with history."[19] In the fifth speech we read, "If a definite religion may not begin with an original fact, it cannot begin at all."[20] God is most clearly manifest in history and in the original facts of any positive religion.

What is divinely posited for Schleiermacher is not immediately the doctrine, but first "the *originality* of the fact which lies at the foundation of a religious communion, in the sense that this fact, as conditioning the individual content of the religious emotions which are found in the communion, cannot itself in turn be explained by the historical chain which precedes it."[21] For Schleiermacher Christianity is a divinely posited religion because in the "one miraculous fact" of Jesus we find the fulfillment of the single decree

---

[18]*On Religion*, 36.

[19]*On Religion*, 80.

[20]*On Religion*, 234.

[21]*Christian Faith*, § 10, p. 50.

of God. Jesus Christ fulfills God's plan and eternal decree.[22] This fact of Jesus implies doctrine. Schleiermacher does not speak of the Incarnation as God's "intervention" as Drey does, but he clearly maintains that Christianity is distinctive from other historical religions in God's eternal decree. "Everything in our world . . . would have been disposed otherwise, and the entire course of human and natural events, therefore, would have been different, if the divine purpose had not been set on the union of the Divine Essence with human nature in the Person of Christ. . . ."[23]

Christianity is a divinely posited reality for both writers. How they speak about the positivity of Christianity is remarkably similar. This positivity, this historical determinacy of the Christian religion discloses the plan of God and the divine decree. This plan of God evident in the positivity of Christianity is concretely configured by these two theologians with the use of the three root metaphors we have mentioned--kingdom of God, life, and education. Whether they consequently agree about the character of doctrine and theology in relation to the positivity of Christianity is a question that will concern us in later chapters.

Drey employs the term positive in a second and older sense; he recalls in his *Kurze Einleitung* a distinction made by earlier theologians between positive theology and scholastic theology.[24] Positive theology, in this sense, denotes a certain orientation in theology: pious reflection on the Scriptures and Church tradition. He mentions Erasmus and Melanchthon among others as examples of this approach. Positive theology is contrasted with scholastic theology which uses the tools of logic, a rigorous argumentative

---

[22]For Schleiermacher on "one miraculous fact" see *Christian Faith*, § 93, p. 381; for his treatment of the single divine decree see 501, 549, 557-558.

[23]*Christian Faith*, § 164, p. 724.

[24]*Kurze Einleitung*, §§ 81-82; Drey suggests this distinction when he treats the role of piety and dialectics in his essay, "Revision des gegenwärtigen Zustandes der Theologie," *Geist des Christetums und des katholizismus*, 88. Also see Tharcisse Tshibangu, *Théologie positive et théologie spéculative* (Louvain: Publications Université de Louvain, 1965).

approach, and speculative reasoning. Drey claims no clear allegiance to this distinction in his own articulation of the positivity of Christianity and theology. Schleiermacher, on the other hand, does not even refer to this understanding of positive theology as distinct from scholastic theology, although he plainly understood his own theological project as quite different from the scholastic, speculative enterprise. Schleiermacher's and Drey's different understanding and evaluation of speculation within theology will concern us later.

Positive is used in a third sense by Schleiermacher and Drey as a designation for the practical and social character of the theological science. Schleiermacher explains in *Kurze Darstellung* that "a positive science is an assemblage of scientific elements which belong together . . . insofar as they are requisite for carrying out a practical task."[25] Theology, jurisprudence, and medicine were positive sciences, as they were for Schelling, Kant, and Fichte. Schelling emphasized the public and external use of these sciences, while Kant, Fichte, and Schleiermacher emphasized their practical purposes.[26] In his 1808 Memorandum on the establishment of Berlin University Schleiermacher wrote: "The positive faculties each arose from the need to establish an indispensable praxis securely on

---

[25]*Kurze Darstellung des theologischen Studiums zum behuf einleitender Vorlesungen*, edited by Heinrich Scholz (Hildesheim: Georg Olms Verlagsbuchhandlung, 1977; original edition, 1830); translations taken from *Brief Outline of Theology as a Field of Study*, trans. and intro. Terrence Tice (Lewiston: The Edwin Mellon Press, 1988), § 1.

[26]See F. W. J. Schelling, *Vorlesungen über die Methode des akademischen Studiums* (Hamburg: Felix Meiner Verlag, 1974); translated by E. S. Morgan, *On University Studies* (Athens, Ohio: Ohio University Press, 1966), 7th lecture. I. Kant, *Der Streit der Fakultäten* (Akademie edition, 1798), 7:22, 30, J. G. Fichte, *Deduzierter Plan einer zu Berlin zu errichtenden höheren Lehranstalt* (1807). Works by Kant and Fichte cited by Pannenberg, *Theology and the Philosophy of Science*, 249.

theory and the tradition of knowledge."[27] Theology as a positive science is not merely one branch of theology, but is constitutive of the entire theological endeavor; the diverse branches are brought together in service of the church by church leaders.[28]

Drey explicitly refers in his own *Kurze Einleitung* to Schleiermacher's discussion of theology as a positive science in *Kurze Darstellung.* Earlier introductions to theology treated the entire area of the science according to its outer limit and inner boundary; they specified what had been treated within this area; they joined the present condition of the science with the rules of this enterprise; and they indicated the best works in the individual branches of the science.[29] Schleiermacher's effort is different and Drey concurs that the theological science is "an organic whole, in which the main task requires understanding and presenting the individual parts in the spirit of the whole, while the whole itself is most naturally connected to its parts."[30] This is more than a formal arrangement. It provides theology's positive foundation and it indicates its practical intent.

---

[27]*Gelegentliche Gedanken über Universitäten in deutschen Sinn, nebst einem Anhang über eine neu zu errichtende, Schleiermachers Werke* (Leipzig: Felix Meiner Verlag, 1911), 4: 579. Pannenberg contends that Schleiermacher's recognition of the practical nature of theology reasserts the claim made by those who used the term positive theology as distinct from speculative theology, see Pannenberg, *Theology and the Philosophy of Science*, 249-250.

[28]*Brief Outline*, § 5: "Christian theology . . . is that assemblage of scientific knowledge and practical instruction without the possession and application of which a united leadership of the Christian Church, i.e., a government of the Church in the fullest sense, is not possible." Edward Farley speaks about this teleological unity as the development of theology within a clerical paradigm; see *Theologia: The Fragmentation and Unity of Theological Education* (Philadelphia: Fortress Press, 1983), 85-88.

[29]*Kurze Einleitung*, p. III.

[30]*Kurze Einleitung*, p. IV, also see § 37.

The Kingdom of God

When Drey and Schleiermacher articulate the positivity of Christianity in its concrete richness, that is, insofar as it is a positive religion in contrast to natural religion, they employ three metaphors: the kingdom of God, organic life, and education. These metaphors work together to provide a narrative structure for understanding the life of the individual Christian and the Christian community as well as the means to configure the grand plot of the history of Christianity and its relation to world history. What we discover in the interplay between kingdom, life, and education is their theological interpretation of the historical narrative of Christianity.

In Schleiermacher's lectures on the life of Jesus and in his *Glaubenslehre* and *Sittenlehre*, Jesus's teaching about the kingdom of God provided an overarching idea which distinguishes the uniqueness of the Christian community.

> We will thus have to regard that what in Christ's teaching is related to the community he came to found as properly central, and everything else as only a development stemming from that central idea [of the kingdom of God]. We cannot however think of the latter development as theoretical in relation to everything that is practical. Every further development of what is and must be in the kingdom of God and also that which is nominally excluded from it are always related to it.[31]

Drey came to a like judgment. "It was the great, all-encompassing idea of the kingdom of God under which he [Jesus]

---

[31]*Das Leben Jesu*, Lectures at the University of Berlin in 1832, ed. K. A. Rütenik *Schleiermachers Werke*, vol. 6 (Berlin: G. Reimer Verlag, 1864), 251-252, (translation mine), see also 261-262. *The Life of Jesus*, trans. S. Maclean Gilmour, Jack C. Verheyden (Philadelphia: Fortress Press, 1975), 235, 245.

sought to make himself understandable through many parables."[32] He contends that "in the teaching of Christ, the way he expressed it himself is not any system properly speaking, at least not a full system, but there lies in it the seed of a system; there lies the ground of an all encompassing system in the idea of the kingdom of God. . . ."[33]

What follows from these judgments by Schleiermacher and Drey is very important: every major doctrine must be related to this cardinal idea of the kingdom of God. As we will discover in subsequent chapters, Drey makes the further claim that all the doctrines are generated out of or deduced from this idea of the kingdom. Although it is not my intention to examine how they articulate the relationship between every doctrine and the idea of the kingdom of God, I do wish to focus on how their use of this metaphor discloses the sacramental character of their understanding of history.

The kingdom of God provides both thinkers with a way to map the grand sweep of sacred history in terms of the relationship between the Old Testament and the New Testament, the distinctiveness of the person and work of Jesus Christ, and the nature and the mission of the Church. Schleiermacher's and Drey's interpretations of the kingdom of God offered a clear alternative to those of Hermann Samuel Reimarus and Immanuel Kant.[34]

---

[32]"Ideen zur Geschichte," 261-262.

[33]"Ideen zur Geschichte," 263-264. Drey adds that, "there lies in these indications [of the kingdom of God] the sufficient and proper summons for development. In this Jesus presented his institution as a world institution, as one which is extending over the entire human race and over all times, through which is given at the same time the historical view of Christianity. There lies in the mysteries pronounced by Christ the substance and the incitement, which concern the ways of providence, the nature of God, the nature and the person of Jesus, the Spirit, and the future."

[34]On uses of the idea of the kingdom of God during the Reformation and modernity, see Emanuel Hirsch, *Die Reich-Gottes-Begriffe des neueren europäischen Denkens* (Göttingen: Vandenhoeck & Ruprecht, 1921); Josef

Like Reimarus, more than a quarter of a century earlier, Schleiermacher and Drey focussed attention on the kingdom of God. But Reimarus understood the relationship between Judaism and Christianity differently. In the *Woffenbüttel Fragments*, which were published posthumously by Lessing between 1774-78, Reimarus interpreted Jesus' preaching of the kingdom solely in terms of contemporary Jewish expectations of a political messianism. "Thus when Jesus everywhere preached that the kingdom of God and the kingdom of heaven had drawn near and had others preach the same thing, the Jews were well aware of what he meant, that the Messiah would soon appear and that his kingdom would commence."[35] The prevailing understanding of the Messiah and the kingdom raised hopes for a temporal and political kingdom in Jerusalem; Jesus "would free them of all servitude and make them masters over other people."[36] With Jesus' death, in Reimarus's estimation, the apostles had to reassess Jesus' teachings and deeds. They came to reject a temporal and political interpretation of Jesus' kingdom, and posited in its stead a belief that Jesus' life and death had established him as the suffering savior of all mankind.[37] In light of this assessment of New Testament Christianity, Reimarus expressed his personal conviction that only

---

Rupert Geiselmann, *Die Katholische Tübinger Schule* (Freiburg: Herder, 1964), 191-210; and Josef Rief, *Reich Gottes und Gesellschaft nach Johann Sebastian Drey und Johann Baptist Hirscher* (Paderborn: Ferdinand Schöningh, 1965), 11-68.

[35]Hermann Samuel Reimarus, *Reimarus: Fragments*, ed. C. H. Talbert, trans. R. S. Fraser (Philadelphia: Fortress Press, 1970), 125.

[36]Reimarus, *Reimarus: Fragments*, 126.

[37]Albert Schweitzer says of Reimarus: "His work is . . . the first to grasp the fact that the world of thought in which Jesus moved was essentially eschatological." *The Quest of the Historical Jesus* (New York: Macmillan Publishing Co., 1960), 23. Schweitzer sees Johannes Weiss's work of 1892 as a vindication and rehabilitation of Reimarus' work, as well as a correct interpretation of the kingdom of God in apocalyptic rather than political terms.

a rational religion could serve humanity; the historical sources and revelations of Christianity should be attacked in order to make room for natural and rational religion.

In another vein, Immanuel Kant constructed a moral interpretation of the kingdom of God. In his *Groundwork of the Metaphysic of Morals* (1785), Kant had spoken of a kingdom of ends as the ideal embodiment of the law under which each rational being exists. This law requires that "each of them should treat himself and all others, never merely as a means, but always as at the same time as an end in himself."[38] The categorical imperative is hereby transposed into the language of the kingdom, but no direct reference is made to the gospels, or to Jesus's announcement of the kingdom. Rather the kingdom is understood only as "a systematic union of different rational beings under common law." This common law is objective and moral.

In Book III of *Religion Within the Limits of Reason Alone* (1793), Kant spoke specifically of the kingdom of God in battle with the kingdom of evil. He takes up the scriptural references to the kingdom of God, but only to distill its rational and moral essence.[39] It was Kant's assessment that

> the sovereignty of the good principle is attainable, so far as men can work toward it, only through the establishment and spread of a society in accordance with, and for the sake of, the laws of virtue, a society whose task and duty it is rationally to impress these laws

---

[38]Immanuel Kant, *Groundwork of the Metaphysic of Morals* (New York: Harper Torchbooks, 1964), 75, 101.

[39]For Kant's views on religion and history, see Kant, *Kant: On History*, ed. L. W. Beck (Indianapolis: Bobbs-Merrill Company, 1957); on purpose and teleology in nature and history, see *The Critique of Judgement*, trans. J. C. Meredith (Oxford: Oxford University Press, 1952). For recent work, see Alfred Habichler, *Reich Gottes als Thema des Denkens bei Kant* (Mainz: Matthias-Grünewald-Verlag, 1991); and, *Kant's Philosophy of Religion Reconsidered*, eds. Philip Rossi and Michael Wreen (Bloomington: Indiana University Press, 1991).

> in all their scope upon the entire human race. For only thus can we hope for a victory of the good over the evil principle.[40]

On the basis of the highest law of duty, an ethical as distinct from a merely juridical commonwealth is formed. Such an ethical commonwealth lives under the highest lawgiver who must know actions and the heart "in order to see into the innermost parts of the disposition of each individual and, as is necessary in every commonwealth, to bring it about that each receives whatever his actions are worth."[41] This commonwealth, Kant contends, can rightly be called a people of God, and is properly designated Church. "An ethical commonwealth under divine moral legislation is a church which, so far as it is not an object of possible experience, is called the church invisible. The visible church is the actual union of men into a whole which harmonizes with that ideal."[42] Kant concludes, "the true (visible) church is that which exhibits the (moral) kingdom of God on earth so far as it can be brought to pass by men."[43]

Kant distinguished between the ecclesiastical faith which originates out of some historical revelation and his pure religious faith of reason and morality. The precise relation of ecclesial faith to the religion of reason is clarified when he states that "historical faith can become an ecclesiastical faith (of which there can be several), whereas only pure religious faith, which bases itself wholly upon reason, can be accepted as necessary and therefore as the only one which signalizes the true church."[44] For Kant there is in history a "gradual transition of ecclesiastical faith to the universal religion of reason."[45] Hence, the coming kingdom of God refers

---

[40]Immanuel Kant, *Religion Within the Limits of Reason Alone*, trans. T. M. Greene and H. H. Hudson (New York: Harper Torchbooks, 1960), 86.

[41]Kant, *Religion*, 91.

[42]Kant, *Religion*, 92.

[43]Kant, *Religion*, 92.

[44]Kant, *Religion*, 105-106.

[45]Kant, *Religion*, 113.

to the rational and ethical state on earth, which "has become general and has also gained somewhere a public foothold, even though the actual establishment of this state is still infinitely removed from us."[46] Kant sought to show how in the historical development of religions this process was well underway, and that the present post-Reformation era is the best age because now the true church lives in moral freedom and not under ecclesiastical rule. For Kant the apocalyptic discourses of John and the Sibylline books present the end of the world as symbolic representations intended to motivate and promote courage to that end. The same is true for Jesus' teaching of the kingdom.

> The Teacher of the Gospel revealed to his disciples the kingdom of God on earth only in its glorious, soul-elevating moral aspect, namely, in terms of the value of citizenship in a divine state, and to this end he informed them of what they had to do, not only to achieve it themselves but to unite with all others of the same mind and, so far as possible, with the entire human race.[47]

Drey and Schleiermacher stand together in their opposition to the interpretations of the kingdom developed by Reimarus and Kant. Certainly they affirmed with Reimarus that there exists common strands between the Old and the New Testament and like Kant recognized and even accentuated the moral and communal character of the message conveyed by the idea of the kingdom of God. But both theologians underscored the more fundamental meaning of the kingdom: the redeeming mediation of God by Jesus Christ through the Church. This commonality connects them with a much older sacramental theological tradition and places them closer to Kant's formulation of "ecclesiastical faith." While Schleiermacher and Drey have a great deal in common in their interpretations of the kingdom of God, their distinctive treatments of this theme warrant separate analyses.

---

[46]Kant, *Religion*, 113.

[47]Kant, *Religion*, 125.

Schleiermacher on the Kingdom of God

The *Glaubenslehre* provides the most fitting point of entry into Schleiermacher's statements about the kingdom of God. This work has the kingdom of God as a dominant point of reference. What he says there corresponds to the statements made in his lectures on *Das Leben Jesu* and in his exploration of the ethical ramifications of the kingdom of God in *Die christliche Sitte*.

In order to understand what Schleiermacher says about the kingdom of God in the *Glaubenslehre*, it is necessary to rehearse certain pivotal moves in the pioneering methodology of that work, even though in subsequent chapters we will return to his method and examine it from the vantage point of his configuration of history. Dogmatic theology for Schleiermacher was not a commentary on scriptural and creedal statements of faith, a catechism, nor a collection of sermons. Instead dogmatic theology should provide a description of the consciousness of the Christian Church, employing what may be called a social phenomenology. To this end, he endeavored to present Christian doctrines as they manifested themselves in religious affections.[48]

This new understanding of dogmatics was explained in the introduction to the *Glaubenslehre*, which provides the context for Schleiermacher's initial discussion of the kingdom of God. Religion, it is argued, is neither a thinking nor a doing, but it is a more basic feeling which serves as the interest in knowing about the object of religious matters and the impulse in religious moral action.[49] Feeling is the domain of piety, but it is not excluded

---

[48]*Christian Faith*, § 15.

[49]Schleiermacher distinguishes feeling as self-consciousness, which is an abiding in the self, from knowing, which passes beyond the self only to return to the self, and from doing, which is a moving beyond the self (*Christian Faith*, § 3, p. 8). He also claims religious feeling provides interest in knowing in religious matters and supplies the motive or the impulse in religious activity; see *Die christliche Sitte*, edited from Schleiermacher's lecture manuscripts by L. Jonas (Berlin: G. Reimer, 1834, 2nd edition, 1884), 22-23.

from connections with knowing and doing. Feeling is an abiding-in-self. As such, feeling or piety is contrasted with knowing as the movement beyond the self to return to the self and with doing which moves beyond the self in action. While these three states of consciousness may be distinguished, in experience they are interrelated. Hence, "it will fall to piety to stimulate knowing and doing, and every moment in which piety has a predominant place will contain within itself one or both of these in germ."[50]

Human consciousness is always simultaneously self-consciousness for Schleiermacher as well as world-consciousness and God-consciousness, rooted in human experiences of freedom and dependency.[51] Doctrinal propositions for him are primarily descriptions of consciousness. Only secondarily and derivatively are they propositions "which assert attributes of God and qualities of the world," which saves the theologian from "the creeping in of alien and purely scientific propositions." Here is a method chastened by Kant's *Critique of Pure Reason*. Within it is no move from *quoad nos* knowledge of God to *quoad se* knowledge, from knowledge of God in relation to us to knowledge of God in God's self.

Dogmatics (*Glaubenslehre*) analyzes this feeling in relation to thinking, and Christian ethics (*Sittenlehre*) takes up this feeling in relation to ethics. Schleiermacher seeks to define the universal and abstract nature of this religious consciousness or feeling as a consciousness of absolute dependence. This religious apprehension is discerned as a basic human experience within diverse kinds and types of positive religions, but it is further specified according to the nature of these religions. Natural and aesthetic religions draw

---

[50]*Christian Faith*, § 3, p. 9.

[51]Human consciousness of self, God, and world is based on the antithesis between receptivity and activity, between the feeling of dependence and the feeling of freedom. "Let us now think of the feeling of dependence and the feeling of freedom as one, in the sense that not only the subject but the corresponding Other is the same for both. Then the total self-consciousness made up of both together is one of reciprocity between the subject and the corresponding Other" (*Christian Faith*, § 4, p. 14).

individuals from an active state of consciousness into a passive state of consciousness, whereas Judaism and Christianity are best understood teleologically, as moving people from a passive state of consciousness to an active state. "Now if the action which is prefigured in the religious emotion is a practical contribution to the advancement of the kingdom of God, the mental state is an elevating one. . . ."[52]

The kingdom of God serves as the teleological motive for both Judaism and Christianity. In Judaism, however, this is expressed "less perfectly" than in Christianity, although no exhaustive reason for this judgment is given in the introduction to the *Glaubenslehre*. Schleiermacher adds that "in the realm of Christianity the consciousness of God is always related to the totality of active states in the idea of the kingdom of God." Moreover, "the figure (*Bild*) of the kingdom of God, which is so important and indeed all-inclusive for Christianity, is simply the general expression of the fact that in Christianity all pain and all joy are religious only in so far as they are related to activity in the kingdom of God, and that every religious emotion which proceeds from a passive state ends in the consciousness of a transition to activity."[53] This figure of the kingdom of God demarcates what is distinctive about Christianity and situates Christianity in relation to the history of religious consciousness.

To grasp the significance of these claims fully one must move beyond the introduction and examine Schleiermacher's analysis of the kingdom of God in the context of his dogmatics proper. For there, Jesus Christ, as historically posited and determinate, specifies the meaning of the kingdom of God, initiates the Christian community, and mediates the conversion of the human subject through the Christian community.

---

[52]*Christian Faith*, § 9, p. 42.

[53]*Christian Faith*, § 9, p. 43.

We find that Schleiermacher describes and analyzes in the *Glaubenslehre* the emergence of the corporate consciousness of grace from the consciousness of sin, and then he traces these phenomena back to the influence of Jesus, who as redeemer brings about this transformed consciousness through the community.[54] What Schleiermacher infers from the graced consciousness of the Christian Church about Christ as redeemer and the founder of the Church, he also correlates with the early testimony about Christ in terms of the threefold office of Christ as priest, prophet, and king. He judges it obligatory, once he has treated the person and work of Christ as redeemer and reconciler "on the basis of our Christian experience," to examine the threefold office of Christ "to preserve continuity with those original presentations, for the first theoretical interpretation of Christianity was based upon a comparison of the new Kingdom of God and the old." Even though he believes that these earliest Christian forms "cannot suffice for us," he suggests that it is incumbent upon every theologian "to show that our conception [of Christianity] is in agreement with that which the earlier Christians formed for themselves, when they represented the offices of Christ as *new* and *intensified* forms of those through which in the old covenant the divine government was revealed."[55] In this way, the kingdom of God provides a *leitmotif*, a grand narrative bridge and transition between the old and the new covenant, and the basic link between his description of ecclesial consciousness and the testimony of earliest Christianity.

Schleiermacher develops several historical themes in the context of defining the nature of the redemption and reconciliation effected by Jesus Christ. Each of these themes is associated with the idea of the kingdom of God. The themes are situated in three contexts. In the first, Schleiermacher depicts the historical dynamics of personal development at work in Jesus and in every Christian. The second centers on Jesus as the historical source of Christian redemption; in

---

[54]*Christian Faith*, §§ 87-88.

[55]*Christian Faith*, § 102, p. 439, emphasis mine.

other words, Christ as the primary sacrament of redemption. The third concerns the historical mediation of redemption through the Church, that is, the Church as the sacrament of Christ.

Schleiermacher discusses the historical dynamics of the kingdom in terms of the human transition from the passive reception of grace to the active response to grace. The result of this grace is that the individual grows in God-consciousness, which is evident in the willing of the kingdom of God. Willing the kingdom of God as the *summum bonum* brings about the correct ordering of goods in the individual's life, and establishes the correct relationship of spirit over flesh.[56] Jesus teaches about the kingdom of God and in his person he embodies this message. Human individuals experience the movement from passive to active in an oscillating fashion insofar as we are both determined and free, influenced and determined by the world as the lure of the flesh yet influenced and spiritually freed by God. Because Jesus is sinless and thus not encumbered by the world and the flesh, his spontaneous activity is constant and provides the source of our relative freedom. The kingdom of God thus entails the emergence of human freedom through Jesus because of his spontaneous activity. The result of the reception of God's grace through Jesus is the overcoming of sensuousness: spirit overcoming flesh. This Pauline motif is employed as the dominant dynamic of the moral life of the kingdom of God in Schleiermacher's ethics.[57]

---

[56]This theme is developed at length in *Die christliche Sitte*, e.g., "The Christian self-consciousness knows however of no communion with God except through the redeemer. Consequently redemption itself through Christ is the highest good. And if this is only presented in the human race through the kingdom of God, the kingdom of God is therefore the highest good or for the individual a place in the kingdom of God. . . . So we have then a purely Christian formula out of which the entire Christian ethics can be presented" (78).

[57]We are leaving aside important questions about the moral dimensions of the kingdom of God mentioned here. In his essay on philosophical ethics Schleiermacher contrasts ethics of duty, of virtue, and of the highest good.

The Christian freedom of the kingdom, spoken of in terms of spirit overcoming flesh, is made possible through the spontaneous activity of Jesus Christ.[58] Jesus perfectly wills the kingdom of God and thus he exhibits the perfection of God-consciousness. In Jesus Christ the ideal manifestation of God-consciousness has become historical.[59] Christ is the exemplar and the ideal.

Schleiermacher's analysis of the transformed Christian community led him to certain conclusions about that community's source and goal. The contours of the Christian experience of redemption can only be understood in relation to the historical source in the redeemer. Christ's person and mission are brought together in his teaching about the kingdom of God. "The source of his teaching was the absolutely original revelation of God in him."[60] In his lecture notes on the life of Jesus we read:

> When we take a look at Christ's teaching activity in terms of its content, we find it summed up in the general formula employed to describe his teaching. The idea of the kingdom of God is not to be separated from that of the Son of God; therefore Christ's teaching

---

He contends that the highest good is the *Himmelreich* toward which all people strive. It is that idea which integrates all of the legitimate goods within a teleological ethics of virtue. This formula contrasts with Kant's approach to the kingdom of God, duty ethic, and the highest good. See "Über den Begriff des höchsten Gutes, (Zweite Abhandlung)" *Friedrich Schleiermachers sämmtliche Werke* (Berlin: G. Reimer, 1834-64), 3, pt. 2: 469-495. For further discussion of Schleiermacher's treatment of the kingdom of God in relation to his philosophical and theological ethics, see Marlin Miller, *Der Übergang*, 54-87, 198-214, and Eilert Herms, "Reich Gottes und menschliches Handeln," in *Friedrich Schleiermacher 1768-1834. Theologe--Philosoph--Pädagoge*, edited by Dietz Lange (Göttingen: Vandenhoeck & Ruprecht, 1985) 163-192.

[58]Schleiermacher's discussion of "Eine Herrschaft des Geistes über das Fleisch" is found in *Die christliche Sitte*, 111, 221-222, 293-294, in *Christian Faith*, § 148, and in *Life of Jesus*, 305, 310.

[59]*Christian Faith*, § 93, p. 377.

[60]*Christian Faith*, § 103, p. 443.

> was teaching about his person and about his mission. All else is a development of this according to the degree of relationship, taken over from the tradition.[61]

Because of the perfect God-consciousness of Jesus, those under his influence find redemption and communion with God and reconciliation with their fellow human beings. Christ's union with God is original and complete; in his followers this union is derived from Christ and is progressive.[62] Jesus' teaching of the kingdom, his perfect willing of the kingdom, and his effecting of conversion to the kingdom of those under his influence, serve as the basis for Schleiermacher's claim in the *Glaubenslehre* that "to ascribe to Christ an absolutely powerful God-consciousness, and to attribute to Him an existence of God in Him, are exactly the same."[63]

The inauguration of the new kingdom of God effected in history by Christ does not make all that is before Christ unintelligible and unimportant. As we have already seen, for Schleiermacher the figure of the kingdom of God bridges Judaism and Christianity and structures the story of the transition from the old to the new covenant. We will examine this transition shortly. But Schleiermacher constructs a further bridge between the kingdom initiated by Christ and the creation of the human race by employing the Pauline Adam-Christ motif. The work of God in the first Adam is not set aside by the work of God in the second Adam. Creation is taken up into the historical significance of the kingdom: with the person and work of Jesus creation is brought to completion. Schleiermacher explains:

> If the impartation of the Spirit to human nature which was made in the first Adam was insufficient, in that the spirit remained sunk in sensuousness and barely glanced forth clearly at moments as a presentiment of something better, and if the work of creation has

---

[61]*Life of Jesus*, 243.

[62]*Die christliche Sitte*, 38.

[63]*Christian Faith*, § 94, p. 387.

> only been completed through the second and equally original impartation to the Second Adam, yet both events go back to one undivided eternal divine decree and form, even in a higher sense, only one and the same natural system, though one unattainable by us.[64]

Jesus Christ is consequently called the second Adam because he is "the beginner and originator of this more perfect human life, or the completion of the creation of human beings."[65] Through Christ creation is perfected and history can be "divided into two stages."[66] Again we read, "He [Christ] alone mediates all existence of God in the world and all revelation of God through the world, insofar as He bears within Himself the whole new creation which contains and develops the potency of God-consciousness."[67]

The kingdom of God provides the dominant motif in the narrative of Jesus' life and mission and the narrative presentation of Christian redemption. On a grander scale, the kingdom of God is linked with Christ as the source of Christian redemption and the fulfillment of the created order. Although the language is not Schleiermacher's own, in this context Christ is portrayed as the sacrament of Christian redemption, for only through the personal mediation of Christ is salvation made possible.

With the death and resurrection of Jesus Christ, the physical, historical, and sacramental mediation of Christ is no longer directly accessible. Even though Schleiermacher had doubts from an early age about a sacrificial interpretation of Jesus' death, he clearly linked the salvific importance of his death to the sacramental mediation of the Christ.[68] Christ dies so that the effective power

---

[64]*Christian Faith*, § 95, p. 389. See the analysis of Maureen Junker, *Das Urbild des Gottesbewußtseins* (Berlin: Walter de Gruyter, 1990), 151-205.

[65]*Christian Faith*, § 89, p. 367.

[66]*Christian Faith*, § 89, p. 367.

[67]*Christian Faith*, § 94, p. 388.

[68]See *Life of Jesus*, 318-9, 323-324; cf. *Christian Faith*, § 104, and Marlin Miller, *Der Übergang*, 115, 147.

of the kingdom of God--the perfect God-consciousness of Christ--can be mediated to individuals to the ends of the earth through the corporate life of the Church. "With the first stirrings of preparatory grace in consciousness, there comes a presentiment of the divine origin of the Christian Church; and with a living faith in Christ awakens also a belief that the kingdom of God is actually present in the fellowship of believers."[69] The Church is now the kingdom of God on earth and the sacrament of Christ. Christian faith and the experience of redemption are made possible by the communication of Christ's sinless perfection and perfect God-consciousness *through* the Church. "There is given to us, instead of His [Jesus'] personal influence, only that of His fellowship, in so far as even the picture of Him which is found in the Bible also originated in the community and is perpetuated in it."[70] The Church serves as the physical and personal medium of Christian salvation.

After developing these interrelated themes--the dynamics of advancing the kingdom in Christ and in his followers, Jesus' inauguration of God's kingdom, and the Church as the mediation of Christ's redemption, Schleiermacher finds it necessary to examine the idea of the kingdom of God as it relates to the threefold office of Christ as priest, prophet, and king, in order to preserve at the same time "that harmony between the old covenant and the new" and "the peculiar quality of Christianity." Schleiermacher feels obliged to correlate his own treatment with this early narrative depiction of Christ's person, work, and commissioning of the Church to show the continuity between the old and the new

---

[69]*Christian Faith*, § 113, p. 528. Schleiermacher speaks of the Church as the kingdom of God because willing the kingdom of God unites the community of believers. "This will for the kingdom of God is the very unity of the whole, and its common spirit in each individual; in virtue of its inwardness, it is in the whole an absolutely powerful God-consciousness, and thus the being of God therein, but conditioned by the being of God in Christ" (§ 117, p. 536).

[70]*Christian Faith*, § 88, p. 363.

covenant and to show the distinctiveness of Christianity in relation to Judaism.

The purpose of any theological depiction of these offices is "to be sought in the comparison they indicate between the achievements of Christ in the corporate life founded by Him and those by which in the Jewish people the theocracy was represented and held together, and this comparison is not even today to be neglected in the system of doctrine."[71] "Christ puts an end through the purely spiritual lordship of His God-consciousness," Schleiermacher argues, to "political religions as well as theocracies."[72] The prophetic, priestly, and kingly offices of Judaism are united in Christ. Any rejection of one or two of the three offices leads to a distortion of Christianity. If Christ is merely a prophet, there is only continuity between Judaism and Christianity and nothing distinctive. If Christ is high priest or king but not prophet, the kingdom becomes magical and loses its moorings in the "living Word." Were Christ merely prophet and priest but not king, there would be union with Christ but no community. If Christ is prophet and king but not priest, the specific content of the original type would be missing. If Christ is only king, there is no immediate relation of the individual to the redeemer "and we would have strayed in the

---

[71]*Christian Faith*, § 102, p. 439.

[72]*Christian Faith*, § 105, p. 473. There are important ramifications here for Schleiermacher's socio-political ethics. In his lectures on the life of Jesus he claims that John's gospel more clearly represents the difference between Jesus' kingdom and the Jewish theocracy than do the synoptic gospels. The fundamental difference is that "the Old Testament theocracy had essentially a political character, whereas the kingdom of God that Christ wished to establish was essentially unpolitical." Lest we think it is irrelevant to politics he added, "it was to be compatible with all political forms, to include all political orders, and so naturally could not itself be a political entity." *Life of Jesus*, 258, 290. For further discussion, see Marlin Miller, *Der Übergang*, 186-214, 232-233, and Richard Crouter, "Schleiermacher and the Theology of Bourgeois Society: A Critique of the Critics," *Journal of Religion* 66 (1986): 302-323.

direction of Roman Catholicism, which makes this relation [of the individual to the Redeemer] dependent at once upon the Church and upon those who direct its government." The three offices are united in Christ, "on whom the kingdom rests," and "what is so bound up together is also complete."[73]

Thus, Christ's heavenly kingdom is differentiated from the earthly theocracy of Judaism. The old and the new are joined and severed. "The meaning of this," Schleiermacher explains, "is that in this kingdom . . . the establishment and maintenance of the fellowship of each individual with God and the maintenance and direction of the fellowship of all members with one another, are not separate achievements but the same; and further, that these activities and the free dominion of the Spirit in knowledge and doctrine do not spring from a different source but from the same."[74] Christ is both the climax and the end of the offices of priest, prophet, and king.

The union of individuals with God and with one another is at the basis of the idea of the kingdom of God in both old and new forms. But in the new kingdom the union is secured not by an external imposition of theocracy, but by the internal influence of the redeemer in and through the community. This new influence results in a new living reality, a new corporate life animated from within. In the lecture notes on the life of Jesus we read: "The prophets were able to think only in terms of a theocracy. They could not think of the divine election . . . apart from a political formulation of it. But Christ from the beginning separated the religious from the political element in his people's destiny. He must have thought

---

[73]*Christian Faith*, § 102, p. 441. This discussion of Catholicism lends further support to his claim in § 24 that in Protestantism "the individual's relation to the Church [is] dependent on his relation to Christ, while [Catholicism] makes the individual's relation to Christ dependent on his relation to the Church." This formulation does not diminish the importance of the Church in Schleiermacher's understanding of history, but it places certain limitations on how the Church is understood.

[74]*Christian Faith*, § 102, p. 440.

of the political element only as something external, as the outer form by which the destiny was expressed, rather than its actual inner content."[75]

Finally, the kingdom of God is related to the world. Schleiermacher maintained that derivative doctrinal statements about the constitution of the world arose partly in order to keep hymnic and rhetorical statements about the world in due proportion and partly "out of the need for fixing the relation between the Kingdom of God and the world." He speaks of the world in relation to the phenomenological description of the church's consciousness in three contexts. First, the world is understood as creation, that is, as the general, presupposed, and constituent experience of the God-world relationship.[76] Second, the world is treated as the locus of evil in relation to the consciousness of sin.[77] And third, in relation to the consciousness of grace, the world is understood in antithesis to the Church as the kingdom of God.[78]

The world for Schleiermacher is thus relative to created humanity as the place of original perfection, and yet has become the place of sin and evil, where flesh rules over spirit in the human heart, where world-consciousness dominates God-consciousness. Thanks to Christ's influence upon the Christian Church, the human purpose is redirected and spirit leads flesh. However, the growth of Christian God-consciousness results in a tension between the Church and world. Schleiermacher explains:

---

[75]*Life of Jesus*, 255-256. In this context the kingdom theme intersects with life motifs--the inauguration of Christ's kingdom is identified with the formation of the new corporate life, where there is an inner animating force. We will analyze the Church as an organic community below. See Miller, *Der Übergang*, 108-118, 140, 159-62, 232-235.

[76]*Christian Faith*, §§ 57-61, pp. 233-256.

[77]*Christian Faith*, §§ 75-78, pp. 315-324.

[78]*Christian Faith*, §§ 113-163. pp. 525-722.

> [I]f, with the appearance of Christ a new thing has entered the world, the antithesis of the old; it follows that only that part of the world which is united to the Christian Church is for us the place of attained perfection, or of the good, and--relative to quiescent self-consciousness--the place of blessedness. This is so, not in virtue of the original perfection of human nature and the natural order, though of course it is thus conditioned, but in virtue solely of the sinless perfection and blessedness which has come in with Christ and communicates itself through Him. With this goes the converse, that the world, so far as it is outside this fellowship of Christ, is always, in spite of that original perfection, the place of evil and sin.[79]

For Schleiermacher the consummation of the Church functions as a future goal to be sought and as an ideal which cannot be attained within history. This judgment is borne out by his conclusion that "faith in the Christian Church as the Kingdom of God not only implies that it will ever endure in antithesis to the world, but also . . . contains the hope that the Church will increase and the world opposed to it decrease."[80]

Schleiermacher's formulation of the relationship between the kingdom of God and the world did not rule out any commerce between the two realms within the historical process. The world as creation is good and necessary for salvation, but the created order requires the influence of Christ for its fulfillment. Moreover, even when the world is defined as those individuals trapped in a web of relationships which are not ordered to the kingdom of God, Schleiermacher professes the strong hope of transforming the world and of bringing all under the influence of the kingdom of God. Thus any tension between Church and world will eventually be overcome; through the "planting and extension of the Christian

---

[79]*Christian Faith*, § 113, p. 527.

[80]*Christian Faith*, § 113, p. 528.

Church" will come about "the divine government of the world."[81] Schleiermacher's openness to that which is good in the world and his hope of transforming the world will prove most significant as we proceed. For his further organic interpretation of the kingdom in history supports a tensive and productive relationship between kingdom and world. The triumph of the kingdom over the world has already begun in history and will arrive in the real future, but this triumph also functions within Schleiermacher's system as an ideal. Thus is the kingdom proleptically present, really manifest in history though incompletely.[82]

Drey on the Kingdom of God

Drey's selection of the kingdom of God motif as central for his theology was made independently of Schleiermacher's usage.[83] There are clear differences in how the idea of the kingdom of God is interpreted in Drey's and Schleiermacher's theologies, which will

---

[81]*Christian Faith*, § 164, p. 723. Also read: "The fellowship of believers or the kingdom of Christ can increase only as the world (as the antithesis of the Church) decreased, and its members are gradually transformed into members of the Church, so that evil is overcome and the sphere of redemption enlarged" (§ 105, p. 469).

[82]To enter into the kingdom of God and to have eternal life are one and the same for Schleiermacher. The final triumph of the kingdom is not the regulative idea of Kant which only lies beyond history and cannot be found manifest within history. See *Life of Jesus*, 310 and *Christian Faith*, §§ 159-163, pp. 703-722. We will discuss Schleiermacher's treatment of eschatology in Chapter V.

[83]Drey's treatment of the idea of the kingdom of God was greatly indebted to the Benedictine professor Marianus Dobmayer (1735-1805). Drey reviewed Dobmayer's *Theologia dogmatica* in *Theologische Quartalschrift* 1 (1819):416-440; 2(1820):38-55, 309-323. On Dobmayer's influence, see Abraham Kustermann, *Die Apologetik Johann Sebastian Dreys (1777-1853)* (Tübingen: J.C.B. Mohr [Paul Siebeck], 1988), 149, 189-199, and passim.

be noted as we proceed. Nevertheless, there are fundamental similarities in the ways that the kingdom of God serves as the *leitmotif* in Drey's and Schleiermacher's configuration of history: it stretches from creation to the end of the world and structures the plot of history in terms of Jewish theocracy, the manifestation of Jesus Christ, and the age of the Church. The reason for the similarity must ultimately reside in their common recognition of the linguistic resourcefulness and theological significance of Jesus' teaching about the kingdom for interpreting history. Drey's discussion of the kingdom of God in the *Kurze Einleitung* predates Schleiermacher's treatment of this theme in the first edition of the *Glaubenslehre*. Drey discusses this work by Schleiermacher on numerous occasions in his *magnum opus*, *Die Apologetik*; it is possible that in this work Drey is also in conscious dialogue with Schleiermacher's treatment of the kingdom of God as found in the *Glaubenslehre*, but this is never explicitly stated.

Drey's most comprehensive published treatment of the idea of the kingdom of God is found in his three volume *Die Apologetik*.[84] There the kingdom of God provides the master idea and the organizing source of all that is distinctive about Christianity. In the first volume, Drey argues for "the necessity of revelation as divine communication and instruction for the purpose of the original development of religious consciousness by means of its content."[85] In this so-called philosophy of revelation Drey analyzes the nature of revelation and the human subject's receptivity to revelation; it also schematizes positive religions throughout history. The second volume examines the historical manifestations and development of

---

[84]Equally comprehensive is his use of the idea of the kingdom as the narrative frame of reference for his dogmatic lectures. See the small selection of a student's notes in Geiselmann, *Die Katholische Tübinger Schule*, 210-223; on Drey's dogmatic lectures in manuscripts and student notebooks and for an analysis of these lectures, see Wayne Fehr, *The Birth of the Catholic Tübingen School: The Dogmatics of Johann Sebastian Drey* (Chico, CA: Scholars Press, 1981).

[85]*Apologetik*, 2:1.

religions of nature ("heathenism") and historical religions (Judaism and Christianity) in an attempt to show the divine character of Christian revelation.[86] The third volume argues for the divine character of Catholic Christianity.

Drey begins this project by discussing the nature of religious consciousness and piety in relation to the gratuitous revelation of God in nature and history. This lays the groundwork for the major argument of the second and third volumes that the idea of the kingdom of God is the definitive revelation of God in Christ and Church.

The overriding assumption for Drey's apologetics, which he plainly articulated in his dogmatic lectures, is that "the idea of the kingdom of God is presented in the form of history, and so, like all history, is comprised of certain periods"; it is "like a drama before our eyes of faith."[87] The turning point of this drama of history is Jesus Christ--his teachings, deeds, death, and resurrection. But this narrative must begin with the original revelation of God in creation.

> Christianity [is] not simply a special religion, but also . . . an institution of the world in its significance and determination, namely, an institution of God in its source, its development, and its perfection. It is founded in the original revelation, further developed in Judaism, prepared in another way and in another manner in heathenism, and appearing at the right moment in its full manifestation in the son of God, Jesus Christ.[88]

God's original revelation in creation develops in religions of nature and in Judaism.[89] Natural religions are multiple and polytheistic, encompassing both familial and national forms. They

---

[86]*Apologetik*, 2:232.

[87]Drey's dogmatic lectures, in Geiselmann, *Die Katholische Tübinger Schule*, 212, 214.

[88]*Apologetik*, 2:225; also see *Kurze Einleitung*, § 27.

[89]Drey's way of proceeding here parallels Schleiermacher's strategy in the introduction to the *Glaubenslehre*.

have dissolved the unity and transcendence of God in a misguided effort to acknowledge God's immanence in the world, and in so doing they have confused the divine with earthly things.[90] In the process they have lost a sense of God's providence in the world, which is the principle of the correct understanding of history. In place of God's providence, they have placed a "dark, inscrutable, ghostly entity: blind fate."[91] "That is why the divine could no longer appear in history to them as the highest and final cause, as the chain of causes and effects bonding for a grand purpose, as the proper unity of the historical drama."[92] Consequently, the divine in history is reduced to a matter of "sporadic manifestation" and "idolizing humans" through a symbolic-mythic worldview. Nature religions for Drey are aesthetic religions which lead to idolatry--the creator is confused with creation.[93] The fundamental problem is that nature religions have deviated from the *Urtradition*. Religious error accompanies sin.[94]

Natural religions are older than historical religions, even though there are historical dimensions in natural religions. What is common to nature-based religions and the historical religion of Judaism is that they both suffer from outside infiltration of different cultural forms through the physical, intellectual, and moral influences of other nations.[95]

---

[90]*Apologetik*, 2:62, also 142-149.

[91]*Apologetik*, 2:67.

[92]*Apologetik*, 2:67.

[93]*Apologetik*, 2:217-218.

[94]*Apologetik*, 2:152-153. In the dogmatic lectures, Drey divides the history of the kingdom of God into four periods: (1) creation, (2) the fall of the human race and its consequences, (3) the restoration of the kingdom of God through the redeeming work of Christ, and (4) the perfection of the kingdom of God. See Geiselmann, *Die Katholische Tübinger Schule*, 192-223 and Fehr, *The Dogmatics of Drey*.

[95]*Apologetik*, 2:69.

The idea of the kingdom of God as understood in Christianity has its roots in Judaism. Drey suggests two principles for interpreting it in Judaism:

> The first principle and viewpoint is that for the purpose of the maintenance and progress of the true religion the revelations of God must connect with the natural history of the Jewish people. And since this history has three periods--preparation, constitution, and political development--so also the divine revelation has its introduction, foundation, and further development. The second principle and viewpoint follows partly out of the first, partly out of the final determination of revelation. This [revelation] was given to the Jewish people . . . , however it was not destined exclusively for that people. On the contrary, its destiny was higher and more general for the entire human race, namely to bring about the perfect religion and redemption.[96]

Drey's entire treatment of Judaism places the formation of the religious community around the institutions of theocracy and the Mosaic Law: priesthood, prophecy, and kingship. What Judaism practices as a national-political religion is in germ the universal-moral religion of Christianity.[97] "The idea of the Mosaic theocracy is the anticipation of an idea that became prominent in Christianity only, that is to say, the idea of the kingdom of God as an ethical commonwealth of God, which could be made accessible and conceivable to the old world and culture only under the veil of a sensuous world state."[98] The three institutions of priest, prophet, and king are combined in the prophetic idea of messianism which is in turn related to a messianic kingdom as the community of a new covenant. According to the prophets, this community will experience a new spiritual worship and pure sacrifice, a moral conversion and atonement for their past sins. Theirs will not be an

---

[96]*Apologetik*, 2:156-57.

[97]*Apologetik*, 2:156, 162, 166.

[98]*Apologetik*, 2:167.

external and legal unity, but an internal unity of spirit and disposition. The fulfillment of the messianic idea is the realization of the moral kingdom of God on earth. This is why Drey states that "Christianity has brought pure idealism into the world."[99]

In the *Kurze Einleitung* Drey argues that Christ "purified that sensible idea of an earthly kingdom of God and world citizenship to the purity and generality of a heavenly kingdom, a moral kingdom in the universe."[100] Christianity does not share in the national and political nature of Judaism, where law and theocracy are the fundamental tenets. Jesus' announcement of the messianic kingdom breaks with the Jewish model. "The fundamental idea of the dignity of the messiah is, according to the basic theocratic principle of the Old Testament, that he should be the full representative of God in his kingdom on earth."[101] But in Christianity we have something different. "The entire Jewish religious doctrine was a revelation of the relationships of the kingdom of God . . . ; the embodiment of Christian religious doctrine is a revelation of the relationships of the kingdom of God from a higher standpoint, for which God had in the meantime prepared and raised humanity."[102] Drey explains this difference:

> Indeed, Christ also makes the idea of the kingdom of God the centerpoint and carrier of all ideas. Yet his kingdom is not an earthly one like the empires of the world, but rather a true kingdom of God, which is in heaven. For this reason it is also called kingdom of heaven. It is indeed, insofar as it admits persons here and now, in this world, but not of this world, for the Spirit which inspires it comes not from this world but from God. Also,

---

[99]*Apologetik*, 2:187.

[100]*Kurze Einleitung*, § 59.

[101]*Apologetik*, 2:188.

[102]*Apologetik*, 2:214. Drey adds that while Christianity is the fullest revelation of God in the historical development of revelation, "Judaism is an essential moment." Christianity fulfills and completes Judaism. See 2:216-217.

> its endeavor is directed not to earthly property and sensuous happiness, but rather to a higher, spiritual, and eternal good, whose acquisition begins during earthly existence, but is completed only at a higher level. It is in a word a purely spiritual and moral kingdom, which recognizes no other Lord than God and his Son, whom he sent, destined not to annihilate the kingdoms of this world, but rather to cultivate them through its religious and moral spirit and destined not to subjugate the peoples of this earth, but rather to unite all through the covenant of love into one people of God under the Lordship of the father of humanity and the king of kings.[103]

Jesus' teaching of the kingdom of God is self-referential in that it reveals him as the messianic figure and Son of God. "The purpose for which God sent his son to humans is in the first place the announcement of the good news of the kingdom of God."[104] Jesus is the fulfillment of the messianic idea, which incorporates the power of the king, the holiness of the priest, and the wisdom of the prophet.[105] Jesus' teaching is evidently divine because it mediates the reunification of God and humankind, the rejuvenation of the moral life, and the universal appeal of this teaching.[106] The central role of Jesus Christ in the drama of the kingdom of God includes his identity as moral example and herald of an ethical kingdom, but as Messiah, incarnate Son of God, and *Gottmensch*,

---

[103]*Apologetik*, 2:212. Drey links the Mosaic notions of theocracy with the pre-Mosaic idea of creation (Schöpfungsbegriffe). What was originally a physical-ethical idea was transformed into a sensible earthly kingdom of God and in Christianity was subsequently transformed into an spiritual and moral kingdom.

[104]*Apologetik*, 2:247.

[105]*Apologetik*, 2:175.

[106]*Apologetik*, 2:252-259.

Christ mediates salvation; he is the primordial sacrament of salvation.[107]

When Drey speaks of Christ's presence in history, he speaks of him as the manifestation and fulfillment of God's providence, the divine decree, and the divine plan. The link between the old and the new kingdom of God, can be traced through the early revelations and prophecies.

> God wanted to maintain and further develop in the descendants of Abraham the original pure religion. The extraordinary providential guiding of them served that purpose, and joined to this was the divine decree to have blessing and salvation go out from the people of Israel to all nations, with all entailing promises and prophecies. This was the economy of the kingdom of God from the beginning, in accordance with which its perfecter, the Christ-Messiah, had to arise and appear among this people. And for the same reason he could find the most worthy instruments for his great purpose nowhere else than in this people who had been fashioned by God for so long and in so many ways.[108]

This is God's plan from the beginning. Christ's transformation of the kingdom is included in the *Uroffenbarung*, for in creation there is already present the movement toward its fulfillment in Christ's mission.[109] Christ effects a "new spiritual creation" which brings to completion the first creation.[110] "Thus the revelation of God

---

[107]In the *Kurze Einleitung* the kingdom of God was identified as the *Grundidee*, but this idea includes the ideas of Incarnation and *Gottmensch* (§§ 32, 224, 230, and 233). The Incarnation is identified as the *Grundidee* of Christianity in *Apologetik* 2:V-VII, cf. 239-240. Does this difference imply a shift in Drey's thinking or does the Incarnation provide an abbreviated way of speaking about the drama of the kingdom of God, which has the incarnate Son of God as its focal point? I am inclined toward the latter. cf. Abraham Kustermann, *Die Apologetik Johann Sebastian Dreys*, 309-311, 314.

[108]*Apologetik*, 2:283.

[109]*Kurze Einleitung*, § 27.

[110]*Apologetik*, 2: 237-238.

in Christ is the revelation in his son, the only begotten, who from eternity was in the father's bosom. . . ."[111]

The divine character of Jesus' life is recognized, according to Drey, in the moral character of Christ; he was sinless, exhibited moral perfection, symmetry, and harmony; and this moral balance distinguishes Christ from religious fanatics.[112] Christ manifests religious consciousness--God-consciousness--to the highest degree. "So appears in Christ not merely the highest religiosity; he himself is the personification of religion."[113] Drey uses the kingdom of God motif as the organizing idea for Christ's person and mission in sections devoted to the divine self-consciousness in Christ (1) in eternity, (2) according to his relationship to God, (3) as son of God, and (4) as one sent by God. "The purpose for which God sent his son to humanity is, in the first place, the announcement of the joyful message of the kingdom of God."[114] Closely connected to the first purpose is "redemption, deliverance of humanity out of the ruin into which they have fallen through sin and disbelief."[115] The third and highest purpose of the message of the son is that everything will become united in and through God. The fourth purpose is that the son comes as judge and rewarder.[116]

Christ's teaching of the kingdom of God is divine because it shows the correct relation between the nature of God and the world. It speaks of restoring the image of God in the human person as the likeness of God. This teaching establishes a moral integrity based on a recognition of one's sinfulness and the forgiveness of sin through grace.[117]

---

[111]*Apologetik*, 2:211.

[112]*Apologetik*, 2:264.

[113]*Apologetik*, 2:266. Drey defines religion in this context as *Gottesbewußtsein*.

[114]*Apologetik*, 2:247.

[115]*Apologetik*, 2:248.

[116]*Apologetik*, 2:248.

[117]*Apologetik*, 2:252-259.

Thus the idea of the kingdom of God unites all three aspects of the work of Christ. First, Christ brings about a moral recreation and reconstruction of the human person. Second, he announces the forgiveness of sin and the gift of salvation. Third, he establishes a religious community on the foundation of his teaching.[118]

> These three goals are united into one, to unite humankind into one great kingdom of God; an idea which was already given with the Mosaic theocracy and which was developed in the Old Testament and in accordance with the political spirit of the old world in the form of an earthly monarchy. But by Christ it was traced to its deeper meaning and has been understood and announced as a spiritual and moral kingdom, as a kingdom of heaven.[119]

The establishment of the Church assures the continuing presence of the kingdom of God on earth. "The institution of a great religious community was intended to give an ethical form to this kingdom, the rebirth of the spirit and the forgiveness of sins serving as its inauguration, holiness and blessedness with God being its higher purpose. This is the work which Christ wanted to accomplish."[120] This church is not the family or tribal community of primitive religions, nor is it a national or state religion. It is a spiritual and moral community that mediates salvation and reconciliation. In the *Kurze Einleitung*, we read, "This idea [of the kingdom of God] appears therefore as the highest, as the one idea of Christianity that carries in itself, and from which arise, all others; and Christ, who universally effects its recognition, is for that reason also the visible head of the kingdom, just as its visible presentation and sensible perception is the Church."[121] The Church as the kingdom of God is the continuation of the fact of redemption accomplished through Christ. "The purpose of each church is

---

[118]*Apologetik*, 2:278-286.

[119]*Apologetik*, 2:280.

[120]*Apologetik*, 2:281.

[121]*Kurze Einleitung*, § 32.

religious life, piety, and union of persons with God. This purpose appears in the Christian Church in its proper form as the idea of the kingdom of God that is meant to be realized in and through it [i.e., the Church]."[122] Thus is the Church for Drey, the primary mediation of Christ's kingdom in the world or, in our words, the primary sacrament of Christ.[123]

As we have discovered, Drey contrasts a sensuous and earthly understanding of the kingdom with a religious and spiritual one. He also writes of a struggle between Christianity and the world, but Drey contends that there is not an absolute opposition between the Church and the world.[124] In fact, as we will learn more clearly in the next chapter, there was an openness to the world and the culture in Drey's understanding of history. Drey believed that the great miracle of Christ would ultimately bring about the "Christianization of the world" and the drama of the kingdom of God would come to completion, but in the meantime there would be conflict, which would sometimes require a rejection of the things of this world.[125]

In comparison we find that both Schleiermacher and Drey employed the idea of the kingdom of God as a key metaphor for discussing the nature of Christianity. Their use of this multivalent idea is meant to be thoroughly historical and thoroughly theological. It provides the grand narrative plot for history. It serves as the bridge and hiatus between the old and the new covenant. The one

---

[122]*Kurze Einleitung*, § 324.

[123]The kingdom of God is also identified with the Church in his 1819 essay, "Vom Geist und Wesen des Katholizismus": "The Church is a brotherhood and a kingdom at the same time; a brotherhood to those who like to follow the promptings of love, to the free ones who know how to rule themselves and how to suppress everything base in themselves; a kingdom to those who raise themselves selfishly against the brotherhood, to the slaves, who are not able to rule the enemy of love, egoism" (in *Geist des Christentums*, 210).

[124]*Kurze Einleitung*, §§ 177-178.

[125]*Apologetik*, 1:216.

who teaches the message of the kingdom of God also embodies its meaning. Jesus Christ through his message and person offers redemption, reconciliation, and a way of personal moral transformation. The Church as the kingdom on earth mediates the redemption effected through Christ. In the course of history, the Church stands in relationship with the world; this world is sometimes a part of the progress of the kingdom (when it is the created order fulfilled through grace) and sometimes it is antithetical to the kingdom (when the world stands with those and for those under the influence of sin and sensuousness). Consequently, the world is a place of ambiguity, not simply evil, not thoroughly good.

Leaving aside their doctrinal differences, most especially in christology and ecclesiology--matters that will concern us later, there are dissimilarities in their construction of a grand narrative plan with the kingdom of God motif as its linchpin. Schleiermacher incorporates the Pauline Adam-Christ motif to speak of the fulfillment of creation in Christ. Drey does not, but his theology explicitly interprets Christ as the fulfillment of the created order. Schleiermacher also utilizes the Pauline motif of spirit overcoming flesh to talk about the inner transformation of the Christian. Drey speaks of an inner personal conversion as central to the drama of Christianity, but he does not use this formula.

We have seen that the kingdom of God serves as a root metaphor and model in Schleiermacher's theology. In turn this root metaphor provides a deep narrative structure for his interpretation of history--in the grand sweep of history from creation to the end of the world, but also for the narrative patterns of individual life experience. The same is true for Drey's theology, but for Drey the narrative character of the idea of the kingdom of God as a *narrative* frame of reference is more pronounced--he speaks of "the history" and "the economy of the kingdom of God"; for him the kingdom of God is "like a drama."

The narrative themes and structures generated from the idea of the kingdom of God serve as stabilizing and renovating factors in their theologies: this figure affirms continuity in history from the beginning to the end, even as it evokes changes, tensions, and an openness to transformation. Their constructions of the plot of the kingdom of God echoed moral themes sounded by Enlightenment thinkers, but in fundamental ways these narratives developed an argument against them--the meaning and role of Jesus Christ and the Church in history cannot wither away. On the other hand, their vision of the kingdom of God and especially their portrayal of Christ, the Church, and the world in this plot, was not simply a reaffirmation of the classical dogmatic heritage. The metaphor of the kingdom of God yielded for them a narrative that rendered more rigid and stagnant ones problematic or obsolete. And yet for both of these theologians the metaphor of the kingdom of God cannot be viewed in isolation; it can only be fully understood in relation to the organic and educational metaphors which work together in their construals of history and in their arguments against alternative visions of history.

Organic Dialectic

Through their treatment of the positivity of Christianity and the idea of the kingdom of God, Schleiermacher and Drey affirmed the fundamental tenets of the dominant theological vision of history in Christianity. This model we have called sacramental because it accentuates the Church's mission of mediating the salvation effected through Christ. Down to the nineteenth century this sacramental model of history was wedded to a classicist worldview, a normative rather than empirical understanding of culture.[126] Time since Christ was understood as all of one kind, homogeneous. The finality of Christ's revelation was acknowledged and historical developments were assumed to have made no substantive impaacton the structure of Christian history. The age of the Church was the

---

[126]See Bernard Lonergan, "The Transition From a Classicist World-View to Historical-Mindedness," *Second Collection* (Philadelphia: The Westminster Press, 1974), 1-10.

time for the spreading of the Gospel to all corners of the earth. For some theologians there was the possibility of logically deducing sacred conclusions from the principles of faith as found in the Bible and church pronouncements, and yet the sacred truths retained a timeless quality; the creedal symbols and the scriptural testimony remained unaffected by the vicissitudes of historical life. With Schleiermacher and Drey we witness the transformation of the sacramental model, a transformation due in large measure to their appropriation of the then emerging organic understanding of temporality, the mind, and reality itself.

In the late 18th and early 19th century the prominence of the mechanistic worldview of the physical sciences was challenged by an organic model of reality. Drawn from the biological sciences, this model became a common source of insight for fields beyond the natural sciences.[127] Johann Gottfried Herder's essay, "On the Knowing and Feeling of the Human Soul," (1778) announced the new age of biologism and confirmed the shift from the prominence of the physical sciences and Cartesian and Newtonian mechanics to the sciences of life.[128] While that essay propounded an organic understanding of the human soul or spirit, it was Herder's *Reflections on the Philosophy of the History of Mankind* (1784-91) which examined the movements of history from an organic perspective.[129] Schelling's *Reflections on a Philosophy of Nature* (1797) was also pioneering in the development of an organic vision, and his *Lectures on the Method of Academic Study* (1802) played an influential role in propagating the organic vision into fields beyond

---

[127]On the shift from mechanistic to organic root metaphors in literary theory see M. H. Abrams, *The Mirror and the Lamp* (New York: Oxford University Press, 1953), 156-225.

[128]"Vom Erkennen und Empfinden der menschlichen Seele," *Herders Werke* (Berlin and Weimar: Aufbau-Verlag, 1982), 3:331-405.

[129]*Ideen zur Philosophie der Geschichte der Menschheit* in *Herders Werke* (Berlin and Weimar: Aufbau-Verlag, 1982), Vol. 4; *Reflections on the Philosophy of the History of Mankind*, abridged trans. F. E. Manuel (Chicago: University of Chicago Press, 1968).

the biological sciences, in particular into philosophy and theology.[130]

Schleiermacher's and Drey's organicism is one of the constant elements in their theology. It provides the impetus for an epochal shift in the understanding of history, revelation, and doctrinal development. As we have seen, the idea of the kingdom of God provided both thinkers with a theological interpretation of history, but their construal of history works also with an organic dialectic.[131] All of history, both Schleiermacher and Drey believed, should be understood organically. However, the history of Christianity in particular as the history of the Church should be understood as an organic process, since the Church (as the kingdom of God on earth) is an organic community and because its organizing ideas (such as the kingdom of God) develop organically. The metaphors of kingdom and organic life work together for Schleiermacher and Drey to produce innovative narrative themes and structures, which precipitate in turn an overall revision of the nature of theology, doctrinal development, and the role of the theologian and church leader in the process of articulating doctrines. Four particular themes in Schleiermacher's and Drey's use of organic metaphors in interpreting history merit attention.

---

[130]F. W. J. Schelling, *Ideen zu einer Philosophie der Natur* in *Schellings Werke* (München: C. H. Beck und R. Oldenbourg, 1927), 1: 653-723. *Vorlesungen über die Methode*; *On University Studies*. Schelling's work had influence not only in Germany, but, through Coleridge, in England as well. For the reception of Schelling's philosophy by nineteenth century Catholic theologians, see Thomas Franklin O'Meara, *Romantic Idealism and Roman Catholicism: Schelling and the Theologians* (Notre Dame: University of Notre Dame Press, 1982).

[131] An organic model of history is often rightly contrasted with a dialectical model. Organic models emphasize growth and continuity; dialectic models accentuate the conflictual character of history. Historically, however, the dialectical model of history emerged with Hegel as a hybrid organic model of history. We use the appellation "organic dialectic" to underscore the tensive quality of the term organic in Schleiermacher's and Drey's interpretation of history.

First of all, Schleiermacher's and Drey's organic interpretation of history accentuates the identity and continuity of Christianity over time by referring to the seed as the source of organic life and identity.[132] So Drey states that "[t]his seed and beginning [of development] lies in the presentation of the teaching of Christ, as he has expressed it himself, at least as it has been expressed according to the report of the evangelists. . . ."[133] Drey also affirms continuity amidst change in the following:

> In the teaching of Christ as he presented it, there is not any system properly speaking, at least not a full system, but there lies in it the seeds (*die Keime*) of a system. There lies in the idea of the kingdom of God the ground of an all encompassing system. There lies in these indications [of the kingdom of God] the sufficient and proper summons for development. In this Jesus presented his institution as a world institution, as one which is extending over the entire human race and over all times, through which is given at the same time the historical view of Christianity.[134]

---

[132]Continuity is accented by Schleiermacher and Drey in certain ways which make no direct appeal to organic metaphors. Drey speaks about the *Uroffenbarung* which Christ fully manifests in time. Schleiermacher writes in an analogous way about creation and the world as being the primordial revelation. Both affirmed the continuity and identity of a divine plan at work in history--Christ is the fulfillment of creation, as the original revelation, and the Church is the mediation of Christ's salvation. For both, the normative character of earliest Christianity was hereby accounted for and the continuity of Christianity was manifest in the piety of the Christian Church throughout the ages. The concept of revelation is treated in Chapter IV.

[133]"Ideen zur Geschichte," 260-261. Eberhard Tiefensee offers a helpful analysis of Drey's handwritten manuscripts on the philosophy of nature in relation to his interpretation of the religious structure of the human person and the religious plan in history. Tiefensee identifies various natural phenomena and theories that Drey investigated and that provided metaphorical resources for his theology; *Die religiöse Anlage und ihre Entwicklung* (Leipzig: St. Benno-Verlag, 1988).

[134]"Ideen zur Geschichte," 263.

Schleiermacher made a similar claim in his lectures on the life of Jesus. He taught that "we are referred by all our sources to a general formula of all Christ's teaching activity, a formula that we have to accept as one that sums up all he taught, as the living seed from which his teaching developed, namely, 'the kingdom of heaven is at hand,' (Matthew 4:17)."[135]

Thus, Christ's teaching of the kingdom of God (which entails for both claims about the redemptive mission and nature of Christ) is a generative and organizing seed of doctrines and theology for Schleiermacher and Drey. This seed of Christ's teaching of the kingdom of God, which discloses the significance of Christ for human history, was planted in the community of the Church. It can be claimed that the Church is the kingdom of God because it continues to carry the seed of Christ's teaching within, and mediates the redeeming and reconciling action of God. The organic understanding of the Church made it possible to affirm the basic unity and identity of Christianity down through the ages. Schleiermacher states, as Drey also affirms, that "Christianity is meant to exist as an organic community."[136] This means not only a community united in the present, but as we shall see in greater detail below, it also means a community organically united though time.

---

[135]*Life of Jesus*, 245. Schleiermacher identifies the kingdom of God motif, dominant in the synoptic gospels, with the Johannine teachings about Jesus as the source of "life." See his reflections on John 5:26: "As the Father has life in himself, so he has granted that the Son also have life in himself. . . . (The) noun "life" in this passage (must be taken) transitively, as the power to communicate life as a life that passes over into others. . . . The communication of life that had its source in him could only take place within such an organic complex and could only so be assured to the whole human history" (286-287). See Marlin Miller, *Der Übergang*, 108-123, 140-169.

[136]*Brief Outline*, § 49; *Die christliche Sitte* states that in the Christian community "everyone must be organically bound and work in organic community, that is, they must be Church" (366).

Second, Schleiermacher and Drey identify the Church as a living organism, which has been given life through Christ.[137] The organic life of the Church and of the substance of its teaching, which identifies and unites this community, develop over time. Such organic development is important and subtle. Organic life is not exhausted by its origins and nature, rather it evolves, assimilating--shaping and being shaped by--multiple external factors, all the while empowered by an internal source of life.

Drey acknowledged that Christianity develops beyond its origins in his use of the term "living tradition."[138] "The ideas of Christianity [are] in themselves something living. . . ."[139] For the tradition of Catholicism to be living, its nature had to develop in ways appropriate to different times and places.

> Christianity, as a positive divine religion, is a temporal phenomenon, a fact. As such, it has a time of origin, a period of existence, and a form in which it was given as a divine revelation. But no fact of any kind is momentary, that is, none is extinguished and disappears

---

[137]Schleiermacher's and Drey's identification of the Church with the kingdom of God is also qualified by their organicism. The Church is the kingdom of God because the seed of its life is the teaching and mission of Christ, but since this kingdom is developing, it always strives toward the final organic fullness of time.

[138]"Vom Geist und Wesen des Katholizismus," 199; *Kurze Einleitung*, § 192; *Apologetik*, 1:381-410, especially 381-382, 398-404; 2:1-17. See Josef Rupert Geiselmann, *Lebendinger Glaube aus geheiligter Überlieferung* (Freiburg: Herder Verlag, 1966), 120-121; and "Die Glaubenswissenschaft der Katholischen Tübinger Schule in ihrer Grundlegung durch Johann Sebastian v. Drey," *Theologische Quartlaschrift* 111 (1930): 49-117, especially 78-86. Geiselmann traces the concept of the "living tradition" back to Sailer, Zimmer, and Fenelon and he rejects the suggestion that Drey borrowed the idea from Protestants Schleiermacher and Neander (78). The latter claim concerning Schleiermacher and Drey is strictly speaking accurate, but it leaves unexplored the similarities in their use of organic metaphors.

[139]*Kurze Einleitung*, § 192. Drey also speaks about *ein lebendiges Wissen* (§ 99) and *die lebendige Erscheinung der Ideen des Christentums* (§ 225).

> again in the same moment it arises. On the contrary, every fact intervenes within the series of, and in interaction with all other facts; expanding itself, restraining or accelerating, or changing its combined effect in narrower or wider circles, thereby attaining its own history.[140]

As this text indicates, Drey's concern with the facticity of Christianity is based on his convictions about the positivity of Christianity. These divinely posited facts are not for Drey merely the occasion of a rational religion which grows in depth and in members throughout history. Instead these facts are historically maintained and developed within an organic community. "The historical character of primitive Christianity . . . is either dissolved in ideas, and thus is present as these ideas, or it perdures as a constant and unbroken fact in the thoroughly empirical phenomenon of the Church and its organic constitution."[141]

Schleiermacher pointed out in his *Kurze Darstellung* that Christianity, like any historical entity, must be viewed as a life in process. "The more any given historical career is occupied in the process of expansion, so that increasingly the inner unity of its life appears only in encounter with other forces, all the more do these forces, in turn, enter into the various individual situations that make it up."[142] He also spoke in language which is similar to Drey's "living tradition."

---

[140]"Vom Geist und Wesen," 195.

[141]"Vom Geist und Wesen," 208. Also see 228-229: "This ecclesial life of original Christianity, with its organic forms, is therefore the enduring type of every Christian church; the constant, uninterrupted, and essentially unchanged continuation of this type is the Catholic Church." That this is not a classicist understanding of Catholic Christianity becomes clear as the argument proceeds.

[142]*Brief Outline*, § 83, see also *Geschichte der christlichen Kirche*, edited from Schleiermacher's lecture notes by E. Bonnell, *Sämmtliche Werke*, Division 1, Vol. 11 (Berlin: G. Reimer, 1840), 20.

> Scripture now stands by itself, for its preservation unchanged guarantees in a special manner the identity of our witness to Christ with that originally given. Yet it would be a mere lifeless possession if this preservation were not an ever-renewed self-activity of the Church, which reveals itself also in living witness to Christ that either goes back to the Scripture or harmonizes with Scripture in meaning and spirit.[143]

It is in this context that Schleiermacher links an organic model and the Pauline body of Christ motif with the threefold office of Christ and thus to the idea of the kingdom of God. He explains that the Church,

> as the organism of Christ--which is what Scripture means by calling it His Body--it [the Church] is related to Christ as the outward to the inward, so that in its essential activities it must also be a reflection of the activities of Christ. And since the effects produced by it are simply the gradual realization of redemption in the world, its activities must likewise be a continuation of the activities of Christ Himself. These we have reduced to the scheme of the threefold office.[144]

---

[143]*Christian Faith*, § 127.

[144]*Christian Faith*, § 127, pp. 589-590. For both Drey and Schleiermacher the ability to talk about an *organic* community, and a *living* tradition is rooted in a theology of the Holy Spirit. The Spirit gives life to the community and sustains the community throughout history. In Schleiermacher's words the Holy Spirit "is promised (in the New Testament) to the whole community, and where communication of the Spirit is spoken of, it comes by a single act to a multitude of people who *eo ipso* become an *organic whole*, who are urged on to like activity and stand in for each other" (§ 121, p. 562). The Holy Spirit is identified with (yet not exhausted by) the common spirit of the organic community. On the relation of the corporate unity of Christianity and of the unity of the human race, see § 121, pp. 564-565. Drey states, "As principle and organ of inner spiritual unity, Christ promised and sent a Spirit to all--not only to the Apostles, but also to the faithful. The Spirit . . . should bind them together from within in their conviction, as the Holy and Christian Spirit of the community (*Gemeingeist*)"

In addition to viewing the "seed" of Christ's teaching as the point of *origin* and *continuity* and the "living organism" of the Church as the vehicle for *development*, a third facet of Drey's and Schleiermacher's use of organic metaphors is that it provides a way of thinking about history in terms of an *organic unity*. Their understanding of organic unity combines two insights. On the one hand, organic unity conveys the great romantic equation of life: the whole is everything and each part must be viewed in relation to that whole. On the other hand, this affirmation of the whole must be balanced with the romantic appreciation of the individual part; each individual historical part--person, event, community, nation--has its own integrity as a part and each part must also be viewed as a reflection of a larger whole. The attempt to discern the organic unity in history requires correctly constructing the relation of part to whole. Consequently, it demands a long view of history and a patient investigation into the deeper dynamics and patterns in historical processes.

Drey states simply that we find an "indivisible unity of Christianity and its history."[145] Every historical development within the church's life must be seen in relation to the whole history of Christianity. Moreover, the Christian church must address itself anew to each new epoch and so it constitutes itself differently from age to age.[146]

Schleiermacher addresses these issues in the *Kurze Darstellung*:

> In the sphere of individual life, every real beginning is sudden and original; but from that point on, everything else is simply a

("Vom Geist und Wesen," 229). Further reflections on their pnuematologies will be given in the final chapter.

[145]"Revision des gegenwärtigen Zustandes der Theologie," reprinted in *Geist des Christentums*, 83-97, 94.

[146]See "Vom Geist und Wesen," 231. Geiselmann discusses this appreciation of the individual as a distinctively romantic element in Drey's theory of development in *Lebendiger Glaube*, 125, 160.

> development of what has already begun. However, in the sphere of actual history, that is, of people's life in common, the two aspects are not so strongly contrasted, and only on account of a preponderance of either is one moment considered in one way and another moment in the other way.[147]

There are many moments that make up the life of a historical entity. Consequently, "[e]very historical whole may be considered not only as a unity but also as a composite, in which each of the different elements has a career of its own. . . ."[148]

Schleiermacher argued that this organic unity throughout history has a twofold character. There is an outer unity based on the historical occasion of its formation, "a fixed fact of history with a definite commencement." There is also an inner unity, the positive modification constituting the specific, determinate nature of a concrete religion--"a peculiar modification of that general characteristic which is common to all developed faiths of the same kind and level."[149] Thus historical theology concerns itself with "the total development of Christianity," not merely with the earliest apostolic or patristic period. "Every historical mass may be viewed (a) on the one hand as one indivisible being and doing in process of becoming, and (b) on the other hand as a compound of innumerable individual moments. Genuine historical observation consists in the combination of both."[150] Schleiermacher further explains:

---

[147]*Brief Outline*, § 71. Martin Redeker argues that Schleiermacher's appreciation of individuality stems from Moravian influences and thus is earlier than his encounter with the romantic circle in Berlin. This may be, but his treatment of individuality is ultimately situated in a broader, organic frame of reference. See Redeker, *Schleiermacher: Life and Thought* (Philadelphia: Fortress Press, 1973), 22, 56.

[148]*Brief Outline*, § 74.

[149]*Christian Faith*, § 10, p. 44.

[150]*Brief Outline*, § 150.

> every fact has historical individuality only insofar as these two are posited as identical: the outer reality as the changing of what nevertheless maintains its identity, and the inner reality as the function of a force in motion. In this manner of speaking, the 'inner' is posited as soul, the 'outer' as body--the whole, consequently, as a life.[151]

Schleiermacher and Drey draw an important apologetic conclusion from their organic understanding of Christianity: Christianity must be understood as a living reality; those who oppose it take a stand against life. Drey explicitly contrasts this presentation of the organic life of Christianity with any Cartesian attempt to establish a *Reflexionstandpunkt*.[152] Similarly, as we have already noted, Schleiermacher in his *Über die Religion* says that the cultured despisers' polemic against the positivity of Christianity is a "polemic against life."[153]

Organic interpretations of Christianity often emphasize the source, kernel, or seed of life. They usually stress organic continuity and development. However, one does not always find a treatment of threats to organic life. The possibility of disease and corruption is the fourth aspect of Schleiermacher's and Drey's use of organic metaphors.[154]

---

[151]*Brief Outline*, § 151. In the *Sittenlehre*, Schleiermacher develops at length an organic understanding of the mission of the Church as intensive and extensive--the mission to bring about the purifying, spreading, and presenting actions of the Church within the individual and in the world; see *Die christliche Sitte*, 324.

[152]"Vom Geist und Wesen," 198. See Walter Kasper, "Verständnis der Theologie damals und Heute," *Glaube und Geschichte* (Mainz: Matthias-Grünewald-Verlag, 1970), 12.

[153]*On Religion*, 232.

[154]Their acknowledgement of bodily "disease" and "corruption" includes, in an epoch prior to the rediscovery of apocalypticism, some concerns raised by apocalyptic visions of history under the rubric of "crisis." Recent theologians who employ apocalyptic themes of crisis sometimes employ organic metaphors of bodily disease, and sometimes psychological metaphors

The dynamic between sickness and health is central to Schleiermacher's discussions of doctrinal development in the *Kurze Darstellung* and in the *Glaubenslehre*, and in his treatment of doctrinal and moral development in *Die christliche Sitte.* For Schleiermacher, the life of the Church can be threatened by disease and corruption in doctrinal, ethical, and institutional matters. "Diseased conditions do occur in historical entities, no less than in organic."[155] In the *Glaubenslehre* he explains, "If we think of the Christian Church as being what we call a moral person, i.e., as being, though of course made up of many personalities, nevertheless a genuine individual life, then it must at once be admitted that in every such life, just as in individual lives in the narrow sense, there is a distinction between healthy and diseased conditions."[156] Why is it that historical entities become diseased? According to Schleiermacher "[w]hen a historical organism appears diseased, this may be based partly on a recession of vitality, partly on the fact that extraneous factors have entered in and have become organized within it for their own sake."[157] The entire enterprise of Church history is thus partially specified by its endeavor "to distinguish between what has resulted from the distinctive force of Christianity

---

of neurosis and psychosis. Both sets of metaphors, organic and psychological, are used to indicate a problem and the need for a change or discontinuity in history. Organic and psychological metaphors suggest different types of analysis and different types of curative response. Compare the use of psychological metaphors in the work of the early Frankfurt School (Theodor Adorno, Max Horkheimer, and Jürgen Habermas) and in the book by liberation theologian, Leonardo Boff, *Church: Charism and Power*, trans. J. W. Dierksmeier (New York: Crossroad Publishing Company, 1985).

[155]*Brief Outline*, § 35.

[156]*Christian Faith*, § 21, p. 95. He goes on to say, in a passage we will examine in the next chapter, that diseased conditions "are always conditions which do not arise from the inward foundation of the life and in its clear course, but are to be explained only by foreign influences."

[157]*Brief Outline*, § 54. The first edition of the *Kurze Darstellung* is comparable to the second edition in its emphasis on disease, even though there are changes in language. See also *Christian Faith*, § 21.

and what is founded partly in the make-up of the various organs thus set in motion and partly in the influence of principles foreign to them, and then to try to gauge the advance and recession of each."[158]

There are times when, because of sickness, the organic whole of the Church needs to be purified.[159] In the *Sittenlehre*, Schleiermacher examined these threats to the condition of the entire Church from an ethical perspective. It is within this ethical context that he discusses certain "corruptions" which have taken place within the church body.[160]

Drey never offered extended discussions of the nature of disease and corruptions in the organic development of historical entities as we find in Schleiermacher's writings.[161] There were times, however, when he addressed past diseased conditions within the church. In his early programmatic essay "Revision des Gegenwärtigen Zustandes der Theologie," Drey speaks of abscesses in the organic community which will either fall off or will require surgical help to remove.[162] The entire document, in fact, is meant

---

[158]*Brief Outline*, § 160.

[159]*Die christliche Sitte*, 118-225, esp. 120-121, 200-205.

[160]*Die chistliche Sitte*, 1-96; also on *Krankheitszustand* and corruptions, see 406-415.

[161]Compare *Brief Outline*, §§ 54-62, first edition text in the footnotes, with *Kurze Einleitung*, §§ 237-247. In the *Kurze Einleitung* Drey does not echo Schleiermacher's use of disease (*Krankheit*, § 56, n. 1, § 57, n. 1) or degeneration (*Ausartung*, § 60, n. 2) as found in the first edition of the *Kurze Darstellung* when speaking about polemics and the threats to doctrine, liturgy, and the life of the Church. Drey uses the word "*Corruption*" to describe how certain Church parties threaten the organism of Christianity (§§ 245, 246, cf. § 129), but more frequently he speaks of errors, using an epistemological and pedagogical category.

[162]"Revision," 91: "For the theologian had lived so far within the Church, that is, in the intuition of the living organism, as it had developed from the indwelling life-principle--and his theology had been a copy of this organism, self-living and faithful, so the reformer had to take flight to other things. He left the living organism because some abscesses had affixed themselves here

to chart a future course for a theology which will respond to previous diseased conditions and can avoid them in the future.[163]

Moreover, in numerous contexts, Drey did contrast living and unliving tradition. This distinction as employed by Drey harkens back to the Scriptural dictum, "The letter kills, but the spirit gives life." Here it is the letter of the gospel severed from the organic community which kills; it is the primitive Christian witness cut off from the whole of the tradition.

> Each original fact either dies out when it has happened and has created a momentary effect, or it yields a remaining product, in which it continues and perdures. In the first case the future generations come to know it only through the common unliving tradition, through writing or legend, in the other it becomes its own living tradition.[164]

For Drey a tradition severed from communal life is an "unliving tradition" or simply a "dead tradition."[165]

For Drey corruption of the living organism of the Church is something which has taken place in the past and can happen in the future, but which every effort must be made to avoid. Corruption can occur when philosophy enters into the living Christian tradition and distorts the Christian message. Yet philosophy in and of itself does not cause corruption of the living tradition. "The development of Christian teaching into ideas in general is not corruption, but

---

and there which either would have fallen off by themselves or at the right time would have been taken off through surgical help."

[163]Drey also speaks about egoism as an enemy of the brotherly unity of the Church which is organic. The Church has the power within it to ward off the attacks of this enemy and also the means of healing it. Such attacks on the living community are countered through education. See "Vom Geist und Wesen," 212.

[164]*Apologetik*, 1:381; see also 1:398.

[165]*Apologetik*, 1:396.

rather the task of science."[166] When Drey discusses heresy and schism in the Church he speaks of it as a corruption caused by "rebellion," "lagging behind," and "indifferentism."[167] Drey's recognition of "lagging behind" as "inertia" or intransigence provides, as we shall see, a significant challenge to a static understanding of truth as unchanging.[168]

The Education of the Human Race

Another key metaphor employed by Drey and Schleiermacher works in concert with their organic model; history is described as a process of education.[169] This idea is not new to Drey and Schleiermacher.[170] In fact, during the period of the Enlightenment, Gotthold Ephraim Lessing wrote the important essay, "*Die Erziehung der Menschengeschlecht*," (1780) in which he described the ages of the world as the process by which God

---

[166]*Kurze Einleitung*, § 192, n. 2.

[167]*Kurze Einleitung*, §§ 246-247.

[168]Drey states that "Lagging behind (*Zurückbleiben hinter*) the truth is inertia (*Trägheit*), the consequence of the extinguished activity of the (religious) principle in its continuing development" (*Kurze Einleitung*, § 240). See John Thiel's insightful analysis of this language in "Theological Responsibility: Beyond the Classical Paradigm," *Theological Studies* 47 (1986): 583.

[169]For recent analyses, see Eberhard Tiefensee, *Die religiöse Anlage und ihre Entwicklung*, 159-185; and Matthias Riemer, *Bildung und Christentum. Der Bildungsgedanke Schleiermachers* (Göttingen: Vandenhoeck & Ruprecht, 1989).

[170]Pedagogical interpretations of Christ and human history can be traced back to the gospels of Matthew and John and also they are found, for example, in the work of Irenaeus, Clement of Alexandria, Origen, and Gregory of Nyssa. Thomas Aquinas describes the historical relationship between the Old and New Law in pedagogical terms.

educates the human race.'[171] Johann Gottfried Herder, the romantic man of letters, also fashioned an understanding of history as a process of education; not *Erziehung* with its overtones of instruction, rearing, and training, but *Bildung* implying the formation and development of character and a cultured person.'[172]

Drey and Schleiermacher employ this central Enlightenment concept, education, with its close affinities with *Aufklärung* and coming of age (*mündig werden*), but in a romantic context. In fact, their interpretation of the education of human race can be understood in connection with their organic model of history. That the education metaphor need not be joined to this organic model is confirmed, of course, by the example of Lessing. But in our authors' work organic and education metaphors operate on parallel tracks: natural development takes place through organic processes; the development of spirit or consciousness occurs through education. For neither Schleiermacher nor Drey are the organic and education metaphors consciously interwoven, but they work together in shedding light on historical processes.

In numerous contexts Drey claims there is "the right and natural concept of revelation--it is for the entire humanity, what education

---

[171]*Lessings Werke*, ed. Kurt Wölflel (Frankfurt am Main: Insel Verlag, 1967), 3:544-563. Enlightenment philosophers have not always been recognized for promoting a historical perspective, as romantic thinkers have been. See Philip Reill, *The German Enlightenment and the Rise of Historicism* (Berkeley: The University of California Press, 1975).

[172]Herder envisioned history as a means of forming character, educating the cultured person. *Auch eine Philosophie der Geschichte zur Bildung der Menschheit* (1774) *Sämmtliche Werke*, ed. B. Suphan (33 vols, ; Berlin, 1877-1913), vol. 5. As early as 1776, four years prior to Lessing's essay on "The Education of the Human Race," Herder wrote, in *The Oldest Documents of the Human Race*, of history as the means whereby God teaches the human race. vol. 7. In his *Reflections on the Philosophy of the History of Mankind* (1784-91), human history was spoken of as a "*Bildungsgeschichte*." See M. H. Abrams, *Natural Supernaturalism* (New York: W. W. Norton & Company, Inc., 1953), 201-204.

(*Erziehung*) is for the individual."[173] The implication in this view of the advancement of world history is that Christianity brings the human race to maturity. Educational development is an indispensable part of this historical progression. "Just as education never ends for the individual human, . . . so is it also with revelation. It remains a need for humankind throughout all periods of their existence, it does not end even in heaven."[174]

Birth, childhood, adolescence, maturity--the stages of a human life are writ large in the process of human history as conceived by Drey. God's plan of education is manifest from the start with creation and through natural and historical religions, God works to educate the reason of human persons so that they might find their redemption in a living community and a living tradition. Maturity is not found apart from tradition for Drey, nor does it entail rejecting the voices of authority from the past or present. Rather, maturity is found in the advancement of the human species through the human reception of revelation. Drey here effectively uses an idea of the Enlightenment against the Enlightenment vision of autonomy and maturity.[175]

Without using Lessing's language, "the education of the human race," Schleiermacher employs education metaphors as historical motifs. The growth of Christian consciousness is the predominant theme in both Schleiermacher's *Glaubenslehre* and *Sittenlehre*. The individual's and community's growth in God-consciousness develops through history and in the various positive religions. With

---

[173]"Aphorismen über den Ursprung unserer Erkenntnisse von Gott--ein Beitrag zur Entscheidung der neuesten Stretigkeiten über den Begriff der Offenbarung," *Theologische Quartalschrift* 8 (1826): 237-284, 266.

[174]"Aphorismen, p. 268. Drey acknowledges his debt to Lessing in numerous contexts. E.g., "Aphorismen," 155. In this regard see Arno Schilson, "Lessing und die katholische Tübinger Schule," *Theologische Quartalschrift* 160 (1980): 256-277.

[175]For passages treating the education motif, see "Ideen zur Geschichte," 243, 245; "Vom Geist und Wesen," 195, *Kurze Einleitung*, §§ 58, 73, 97; *Apologetik*, 1:140-150, 2:162.

Christianity, through the perfect God-consciousness of Christ, a new epoch in the realization of this God-consciousness has dawned. The growth in God-consciousness continues throughout history within the Church.

In the *Sittenlehre* Schleiermacher suggests that perhaps it would be best to think of the Church as a school. His entire project in Christian ethics was to record the growth of God-consciousness in its intensive and extensive modes of presence. On the one hand, the individual and community must be purified and healed within through a divinely mediated education. On the other hand, the Church moves beyond itself, addressing anyone, even the "cultured" (*Gebildeten*) despisers, inviting them to join in the educational process of Christian formation.'[76] Schleiermacher cautions, however,

> we are not understanding the expression school as . . . in the cultivation of aptitude and skills. Instead, if we say the Church should be organized as a school aimed at the increase of character, we mean by this only that it should be an institution which preserves itself by exciting its principle in each member ever anew, and which is in this way constantly developing itself further in them and through them; this is what lies essentially in the concept of a school.'[77]

'[76]This is, of course, the great ironic ploy of *Über die Religion*: religious education (*Bildung*) is found wanting in the educated despisers of religion (*die Begildeten unter ihren Verächtern*). Schleiermacher discuss the role of the state in education in *Die christliche Sitte*, 440-444.

'[77]*Die christliche Sitte*, 389. Schleiermacher discusses here the educational process as an aspect of the spreading action of the Church. "The Church as a school aimed at raising the activity of the will is nothing other than an Institution of a common [and] enduring morality" (390). "The development of the Christian conscience . . . has always revealed itself through the formation (*Bildung*) of a proper language" (393). "The Church considered as a school constitutes two great systems, on the practical side--morals, on the theoretical side--language" (395). Schleiermacher also discusses preaching and liturgy as a form of moral and linguistic training. He

Both Drey and Schleiermacher voice confidence in the process of education. But there are genuine obstacles in this process. Drey speaks of the problems of childishness: those who play with words, historical facts, distinctions, and concepts in a manner which promotes little insight and hinders education.[178] More importantly, both Schleiermacher and Drey recognize the dynamics of creativity and error in the process of education. This is a crucial ingredient in their discourse on heresy and orthodoxy as we shall discover. But what should be pointed out at this stage is that both theologians state clearly that in the history of the human race erroneous ideas must be contested by the truth.[179] At the same time they maintain that these ideas serve a positive purpose in the educative process of doctrinal development.[180] Erroneous thinking is not always identifiable from the start and therefore there is a need to create a environment where, through dialogue, truth can emerge.

In summary, Schleiermacher and Drey narrate history by affirming the positivity of Christianity and by describing this positivity in terms of the metaphors of the kingdom of God, organic life, and a pedagogical process. It is the cumulative and interactive character of these motifs which discloses their distinctive configurations of history. Their precise construals of the kingdom of God, the life of the Church, and the process of education result in a vision of history which draws from classic theological motifs

---

adds that this education is not only popular, but also scientific (398).

[178]"Revision," 95.

[179]For Schleiermacher and Drey, determining the truth about religion and disputing error is a constitutive dimension of apologetics, polemics, and also included in the dogmatic task determining the truth of Christianity in relation to heresy.

[180]*Brief Outline*, §207, *Kurze Einleitung*, § 193. Geiselmann spoke about the polarity and dialectic of truth and error in Drey's understanding of doctrinal development in "Die Glaubenswissenschaft," 91, 94, 100-103 and in "Das Problem der Dialektik in der Katholischen Tübinger Schule," in *Die Katholische Tübinger Schule*, 369-374.

and convictions, while it also forges a new understanding of history and doctrinal change. These theologically potent metaphors and narratives provide the framework for thinking about God's revelation in history and doctrinal development; they also serve to persuade others--harsh critics of Christianity and defenders of a stale and static understanding of Christian truth--that *the* Christian narrative, that is, *their rendering* of the Christian narrative, demands otherwise. The argument does stop at the level of narrative. But before we can examine the precise warrants and criteria for doctrinal criticism, reform, and development, it will be important to explore in greater detail how an organic vision of history constitutes, for Schleiermacher and Drey, the axis of development.

CHAPTER II

INNER AND OUTER AS THE AXIS OF DEVELOPMENT

The use of organic metaphors in Schleiermacher's and Drey's theological interpretations of history proves to be decisive for their understandings of ecclesial and doctrinal identity and change. These metaphors provide a model for interpreting events and texts that made previous approaches to historiography and hermeneutics no longer sufficient.[1] Both theologians criticize a chronicle approach to history, while commending an organic model that combines speculative and empirical perspectives. In their organic constructions of history, both theologians detect a tension or dialectic between inner and outer elements at work in the development of doctrine as constitutive of the unfolding of the kingdom of God. This dialectic is crucial in their work, even though their formulations differ noticeably; it informs their specific

---

[1]An organic model is sometimes identified with a *Lebensphilosophie*. See, e.g., Albert L. Blackwell, *Schleiermacher's Early Philosophy of Life: Determinism, Freedom, and Phantasy* Harvard Theological Studies 33, (Chico, California: Scholars Press, 1982), 58, 86, 88. Even though this is an apt description of their views, neither Schleiermacher nor Drey speak of their own positions in this way. Wilhelm Dilthey, influenced by his study of Schleiermacher and German romanticism, introduced *Lebensphilosophie* as a philosophy of human life in all of its social and cultural ramifications. See, *Dilthey: Selected Writings*, ed. H. P. Rickman (Cambridge: Cambridge University Press, 1976), 20-23.

treatments of the role of theology in the reforming and developing of doctrines and the specific criteria they employ to judge adequate formulations of doctrinal matters.

In this chapter we will examine Schleiermacher's and Drey's reflections on hermeneutics and historiography. We will explore aspects of their organic visions of history insofar as they bear on doctrinal matters. Specifically, we will analyze the inner and outer dynamic within doctrinal development as they articulate it in their statements about biblical hermeneutics and church history. We will conclude this chapter by exploring how this dynamic provides the framework for their statements about doctrinal orthodoxy, heterodoxy, and hyperorthodoxy.

History as Chronicle

An organic construction of history clarifies the inadequacy of a chronicle approach to history, which offers only a sequential ordering of events, persons, and facts. Schleiermacher judged that a chronicle was ill-equipped to present any historical reality, including the history of Christianity. In his 1806 lectures on Church history, Schleiermacher criticized a chronicle approach for offering merely "the collection of individual events."[2] Such an approach is surely antiquarian: "the motivations can only be idle curiosity."[3] It is "without inner unity," and can distinguish nothing determinate about the historical reality in question. Fifteen years later his judgment had not changed: a chronicle provides "an atomistic presentation" which examines "everything most external."[4] A chronicle isolates each external point; there is only an accidental relationship between the individual moments, a mechanistic connec-

[2] *Geschichte der christlichen Kirche*, 623.

[3] *Geschichte der christlichen Kirche*, 623.

[4] *Geschichte der christlichen Kirche*, 2.

tion of facts, which are combined in order to obtain a sense of "contemporaneousness and succession."[5]

Drey makes similar claims about history as chronicle, though with considerably less commentary, in his *Kurze Einleitung*. Chronicle is distinguished from "history proper" (*die eigentliche Geschichte*) because it only presents the individual facts and does not construct these facts into an intelligible order. Drey observed that "most of the merely historical sources for the history of Christianity dating from antiquity and the Middle Ages are in the form of mere chronicles."[6] What historical theology requires is a vision of history which can adequately present the intelligible order within history.

Historical Construction

Discerning the intelligible order in history is the task, Drey suggests, of a "historical construction." This formulation is derived directly from F. W. J. Schelling's *Vorlesungen über die Methode des akademishen Studiums*. In the eighth through the tenth lectures the German idealist philosopher Schelling treated history as that which, like nature, springs from an eternal unity, a primal knowing (*Urwissen*) of the Absolute. The apparently contingent and accidental events of history are able to be constructed through leading ideas into an eternal and absolute necessity.[7] This historical construction provides an order to the given and actual events of empirical reality from the "higher viewpoint" of either

---

[5]*Brief Outline*, §§ 246, 153; see also §§ 157, 182, 252. The beginning of the *Life of Jesus* lectures reiterates this contrast between chronicle and history.

[6]*Kurze Einleitung*, § 218.

[7]*Vorlesungen über die Methode des akademischen Studiums* (Hamburg: Felix Meiner Verlag, 1974). We will usually cite from the English translation by E. S. Morgan, *On University Studies* (Athen, Ohio: Ohio University Press, 1966), 87-88.

philosophy or religion. This "higher viewpoint" offered by the sciences of religion and philosophy is superseded by the "absolute standpoint" offered by the academic discipline of history, which is an art, not a science. History provides the synthesis of the given and the actual (from the empirical realm) with the ideal (from the speculative sciences of philosophy and religion).

In 1819 Drey drew from Schelling's basic understanding of historical construction. "Every historical study has two elements--that which one wants to experience and, if one has experienced it, knows;--and that through which one experiences each [the former] and how one knows it afterwards. The first is the object itself, the other is the historical construction of the object."[8] Drey makes this distinction in his presentation of the nature of historical theology, which includes exegesis and the presentation of the history of the Christian church. In each of these disciplines the object which is sought can only be ascertained through historical construction.[9] What we find in these historical endeavors is that "the religious concept (or the sum of them [religious concepts]) leads back to an original fact as an immediate certainty, as the demonstrative authority for the concept; then the construction is simply historical. . . ."[10]

Drey contends that in historical theology, "in the treatment and joining of individual facts here, as generally in history, only the common historical construction can prevail, which distinguishes the material of the fact, the perceptible change from the power through which it is effected."[11] This is what makes history in general more than mere chronicle.

> Since history in general is a whole constructed (*zussamengesetzt ist*) out of endless individual parts, consequently, the student of history cannot begin by looking at those individual parts, and constructing

---

[8]*Kurze Einleitung*, § 67.

[9]*Kurze Einleitung*, §§ 67, 69.

[10]*Kurze Einleitung*, § 46.

[11]*Kurze Einleitung*, § 218.

> from there the whole. On the contrary, he must rather start by seeking to procure as true an image of the whole as is possible, in order later to rectify and to elaborate on the individual features within it.[12]

Historical construction is then for Drey the basic requirement of his organic interpretation of history. This construction is organic because it seeks to find the organic unity of the multiple individual events of history through an idea or an arrangement of ideas. This organic construction is idealistic because it seeks to identify the manifestations of ideas at work in history and the multiple influences at work in the historical unfolding of those ideas, which have their ultimate source in the *Urwissen* of God.

The task of historical construction, when pursued in the province of theology, was coupled for Drey with a scientific construction. "The concept--at first derived out of historical tradition and also revelation--is brought back to an idea, that is something immediately certain by virtue of an intuition of reason: then is the construction philosophical, properly scientific; and the knowledge and the certainty there are of the same kind."[13] Thus construction within theology can be attempted in two different ways: "in the merely historical through reflection, or in the scientific through construction out of ideas."[14]

---

[12]*Kurze Einleitung*, § 214.

[13]*Kurze Einleitung*, § 46. Drey's distinction between historical and scientific construction is treated again in Chapter III. For further analysis, see Fehr, *The Dogmatics of Drey*, 150-161.

[14]*Kurze Einleitung*, § 56; The former historical approach is the approach of theological supernaturalism, because it is "not a knowledge of the things believed before, but rather merely a knowledge of and concerning faith." The latter, scientific approach is described as theological rationalism because it seeks "a knowledge of that which is believed, hoping to transform faith into knowledge." Drey delineates two additional approaches. The mystical approach bypasses historical faith as dead and inexplicable and pursues an immediate vision in inner experience. Naturalism on the other hand "excludes all positive organization and all cooperation of God in the

Schleiermacher's approach to history has a basic similarity with Drey's (and Schelling's): history requires an organic construction that combines empirical and speculative perspectives.[15] This contention is advanced in Schleiermacher's earliest lectures on history in 1806:

> History is everything which science includes in the perceived time. Therefore the organization of nature as a process is natural history; the organization of spirit as a process is moral history; the identity of both as a process is world history. Its essence is the absorption of time in the idea. Therefore in it all opposition between the empirical and the speculative is cancelled [*aufgehoben*], and the full appeasement overall [is given] only in the historical view.[16]

For Schleiermacher the presentation of history includes two basic elements, spiritual powers and principles, and empirical materials.[17]

---

generation of religion . . ." (§ 46). One could argue that Drey attempts in his own model of history to combine the legitimate aspects of at least the first two approaches if not of all four approaches. For further analysis of supernaturalism and rationalism, see Chapter V.

[15]The task at this point is to clarify the similarities between Schleiermacher and Drey on historical construction. Their similarities will be placed, as we proceed, in relation to fundamental differences about how the empirical and speculative are combined in their assessments of the scientific nature of history and theology. These differences can be traced back to the differences between Schelling and Schleiermacher, as reflected in his review of Schelling's *Vorlesungen über die Methode* in the *Jenaische Litteraturzeitung* 1 (April 21, 1804): 137-151, reprinted in *Aus Schleiermachers Leben in Briefen*, ed. L. Jonas and W. Dilthey (Berlin: George Reimer, 1863), 4: 579-593. Two years after this review, Schleiermacher lectures on Church history and offers his methodological comments on historiography, undoubtedly mindful of Schelling's position.

[16]*Geschichte der christlichen Kirche*, 624.

[17]See Hanna Jursch, *Schleiermacher als Kirchenhistoriker* (Jena: Verlag der Frommannschen Buchhandlung, 1933), 60; for background, see Wilhelm Pauck, "Schleiermacher's Conception of History and Church History," in *Schleiermacher as Contemporary* ed., R. W. Funk, *Journal for Theology and*

As attested by his lectures on Church history, he, like Schelling, combined these elements through "the higher view" offered by "historical construction":

> Historiography must have entirely the character of art, indeed the scientific presentation has secured this only insofar as it approaches the historical form. In chronicle and in pragmatic history this character can only be something artificial, external, and stuck on. How can one therefore be afraid . . . that in the higher treatment history lacks the living fullness and does not present the movement of the individuals? This appears to be possible only if one considers the higher view (*die höhere Ansicht*) as a later one that stole its way in coming from philosophy and that brings in a foreign purpose and can thus ruin the essence. This is not the case, rather the higher view is--also considered in historical perspective--the original. For history stems from epic poetry and from mythology, and these arise obviously out of the identity of manifestation and idea.[18]

Church, vol. 7 (New York: Herder & Herder, 1970), 41-56; and Kurt Nowak, "Theorie der Geschichte. Schleiermachers Abhandlung "Über den Geschichtsunterricht" von 1793," in *Schleiermacher und die wissenschaftliche Kultur des Christentums*, eds. G. Meckenstock and J. Ringleben (Berlin: Walter de Gruyter, 1991), 419-439.

[18]*Geschichte der christilichen Kirche*, 624. His reference to pragmatic history deserves comment. Pragmatic history is for him the "explanation of the present out of the past, actually in a psychological manner." He judged it inadequate because it fails to present the genuine unity of history and it offers a false necessity in the movement from individual events in the past to individual events in the present (4-5, 11, 624). His judgment is not easily reconcilable with Drey's judgment that historical construction employing an organic model of history yields the pragmatism of history. See *Kurze Einleitung*, § 218. Drey implies that historical construction is pragmatic because it recognizes the teleological and moral direction of historical processes. Schleiermacher would not disagree with this. Schleiermacher's rejection of "pragmatic history" seems close to Schellling's verdict: pragmatic history is subjectivistic because it seeks an accidental and unharmonious unity of history at the level of empirical facts for the sake of the historian's didactic or political purposes. This is contrary to the objective movement of history

For Schleiermacher the historical endeavor rests on the belief that "the whole appears only in individuals." The form of the whole's essence as the idea changes back and forth between "the spreading of the inner spirit in the whole mass and the strong coming forward of the same [spirit] in individuals, which again cannot be shown other than in individual parts."[19] The service of history is performed in this art: "to make the individuals immortal, both raising them forth, and letting them be buried in the mass."[20] Historians must learn from the work of epic poetry and mythology, for in their work we find the original attempts to discern "in the events the unity of idea and manifestation in a process of becoming (*als werdendes*)," even though Church history ultimately "depends most loosely on that mythical origin."[21]

Hence, Schleiermacher maintains that Church history must attempt to find through a historical view the "unity between speculation and empiricism."[22] This unity is an organic unity because each of "the individual organic parts of the ethical construc-

---

discerned through historical construction. Drey could have agreed, but does not explicitly. See F. W. J. Schelling, *On University Studies*, 104-105. On Drey and pragmatic history, see Geiselmann, *Lebendiger Glaube*, 128, 132.

[19]*Geschichte der christlichen Kirche*, 625.

[20]*Geschichte der christlichen Kirche*, 625.

[21]*Geschichte der christlichen Kirche*, 625. This attempt to find the unity of idea and manifestation is only a poetic inclination, and more clearly tends toward philosophy. Together philosophy and poesis form a circle in their endeavor to construct history. Let us recall that for Schelling, history is known from a "higher viewpoint" in the sciences of philosophy and theology, whereas the discipline of history is an art, not a science, which allows the ideas to be disclosed in the narrating of real events. Schleiermacher rejects Schelling's deductive approach to philosophy and theology proceeding from the *Urwissen* of God and seeks to combine the empirical and speculative in a manner that realizes the critical and poetic character of historical judgments. Cf. Schelling's *On University Studies*, 82-110, and Schleiermacher's review, *Aus Schleiermachers Leben in Briefen*, 587.

[22]*Geschichte der christlichen Kirche*, 625, 3rd lecture.

tion" must be seen as they behave in relation to one another as a system of life action.[23]

Schleiermacher addressed these issues again in his lectures on Church history during the 1821-1822 winter semester, fifteen years after his initial lectures. Here he draws a distinction, not between an empirical and a speculative view of history, but between presenting (*darstellenden*) and receiving (*aufnehmenden*) or comprehending approaches (*auffassenden*). Chronicle is judged here as merely "presenting" an aggregate of individual moments--external, atomistic elements sequentially isolated. As material for history it is fine, but "it has no other worth than this."[24]

One cannot receive from the external sequence of events, Schleiermacher insists, the guidance one needs to construe the results.

> If I should construe the results out of the external facts, I ask myself, which are the persons who have so acted? That is an internal matter; and if this is not given to me, I first must make for myself out of the presented series of moments an image of the persons, and only then can I construe the historical success. Something essential is lacking if we have only the external historical process.[25]

---

[23]*Geschichte der christlichen Kirche*, 625. This is the only place I have found where Schleiermacher speaks about this organic unity of history as an "ethischen Construction." Still, Hanna Jursch corroborates my judgment: "The organic treatment which seeks to grasp the idea and [the empirical] manifestation in its identity is the only method that corresponds to Schleiermacher's concept of history." *Schleiermacher als Kirchenhistoriker*, 76-77. Moreover, Hermann Süskind confirms my contention that Schleiermacher agrees to a certain degree with Schelling on the relationship of the empirical and the speculative in historical construction, *Der Einfluß Schellings auf die Entwicklung von Schleiermachers System* (Tübingen, 1909), 188, 190.

[24]*Geschichte der christlichen Kirche*, 3.

[25]*Geschichte der christlichen Kirche*, 4.

Schleiermacher argues that we are not left with the merely external development of history in order to answer "How has B developed out of A?" Moreover, we do not simply posit a causal connection which rests in persons, nor affirm instinct, natural necessity, or accident as the inner something which moves them in a certain direction as a group. Historical inquiry properly understood aims at the inner something, but not as it is for itself, but "as it develops in time." This is an "organic treatment of history."[26] Within such a treatment, Schleiermacher asks, "what is the relationship between the presenting and the receiving?" One's judgments about history influence how one sees the events interrelated. Different faiths may have different perspectives. "Therefore in the organic treatment of history, it [the way one construes history] depends especially upon the identity of the fundamental beliefs, and this is especially so in Church history."[27]

Thus, Schleiermacher claims that the presenting approach appreciates the distinctiveness of the individuals for the sake of the latter historical intuition in the comprehending approach. Both must be united in practice. In order to make any such historical judgments it must not be denied that "the historical spirit [is] a product of the age; one must first have been involved in the general life and have lived through an era."[28]

In their organic presentation of history, Schleiermacher and Drey strive for an intuition of the whole in relation to the individual parts.[29] Schleiermacher treats this oneness or whole in

---

[26]*Geschichte der christlichen Kirche*, 5.

[27]*Geschichte der christlichen Kirche*, 5-6. When considering the historical complex of the Christian churches, Schleiermacher is in need of "a twofold historical treatment: 1) one separating individuals, [and] 2) the integration of all individuals. We cannot part from either of these two sides, for the latter is the living intuition (*die lebendige Anschauung*), and through the first arises the clarity and the liveliness and due respect for the individuals" (14). Cf. *Brief Outline*, §§ 69-79.

[28]*Geschichte der christlichen Kirche*, 14.

[29]*Geschichte der christlichen Kirche*, 15. *Kurze Einleitung*, §§ 214, 224.

his earlier work as the idea and essence, and in his later work in terms of the specific essence of Christianity and the consciousness of the Christian Church (or in the case of the writings of individuals it is the individual consciousness in relation to the manifold moments of the person's life).[30] Drey speaks of the unity of the history of Christianity in the idea which is objectively in the Church and subjectively appropriated by individuals within the Church. In the case of each author, the attempt to hold together the organic unity of Church history with the changing and developing doctrinal formulations generates a key distinction between inner and outer aspects of the history of the Church.

Inner and Outer Dimensions of History

Schleiermacher's and Drey's organic model of history is the immediate context for their distinctive formulations of an inner and outer axis for doctrinal development. As we indicated in the previous chapter, an organic model discloses, on the one hand, that the seed provides the internal source of identity and continuity of organic life; and, on the other, that organic life stands in a tensive and productive relationship with external factors: sometimes nourished or threatened, at other times acting upon the organism's environment in supportive or unsupportive ways, all the while deriving its source of energy from within. Whether this organic model is used to illumine individual persons or communities, it provides a source of insight into the complex dynamic of inner and outer factors in the process of identity formation.

Schleiermacher and Drey formulate this inner and outer axis of development in their reflections on hermeneutics and historical theology. I wish to focus on two uses of an "inner" and "outer"

---

[30]Süskind contends that Schelling offers a one-sided "timeless intuition of an unmoving unity," while Schleiermacher attempts to include alongside of this intuition "the knowledge of (the concept's) changing essence." *Der Einfluß Schellings*, 190-192.

distinction that are operative in their works, both of which have a direct bearing on their theories of doctrinal development.[31] In the first usage, consciousness and language are related as inner and outer. As we shall discover, the discourse and praxis of individuals and communities outwardly presents or expresses inner consciousness, but inner consciousness expresses itself in terms of traditions of discourse and praxis. There is a dialectical relation between consciousness and language: communal discourse not only expresses, but also shapes and identifies communal consciousness. Communal discourse is judged normative when it adequately expresses ecclesial consciousness or the objective faith of the Church.

In the second usage, a specific community's discourse and praxis are inner in relation to outer cultural forces. Communal language and communal action are evaluated not only as to whether they are suitable outer presentations of inner faith consciousness of the Church, but also as to how they accord with the "outer" forces of the present state of philosophical and scientific discourse and socio-political action.

To reiterate: in the first instance, language and action are outer in relation to inner consciousness, and, in the second instance, communal discourse and praxis are inner in relation to modes of discourse and action outside of the designated communal discourse and action. The crucial point for our investigation is that a community's discourse, such as religious discourse, is outer in

---

[31]There are other uses of this distinction in their writings which sometimes have a direct connection and sometimes an indirect or questionable connection with the two uses we will identify. So, for example, in Schleiermacher's lectures on the life of Jesus, he distinguishes between the outer or external rule in a theocracy in contrast to the inner rule within the Christian community. Cf. Marlin Miller, *Der Übergang*, 114, 234. Drey distinguishes the inner coherence of revelation (as a system) which is indivisible from the outer manifestations of its development. Cf. Kustermann, *Die Apologetik*, 272-273, 303-304, 317 and passim. Tiefensee explores this inner and outer distinction is relation to Drey's use of an organic model; *Die religiöse Anlage* 39, 42-45, 57-60, 90.

relation to the community's consciousness (the first meaning) and inner in relation to outer foreign modes of discourse (the second meaning). If the subtleties of each claim are not recognized, distortions in interpretations can occur.[32]

These uses of inner and outer are found in Schleiermacher's reflections on hermeneutics and historical theology. The first meaning of inner and outer is formulated in his manuscripts on hermeneutics: the inner realm is consciousness or ideas which stand in a close relationship with linguistic expression or speech as the outer realm.[33] Language is the empirical reality, while the subjective formulation of ideas or "intuitions" is speculative.[34] Accordingly, hermeneutics is divided by Schleiermacher into a technical approach which attempts to recreate the subjective

---

[32]Some interpreters of Schleiermacher have failed, in my judgment, to render adequately one of these two claims. Wilhelm Dilthey and Hans Georg Gadamer overemphasized the psychological approach to interpretation at the expense of the grammatical approach. Heinz Kimmerle strives for a balanced treatment, but concludes that the grammatical and the objective wanes in Schleiermacher's later writings. Manfred Frank has offered a corrective in *Das individuelle Allgemeine. Textstrukturierung und Textinterpretation nach Schleiermacher* (Frankfurt am Main: Suhrkamp, 1985). Gadamer has more recently stated that "perhaps I overemphasized Schleiermacher's tendency toward psychological (technical) interpretation rather than grammatical-linguistic interpretation." (*Truth and Method*, 565). George Lindbeck, Ronald Thiemann, and Bruce D. Marshall emphasize the psychological and expressive character of Schleiermacher's approach to religious language and fail, in my estimation, to point out the subtleties of the inner/outer distinction and the weight given to the linguistic heritage of Christianity, especially the kingdom of God motif, in the *Glaubenslehre*, the *Sittenlehre*, and in *Das Leben Jesu*.

[33]In Kimmerle's terms, "thinking and speaking are to be distinguished as ideal and appearance." Schleiermacher, *Hermeneutics: The Handwritten Manuscripts*, ed. and intro. H. Kimmerle, trans. J. Duke and J. Forstman (Missoula, Montana: Scholars Press, 1977), 37.

[34]"[L]anguage, in its formation, is related to an intuition (*Anschauung*): the range of every word is determined by an intuition" (*Hermeneutics*, 71).

movement from ideas to expression and a grammatical approach which examines the objective formation of language over time.[35]

Grammatical interpretation is concerned with the objective formation of language over time and the common characteristics of discourse within a culture. This approach accords to language its own independent status as an object of study. It also shows the importance and power of linguistic traditions in Schleiermacher's hermeneutic theory. Thus, "[i]f every spoken statement is understood with the artist as the center, then everything that is given and available in the value of the language disappears, except insofar as it grasps the artist and determines his thinking."[36]

The importance of grammatical interpretation for Schleiermacher and its significance for his theology throughout his career must be more fully appreciated. It is most clearly evident in his sense of fidelity and obligation to the kingdom of God theme as it developed in earliest Christianity, as well as to the creedal heritage of the Protestant Church. He emphasizes these linguistic traditions, even as he recognizes the ability of Christian communities to employ new language in theology and doctrinal formulations. Thus he maintains that "Christianity has created language. From its very beginning it has been a powerful linguistic spirit, and it still is."[37]

"Technical interpretation attempts to identify what has moved the author to communicate."[38] This approach inquires into the

---

[35]The technical approach is needed because: "On the one hand, an author finds himself guided by the power of the subject matter. This is the objective side. On the other hand, the author is free. This is the subjective side" (*Hermeneutics*, 62).

[36]*Hermeneutics*, 49-50.

[37]*Hermeneutics*, 50.

[38]*Hermeneutics*, 147. Schleiermacher states that hermeneutics is a *Kunstlehre*, a technology, which suggests that the technical branch of hermeneutics is the dominant one. However, this designation can also support his contention that "interpretation is an art," which requires an oscillation between grammatical and technical interpretations. Cf. Paul

inner conscious life of the author in order to ascertain the author's individuality and "genius." What Schleiermacher described as the technical branch of hermeneutics he later calls a psychological approach, and in his academic address of 1829 he suggests that this psychological approach is associated with a divinatory method. "A divinatory method enables us rightly to reconstruct the creative act that begins with the generation of thoughts which captivates the author and to understand how the requirement of the moment could draw upon the living treasure of words in the author's mind in order to produce just this way of putting it and no other."[39]

Schleiermacher contends that an adequate interpretation requires an oscillation between the technical and the grammatical, between an intensive inquiry and an extensive one. What this means is that the interpreter must cultivate a talent for language, which corresponds with the extensive impact, and the talent for knowing persons, which corresponds with the intensive direction.[40] He insists however that "understanding takes place only in the coinherence of these two moments."[41] "It is necessary to move back

---

Ricoeur, "Schleiermacher's Hermeneutics," *The Monist* 60 (1970): 181-197.

[39]*Hermeneutics*, 192.

[40]"The grammatical and technical approaches require that their interpreters develop an extensive and intensive linguistic talent and an extensive and intensive knowledge of humans. One must be able to reconstruct discourse historically and technically, objectively and subjectively. "Historically objective means comprehending the behavior of discourse in the entirety of language and of knowledge enclosed therein as a product of language. Divinatory objective means anticipating how the discourse itself will become a stage of development for language. . . . Historically subjective means knowing how discourse exists as fact in the heart, divinatory subjective means suspecting how the thoughts which are contained therein will develop still further in and for the speaking person." *Hermeneutik*, *Sämmtliche Werke*, part 1, 7: 32.

[41]*Hermeneutics*, 98, cf. 68, 97-99, 190-191, 215.

and forth between the grammatical and psychological sides, and no rules can stipulate exactly how to do this."[42]

When interpreting individual classic texts, like Plato's dialogues, or the biblical writings of Paul, or the different gospels, the interpreter uses the technical approach to focus on the individual author, and the grammatical to examine the writer's linguistic environment. Thus, one examines how a language influences a thinker and how a thinker shapes and influences the usage of language.[43] Schleiermacher employs this oscillating method in his lectures on the life of Jesus. We find there an attempt to reconstruct the consciousness of Jesus through a technical method of divination, while simultaneously pursuing the grammatical approach by analyzing the kingdom of God in its many meanings in the Old Testament and in the gospels.

When Schleiermacher turned his attention to the development of the Christian church and doctrine, no individual consciousness could be isolated for a technical approach.[44] Consequently, historical theology seeks a description of the consciousness of the Church in relation to the Church's linguistic heritage (i.e., doctrines) and the Church's life (i.e., the life of common action).

---

[42]*Hermeneutics*, 100. Since "in order to complete the grammatical side of interpretation it would be necessary to have a complete knowledge of language," and "in order to complete the psychological side it would be necessary to have a complete knowledge of the person," neither of which is possible, the oscillation between the two approaches is recommended.

[43]Schleiermacher says in the *Brief Outline* that "the New Testament writings are especially difficult to interpret, both on account of their inner contents, and on account of their external relations" (§ 135). The inner contents are easily misunderstood because the individual writers communicate "particularly unique religious ideas" in a distinctive fashion. The external relations of circumstance are hard to determine because they are usually only reconstructed on the basis of the writings themselves.

[44]We will examine the theory of genius in greater detail in Chapter IV. See Jursch on the relationship between the individual and the group. See *Schleiermacher als Kirchenhistoriker*, 68.

Historical theology pursues this approach as it treats primitive Christianity in exegesis, the entire career of Christianity in church history, and the state of the Church in the present in dogmatics.

Schleiermacher contends that although one can legitimately divide Church history into the history of Christian doctrine and the history of Church life, "if we take the entire domain that has been given to us as the historical result of the new life, which through Christianity came into the human race, actually the one cannot be separated from the other."[45] This history of Christian doctrines and Christian life are united in their origins: "Christ is the beginning of a new period in world history."[46] Attention must be given to Christ in regard to "how this power has historically developed in the organism, namely the Christian Church, which it, that is, the power, has constructed out of itself."[47] On this basis, "[e]verything which we have mentioned heretofore, that is, Christian life and teaching, is outer reality; the Christian Spirit is inner reality, and our question is how has this [life and teaching] developed from the inner reality outward to historical expression?"[48] As we find in this passage, Schleiermacher is not always consistent in his use of inner and outer: although language (i.e., teachings) and life (i.e., life of activity) constitute the outer realm, it is not consciousness, individual or communal, that is the inner reality in this formula, rather it is the Christian Spirit.[49] In the strict sense this need not be viewed as a radical inconsistency,

---

[45]*Geschichte der christlichen Kirche*, 11. See also, *Brief Outline*, §§ 87, 90, 162, also note 105.

[46]*Geschichte der christlichen Kirche*, 15. Cf., *Brief Outline*, §§ 72, 78.

[47]*Geschichte der christlichen Kirche*, 15.

[48]*Geschichte der christlichen Kirche*, 15.

[49]On the nature of Christian "life" as constituted by the activity of the Church, see *Geschichte der christlichen Kirche*, 12-13. In the *Brief Outline*, § 90, Schleiermacher distinguished the history of doctrine from the history of the community (originally polity). This corresponds to the history of Christian life, which includes polity and worship.

for the Holy Spirit, the Spirit of Christ, the common Spirit works upon or within ecclesial consciousness.

It follows that "a spiritual power already meets with the outer reality and should penetrate it" in a historical production.[50] "The Spirit came in original and creative ways into the human race, and has united itself with it, however in such a way that from the beginning it was something foreign."[51] Through an intensive movement, the Christian Spirit penetrates and "takes up possession" (*Besitz genommen*) within the conscious life of the community. The Christian Spirit spreads itself extensively through the Christian community. Christian history must include both inner and outer dimensions together.[52]

Throughout the history of Christian life (action) and doctrine, Schleiermacher discerns a unity of consciousness over time, but a diversity of outer expressions. We read in the *Kurze Darstellung* that every historical mass is composed of "one indivisible being and doing in process of becoming" and "a compound of innumerable individual moments." Together these facts disclose "a single picture of the inner reality (*das Innere*)."[53] Thus he contends that "every fact has historical individuality only insofar as the two are posited as identical: the outer reality as the changing of what nevertheless maintains its identity, and the inner reality as the function of a force in motion."[54]

Schleiermacher maintains that this inner identity of Christianity throughout time constitutes "a particular mode of faith, i.e., a particular way of being conscious of God (*eine bestimmte Glaubensweise, d.h. eine bestimmte Gestaltung des Gottesbewußtseins*)."[55] This *Glaubensweise* continues in its identity

---

[50]*Geschichte der christlichen Kirche*, 16.

[51]*Geschichte der christlichen Kirche*, 16.

[52]*Geschichte der christlichen Kirche*, 16.

[53]*Brief Outline*, § 150.

[54]*Brief Outline*, § 151.

[55]*Brief Outline*, § 1.

throughout the history of the Church, even though there are different outer concrete presentations of this inner identity at different times throughout this history in accordance with the requirements of historical communities.

So on the basis of the first meaning of inner and outer, Schleiermacher views the *Glaubensweise* of the Christian Church as the inner conscious identity of the Church which is presented outwardly in discourse and praxis. These are the doctrines and ecclesial actions that constitute the linguistic and practical heritage of Christianity. However, Schleiermacher employs a second meaning of inner and outer when he claims that ecclesial discourse and praxis, which express the "inner" identity of the ecclesial community, also stand in a tensive and productive relationship with "outer" and "foreign" scientific, philosophical, and socio-political factors. This usage is suggested in the *Kurze Darstellung*: "The more any given historical career is occupied in the process of expansion so that the inner unity of its life appears more and more only in encounter with other forces, all the more do these forces, in turn, enter into the various individual situations which make it up."[56] Outer in this context does not mean language in relation to inner consciousness, but external intellectual discourse and socio-political praxis that influence Christian discourse and praxis.

The two different meanings of inner and outer provide the axis of doctrinal development in Schleiermacher's theology. In his statements on doctrinal development either set of meanings can be involved. The first meaning is indicated when he speaks of the "cultivation" of doctrine that is achieved through the clarification of pious self-consciousness.[57] Accordingly, he says that "[c]onceptions of doctrine are developed, on the one hand, through continual reflection upon Christian self-consciousness in its various aspects, and on the other hand, through the continual effort to fasten down

[56]*Brief Outline*, § 83.

[57]*Brief Outline*, § 166.

its expression precisely and with more general agreement."[58] Christian self-consciousness is inner and the linguistic expression is outer. An outer doctrinal expression is evaluated in light of whether it adequately clarifies ecclesial consciousness for the present time. This requires comparing it with a description of the present ecclesial consciousness. Equally important in this evaluation is a comparison of the doctrinal expression with previous linguistic expressions of that consciousness. Schleiermacher believes that adhering only to "the utterances of primitive Christianity . . . retards the development of Christianity,"[59] but he nonetheless maintains that new doctrinal formulations must cohere with the web of beliefs disclosed by the Protestant creeds and the Bible, notably the biblical language of the kingdom of God as it reveals redemption through Jesus Christ and is mediated by the Church. Thus, it distorts Schleiermacher's view of Christian discourse to say that he is an "experiential-expressivist" (i.e., that doctrines for him only or primarily express and do not shape Christian consciousness) or to suggest that Schleiermacher's is a simplistic instrumental theory of language.[60] We find that for Schleiermacher there is a dialectical relationship between the inner consciousness of the Church and the linguistic heritage of the Scriptures, ecclesial creeds, and doctrinal formulations.

---

[58]*Brief Outline*, § 177.

[59]*Brief Outline*, § 181.

[60]George A. Lindbeck, *The Nature of Doctrine* (Philadelphia: The Westminster Press, 1984), 31-32. David Tracy does not speak explicitly of Schleiermacher but of the romantics who share with positivists an "instrumental theory of language," wherein "the real thing is purely prelinguistic: either my deep feelings or facts." *Plurality and Ambiguity* (San Francisco: Harper & Row, 1987), 48-49. For philosophical background on expressivism, see Charles Taylor, *Hegel* (Cambridge: Cambridge University Press, 1975), chapter 1; idem., *Sources of the Self: The Making of the Modern Identity* (Cambridge: Harvard University Press, 1989), 368-390, 427, 580, n. 26.; Gadamer, *Truth and Method*, 212-213, 217, 335-336, 467, 502-505.

According to the second usage of inner and outer, the "continual effort to fasten down the expression of [doctrine] precisely" requires not only comparing the "outer" language with the "inner" consciousness; it also requires attentiveness to "outer" and "foreign" modes of discourse as they bear on the "inner" discourse of ecclesial faith. Doctrinal developments are partially inspired or influenced by outer sources. "From without the cultivation of the Church's life [i.e., ecclesial praxis] is determined (*mitbestimmt*) above all by political circumstances and by the whole condition of society, whereas the development of doctrine is determined by the whole state of science and especially the prevailing philosophical views."[61] Philosophical and scientific advances are "foreign" elements which must be taken into consideration insofar as they have a bearing on the formulation of doctrine.[62]

Thus historical theology construes how the inner consciousness of the Church and the outer sphere of Christian discourse are interdependent, as well as how the inner sphere of Christian discourse and praxis is affected by outer influences and currents of life and thought. One needs to employ both meanings of inner and outer in order to grasp fully Schleiermacher's description of historical theology as that discipline which "ought above all to distinguish between what has resulted from the distinctive force of Christianity and what is founded partly in the make-up of the various organs thus set in motion and partly in the influence foreign to them, and then to try to gauge the advance and recession of each."[63]

Clearly the specific disciplines of historical theology--exegesis, Church history, and dogmatics--are concerned with different periods in the history of the Church, but all three branches of historical theology must determine the inner and outer influences upon the

---

[61]*Brief Outline*, § 167. This interpretation of inner and outer supports Tice's decision to translate "mitbestimmt" by adding "from without" to "determine".

[62]*Christian Faith*, § 21.; *Brief Outline*, § 177, n. 126.

[63]*Brief Outline*, § 160.

historical changes in Christian life and doctrine. Both sides of the dynamic relationship between inner and outer are necessary for doctrinal development; but either side of this axis of development is susceptible to problems and could be the source of misguided changes.[64] These problems will be treated in the next section.

In sum, Schleiermacher contends that the interpretation of doctrinal discourse and the promotion of development cannot proceed in a manner simply analogous to the technical branch of hermeneutics, as that mode of interpretation is presented in his occasional pieces on the subject. This would result in a overemphasis on the subjective and psychological elements in the developmental process. A more adequate presentation of Schleiermacher's work must explore the technical as the subjective side of hermeneutics in the area of theology, and the grammatical as the objective side. In so doing we find that Schleiermacher's organic vision of history yields hermeneutical and historical principles, which he consistently employs in his study of revelation and doctrine. First, he invariably treats the creedal and biblical language as it develops objectively within the Church and within dogmatic theology. Second, he seeks to show how the language of faith has its subjective source, its genesis, in the consciousness of Jesus and in the consciousness of the Church. And third Schleiermacher is always open to extraneous influences on doctrinal changes, but never uncritically.

Drey's work employs the pivotal distinction between inner and outer, with the same double meaning that pertains in Schleiermacher's theology. Drey did not include dogmatics under the umbrella of historical theology, as Schleiermacher did, but instead places it alongside of apologetics as scientific theology. The historical investigation of Christianity is divided into biblical exegesis and historical theology. Historical theology treats the entire post-biblical life of the Christian church in its development.

---

[64]*Brief Outline*, §§ 54, 177; also read: "Completely external circumstances of life cannot constitute the true basis for important decisions as to how doctrine is to be conceived" (§ 179, n. 128).

It is in his discussion of hermeneutics that Drey distinguishes between the objective character of language and the subjective influences on language.

> Language is equally indispensable for thinking and for expressing thoughts to one another. Consequently, each person can only form his thoughts in his language as it is, yet in relation to others he must denote it again in the same way. Thus the proper objective character of language is the most general law for the author in expressing his thoughts; it is the most general law for the interpreter in uncovering the same thoughts out of the words of the writing.[65]

The relationship between language and human thought is the relation between objective and subjective.

This distinction between objective and subjective provides the framework for Drey's three principles of hermeneutics: the grammatical, the historical, and the individual. The grammatical principle of interpretation is required because of the objectivity of language and its universality in forming the author. The similarities with Schleiermacher's grammatical branch of hermeneutics are clear.[66]

---

[65]*Kurze Einleitung*, § 156.

[66]*Kurze Einleitung*, §§ 160-161. Drey mentions Schleiermacher with respect to hermeneutics twice. (1) Even though Drey did not agree with his Protestant position that the canon remained open to additions and deletions (the task of higher criticism for Schleiermacher), he concurred that "it is more important to determine whether a piece of writing is canonical or not than to determine whether it is to be assigned to this or that author, in which case it could still be canonical no matter what decision is made." *Brief Outline*, § 100. Drey quotes from 1st edition, see Scholz ed., 47, n. 1, § 15. Cf., *Kurze Einleitung*, § 165, "canonicity is fully independent from the demonstrable authenticity of a moral religious book." (2) Drey also quotes Schleiermacher favorably in support of his conviction that exegesis requires a *Kunstlehre* or *Auslegungskunst* in order to acknowledge the authority of the text, for "whoever wants to possess the rules of interpretation only as an

The historical principle of interpretation is required because "[language] is not so objective and universal that it could not be subjected to and altered by the subjective power of the spirit and the specificity of independent will."[67] Language and humanity have histories which serve one another and cannot be separated. Hence, when interpreting a text written by an individual, one must understand how the author speaks out of the spirit of his epoch, his nation, and his audience.[68]

Drey does not wish to suggest that a given text can be reduced to the general and objective power of language, nor that the author is merely a product of his or her age. This is why hermeneutics requires an "individual principle" that will enable one to understand the writings correctly as they came from an individual.[69] This mode of interpretation is the most determinate and the highest and it is equivalent to Schleiermacher's technical branch of hermeneutics.

In this treatment of objective and subjective dimensions of hermeneutics, Drey suggests, but does not expressly state, the distinction between inner and outer as a distinction between inner consciousness or ideas and outer language as the empirical expression of the ideal or inner reality. We shall find this developed in his treatment of historical theology.

One noteworthy difference between Drey's and Schleiermacher's formulation of hermeneutics is that Drey insists that biblical hermeneutics requires a special recognition that this book is "a divine revelation . . . , a word of God."[70] Schleiermacher's *Brief*

---

aggregate of observations, must be left with a strange unclear feeling." *Kurze Einleitung*, §. 170, quote taken from 1st edition of *Kurze Darstellung*, see Scholz ed., 53, n. 2, § 27.

[67]*Kurze Einleitung*, § 157.

[68]Although Schleiermacher does not speak of a historical branch of hermeneutics in his hermeneutic manuscripts, in the *Kurze Darstellung* he clearly suggests a historical task as a facet of the hermeneutical enterprise.

[69]*Kurze Einleitung*, § 158.

[70]*Kurze Einleitung*, § 159.

Outline did not speak of "revelation" requiring a special hermeneutic principle, rather he states that "the special hermeneutics of the New Testament can consist only of more precise determinations of the general rules of hermeneutics, made however with reference to the particular situation of the canon."[71] This does not deny revelation, nor does it reject the specific treatment required by revelation because of its subject matter. Drey argues, on the other hand, that divine revelation is found "not in relation to the (subjective) meaning of the author, by which he has comprehended and presented a given word of God." In the case of subjective meaning, theologians utilize the three principles of hermeneutics in order to understand words and sentences which make up a work. However, "the (objective) significance of the revealed ideas" requires a further principle of interpretation:

> [I]deas are given through revelation--admittedly, they are given in a certain temporal form, and this must at first be understood in accordance therewith. But, their whole significance, their whole power to awaken religious life, and their determination to do that, cannot be limited to that special form, nor to the organ of one human person. Each revelation is ambiguous in regard to its determination and kind.[72]

In comparison with Schleiermacher's position, what is distinctive about this formulation by Drey is his insistence on the objective character of revelation as it is found in the whole of the Bible. This should neither be underestimated, nor unfairly exploited. This characteristic is important for Drey because it provides the "objective" pole for his theology of revelation and his position on the nature of dogmatic propositions, which he believed crucial for Catholic theology. Yet it would be wrong to argue that Schleiermacher denies that revelation has an objective status, even though he does not speak explicitly about "objective revealed ideas."

---

[71]*Brief Outline*, § 137.

[72]*Kurze Einleitung*, § 159.

The idea of the kingdom of God and the evangelical confessional documents are valid and thus objective for Schleiermacher insofar as they clearly presented the Christian faith of the past and the present. This raises questions about the nature of revelation and the criteria for doctrinal development and reform, which will concern us in the next chapter.

For Drey divine revelation of the Bible cannot be fully understood with the general principles of hermeneutics; it must be complemented with a spiritual interpretation.

> [A]bove the letter of the Bible hovers its spirit, that spirit which has touched the heart of the authors in the hour of religious elevation, that allowed them to look into the inner realm of the holy, and that inclined them to announce what had been manifested to them. This spirit has formed the letters of their words, yet it has not entered into the letter, nor been fettered to it. For this reason the meaning of the word might very well be found through the learned art (of hermeneutics), but the composing spirit cannot be driven forth from the letter. That means there is a higher understanding of the Bible, stemming not from the sensible, but rather from the spiritual, and this is only mediated through the same spirit in the heart, which originally moved the author in the writing process. Without this spirit only the shell will be understood, but not the heart of its meaning.[73]

Drey conceived of historical theology as that which dealt specifically with the post-biblical history of Christianity. He believed the Catholic view of historical theology recognizes "the knowledge of the further development of Christianity as equally important and necessary as its original history."[74] It was within this branch of the theological encyclopedia devoted to the continuance (*Fordauer*) and development (*Entwicklung*) of Christianity that Drey

---

[73]*Kurze Einleitung*, § 173.

[74]*Kurze Einleitung*, § 174. This judgment of Protestants fails to account for the positions articulated by theologians like Schleiermacher and F. C. Baur, among others during this period.

introduced the distinction between the inner history and the outer history of Christianity. By way of contrast, Schleiermacher spoke of inner and outer dimensions in the history of Christianity, but not of inner history and outer history.

The entire history of Christianity requires acknowledging a "higher concept of history as the striving and weaving of a sole principle, of one Spirit which bursts forth among the spirits of the time in order to create its own [i.e., time], which by its own force attracts everything into its circle, forming that which can be formed after itself [i.e., the Spirit], destroying that which resists it."[75] However, it must also be recognized that "each historical interpretation and presentation of the manifestations of Christianity out of another principle than out of the one indicated contradicts Christianity, is unchristian and untheological."[76] Thus, Christianity is in the world, and its development in marked by a "history of conflict," because "this history, although in its principle is purely Christian, in its manifestations is set together out of two elements."[77] Herein lies the basis for Drey's distinction between inner history and outer history: the inner spirit of Christianity freely develops and manifests itself externally in the world.[78]

The inner history of Christianity examines the history of Christian doctrines and the actions of the Church and also traces and evaluates the influences which have had an effect on the development of ecclesial doctrines and praxis. This inner history presents the "embodiment" or "essence" (*Inbegriff*) in doctrine and praxis as the most perfect manifestation of "its inner reality" (*sein Inneres*) in history. But it also traces the various worldly influences on doctrines and praxis. It follows that within Drey's inner history of Christianity both meanings of inner and outer, as we discovered and described them, are operative: doctrine and praxis are the

---

[75]*Kurze Einleitung*, § 175.

[76]*Kurze Einleitung*, § 175.

[77]*Kurze Einleitung*, § 176.

[78]*Kurze Einleitung*, § 177.

outer objective presentations of the inner reality; doctrines and praxis as the objective presentations of Christianity are the inner reality that is in a dynamic relation with outer cultural influences.

The outer history includes the destiny of Christianity in the world; its introduction, expansion, and preservation.[79] Christianity struggles with the spirit of the world as it seeks to influence the world. The essence of outer history concerns phenomena that have objective reality in their own right, but "in this outer history the spirit of Christianity must show itself as it does in the inner."[80] However, outer history depicts Christianity actively struggling with and confronting the world as well as resisting the spirit of the world and suffering as a consequence. In all of this, the history of Christianity must answer the question: "What has Christianity experienced in the world as such and what has it effected?"[81]

Inner history is the focal point for charting doctrinal development. The inner history of Christianity concerns "the spirit of Christianity, [whose] basis is its ideas as a phenomenon of the world, [and which] accordingly articulates itself immediately in the constant development, assimilation, and uniting of these ideas to a whole, which is treated as the common good of the Christian world,

---

[79]*Kurze Einleitung*, § 180.

[80]*Kurze Einleitung*, § 177.

[81]*Kurze Einleitung*, § 178. The outer history of Christianity is a part of world history, but religious and Christian principles are never adequately presented by a purely profane presentation of world or universal history. Outer history has three goals: (1) to examine "the conditions of the world in general and of individual peoples in particular in the time immediately before the introduction of Christianity (§ 181); (2) to treat "the powers and means through which Christianity forced its way in, has spread and maintained itself" (§ 182); (3) to clarify "the opposition which Christianity has faced, its causes and effects, how it [i.e., Christianity] withstands it, by what means it has overcome it" (§ 183). Outer history includes the history of persecution, martyrs, and apologetics; it also covers the effects of Christianity upon the world in human affairs, such as in art, science, and civil affairs.

as the common doctrine of Christians."[82] Hence, the history of doctrines serves as the first main part of the inner history of Christianity. This inner history of the Church includes two parts: doctrine ("in itself something abstract") and morals ("as the effect of doctrines") insofar as they both are present in the Church. The practical and the theoretical are intrinsically connected and must be interrelated when treating historical changes in discourse and praxis. However, there can be use for distinct inquiries into the history of doctrine and the history of ethics.[83]

For Drey, "the history of Christian doctrine must be treated as the continuous, unbroken solicitation of Christian ideas on the human spirit," which can be identified as "the essence of Christianity."[84] But besides the element of conformity of the development of ideas within Christianity, there are external influences and stimuli at work. Consequently, besides determining the unbroken thread of the idea or essence, the second main task of the inner history of Christianity is "to trace those influences and to show which part they have had on the respective formation and development."[85] While the Bible presents doctrines that can be identified as the inner idea and essence of Christianity, alternately the *study of the Bible* has been an external influence on the development of doctrine. In addition, philosophical and scientific ideas are generally active as external incentives to this development.

---

[82]*Kurze Einleitung*, § 189.

[83]Drey uses the distinction again. "The life of the Church has . . . two sides, an inner and an outer; the latter is conditioned through the first, therefore it has its religious and Christian character from it; furthermore, morals (*Sitte*) must be treated as the product of other maxims. The inner history of Christianity, while it turns from its doctrines to its life, thus has to explore and present the development and formation of Christian cult and Christian ethics" (§ 195).

[84]*Kurze Einleitung*, § 190.

[85]*Kurze Einleitung*, § 191.

Likewise, political factors can influence the history of Christianity.[86]

The development and formation of Christian doctrines, Drey concludes, takes place "through the inner action of the Christian principle under the stimuli of outer influences"--i.e., various, different "ways of thinking."[87] Christian morality as a way of life is influenced by modes of action outside of the Christian community. Hence, "just as Christian doctrines are modified according to the generally predominant forms of presentation in different times, so also [moral considerations] are modified according to predominant practical maxims and external relationships to the human society in different times."[88]

In the same year that the *Kurze Einleitung* appeared, Drey published a four-part essay, "Vom Geist und Wesen des Katholizismus." Here he sought to articulate the relationship between primitive Christianity and Catholicism and toward this end he employed the inner and outer distinction.

> Christianity as a positive divine religion is a temporal manifestation, a fact. As such it has a time of origin, a time of existence, and a form in which it was given as a divine revelation. However, no fact of any kind is momentary, that is, none dies out and disappears in the same moment as it arises. Rather, every fact intervenes in the sequence and combination of all other facts. It expands and slows

---

[86]*Kurze Einleitung*, § 192.

[87]*Kurze Einleitung*, § 196, cf. §§ 190-191. In "Revision des gegenwärtigen Zustandes der Theologie," Drey argues that there is a need in theology for a balance between an internal mystical source of theological development and a dialectical or philosophical source. He detects this balance in the early Middle Ages: "arising out of the impulse of the living religious intuition, [theology] had to be religious and Christian according to its inner essence; however as a striving to unfold the inner religious world also to the external, to given form to it as a concept and a word, it [i.e., theology] had to become dialectics" (88). A decadent Scholasticism and a misguided Reformation lost this balance and their contact with the living tradition.

[88]*Kurze Einleitung*, § 196.

> or accelerates, or changes its combined effect in what may be narrower or wider circles, and thereby arrives at its own history.[89]

Catholicism is the continuation of this primitive Christianity in an uninterrupted, objective, pure, and consistent manner. While Drey affirms the spiritual unity and continuity throughout the time of the Catholic Church, he also contends that change is required. Consequently, the Church should consider "how it has formed this essential nature according to the spirit and needs of the times, places, and human persons, and how it might form itself further; it [the Church] considers this as something non-essential, but not exactly as something accidental."[90] Drey makes the same point when he states that just as the Church "delivers the same word of Christ but at different times and among different human persons with different wording and with different emphases, so too it forms itself outwardly differently from age to age, but always in accordance with the needs of the people and with what their goals require, and with the spirit of the times."[91]

In keeping with their beliefs about the nature of the kingdom, its relationship to the world, and its organic unfolding in history, Schleiermacher and Drey both affirm that doctrinal changes occur through a complex interaction between inner and outer factors. Christian identity and continuity are based on the internal unity of faith. Doctrines authoritatively express the inner identity of Christianity. Yet, these doctrines must be formulated so as to be consistent with the current state of scientific and philosophical dis-

---

[89]"Vom Geist und Wesen," 195.

[90]"Vom Geist und Wesen," 230-231. For something to be contingent, but not accidental, is important for Drey. He argues that aspects of Catholicism are (relatively) necessary and contingent, not accidental and unnecessary. This may be why he spoke of the pragmatic character of history: past facts are viewed as the necessary causes of present conditions. This manner of argument is foreign to Schleiermacher for theological and historiographical reasons.

[91]"Vom Geist und Wesen," 231.

course. Outer or foreign modes of intellectual discourse are important for both theologians, but they are neither the sole nor the primary source or criterion for evaluating doctrinal discourse.

Besides these important similarities, there are basic differences between these two figures on the nature and interrelationship between inner and outer elements in the process of doctrinal development. Inner and outer *history* is Drey's vocabulary, but it is easily related to Schleiermacher's second usage of the distinction. It is actually within inner history that Drey speaks of the tensive and productive relationships between inner history and outer history as they bear upon issues of doctrinal development. Outer history remains concerned with the narrative of the struggle between the Church and the world and the ways in which the Church has influenced the world in art, science, and in social relations.

We have also noticed that Drey emphasizes the objectivity of language and revelation more than Schleiermacher does. On this basis some might conclude that Schleiermacher's view of revelation is subjectivistic and ultimately relativistic, and is therefore unable to account for the truth status of doctrines, whereas Drey's view of revelation, girded by his objective idealism, can. This contrast will concern us as we examine their visions of theology and the specific criteria they use to evaluate doctrinal formulations, but at this juncture such a comparative judgment fails to do justice to the strong similarities in their understandings of the inner and outer dynamic of history and their comparable commitment to determine and defend the veracity of the essence of Christianity.

Fixed and Moving Elements: Orthodoxy, Heterodoxy, and Hyperorthodoxy

Schleiermacher's and Drey's analyses of heresy and orthodoxy build on the various claims we have examined thus far. As we have seen, their interpretations of history emphasize the centrality of the Church as the manifestation of the kingdom of God in the world. For both thinkers the Church is opposed to the world insofar as it does not advance the kingdom and yet open to the world as God's good creation and as the arena for the unfolding of the kingdom. They both use organic metaphors when describing the Church-world relationship, specifically when it comes to considering Church doctrine and practice in relation to broader cultural patterns of thought and behavior. This results in presenting the relationship between the Church and the world as a complex one: ambiguous, tensive, and productive. They remain open to inner and outer sources of change, while insisting on ecclesial identity and continuity. Collectively these claims provide the framework for their analysis of orthodoxy, heterodoxy, and hyperorthodoxy.

For Drey and Schleiermacher there is something abiding about Christianity that does not change essentially over the course of history; at the same time, Christianity must necessarily change in some way in order to fulfill its own historical destiny. They acknowledge immutable and mutable components of Christianity, essential facets and those not essential, fixed and moving elements.[92] Drey is clearly mindful of and influenced by the distinctions Schleiermacher makes between essential and non-essential and fixed and moving. However, it is within this context that Drey distinguishes himself from Schleiermacher's position.

There are certain abiding elements in Christianity that both Drey and Schleiermacher acknowledge. Corresponding to the first usage of the inner and outer distinction, both argue that there is a constant unity of ecclesial consciousness that is determined by the content of the Christian faith throughout the history of the Church.

---

[92]Their manner of describing doctrinal development--as a change of form, but not of substance--has been criticized for not adequately taking into account the inseparable link between language and experience, historical location and the subject matter of belief. See Elizabeth Schüssler Fiorenza, "To Reject or to Choose?," *Feminist Interpretation of the Bible*, ed. L. M. Russell (Philadelphia: Fortress Press, 1985), 131; Francis Schüssler Fiorenza, *Foundational Theology*, 276-284; John Clayton, "Was ist falsch über Korrelationstheorie?", *Neue Zeitschrift für Systematische Theologie* 16 (1974): 93-111.

Ecclesial consciousness remains the same; the articulation of this consciousness may be more or less adequately expressed and this consciousness should be articulated differently at different times and places. Schleiermacher associates this unity of ecclesial consciousness with a *Glaubensweise*, while Drey speaks of the *lebendige Überlieferung*.[93] They also speak of this abiding faith consciousness in terms of the universal and constant essence of Christianity.[94] Thus, while this essence is unchanging because it corresponds with the eternal decrees of God for salvation, it is formulated differently throughout the Church's history.

In accordance with the second usage of the inner and outer distinction, both theologians recognized certain forms of Christian discourse and practice which remain stable. These stable elements interact with outer cultural influences. In doctrinal matters, these linguistic traditions should not be ignored. The biblical language, especially the language of the kingdom, and the confessional statements, provide a web of beliefs in their theological writings.

In addition to the biblical and creedal traditions, both saw certain enduring elements in the Church which correspond with the prophetic, priestly, and kingly aspects of the kingdom of God as essential for the lasting salvific essence of Christian identity.[95] For Schleiermacher the prophetic dimension resides in the Holy Scripture, and the ministry of the Word of God; the community's priesthood maintains baptism and the Lord's supper; and the kingly practice upholds the power of the keys, understood as the legislative and administrative power in the Church.[96] Drey agrees with Schleiermacher's position that these were "essential and invariable features of the Church." However, he disagrees about the precise nature of these elements: the Word of God requires the teaching

---

[93]See the next chapter for more on these terms.

[94]Drey also speaks of the idea of Christianity as unchanging.

[95]*Christian Faith*, § 127, p. 590; *Apologetik*, 3:97-105.

[96]*Christian Faith*, §§ 127-147. In *Brief Outline*, § 47, Schleiermacher discusses the canon and the sacrament as part of the essential, unchanging character of Christianity.

office of the Church; the list of authentic sacraments extends beyond baptism and the eucharist; and the ministry of the keys justifies the hierarchical character of the Church.

The changing elements of Christianity can likewise be viewed on the basis of both senses of inner and outer. In the first sense, ecclesial consciousness determined by the content of Christian faith --Schleiermacher's *Glaubensweise* and Drey's *lebendige Überlieferung* --is understood differently by different individuals and groups at different times and in different places and thus new linguistic formulations are needed. The faith consciousness does not change, otherwise it would no longer be considered genuinely Christian. However, further reflection upon the consciousness of the Church can warrant doctrinal development.

In accordance with their second meaning of outer as outer discourse and praxis, changes and movements within Christianity are inspired by changing schools of thought, new insights in the sciences, different philosophies as well as regional and political conditions. Variable elements are at a more basic level indicative of the power of the world upon the Church. The Church is open to the world and it can be nourished by cultural products from the world, even though these products must constantly be tested, because the Church struggles with the world, and the world stands to the Church as flesh to spirit.[97] The conditions of time, space, and sin influence language and thought, and for Christianity they influence how doctrines are understood and expressed. On the basis of their openness to outer cultural influences, Schleiermacher and

---

[97]*Christian Faith*, § 153. On this basis Schleiermacher distinguishes the invisible Church as "the totality of the effects of the Spirit as a connected whole; but those effects, as connected with those lingering influences of the collective life of universal sinfulness which are never absent from any life that has been taken possession by the divine Spirit, constitute the visible Church" (§ 148, p. 677). Consequently, "error is possible in the visible Church and therefore in some respects actual . . . everywhere, alike in the formation of religious ideas and in the religious formation of purposes, and possible on every point" (§ 153, p. 687). Cf. *Kurze Einleitung*, §§ 176-178.

Drey are rightly credited with introducing a mediating theological method: contemporary cultural interpretations of human experience or consciousness become an explicit, but not unchecked, source for doctrinal development.

There are fixed and moving elements in the living organism of the Church, which has the Holy Spirit as its principle of life. Fixed and moving elements are indicative of both the antithesis of the Church to the world and its openness to the world for the sake of nourishment, mutual transformation, and ultimate fulfillment. The dynamic relationship between fixed and moving elements stands at the center of their respective discussions of orthodoxy, heterodoxy, and hyperorthodoxy.

Schleiermacher envisioned a constructive tension between orthodoxy and heterodoxy. Both positions have their merits and both are susceptible to problems. In the first edition of the *Kurze Darstellung*, he spoke of orthodoxy in terms of the existing and fixed elements of doctrine, whereas heterodoxy was open to the moving elements and to new presentations of the essence of Christianity.[98] This basic distinction between orthodoxy and heterodoxy was maintained in the second edition. However, Schleiermacher no longer speaks of the "existing" and "fixed" in orthodoxy. Instead, orthodoxy entails "holding fast to what is already generally acknowledged, along with any inferences which may naturally follow."[99] What are fixed or generally acknowledged are the various modes of discourse which present the Christian ecclesial consciousness, be they canonical Scriptures, ecclesial confessional statements, or theological positions.[100] However, what is generally acknowledged or fixed is always open to reevaluation. Although we will need to examine in more detail the normative status of these diverse types of discourse in the following chapters, it is possible now to grasp that for Schleiermacher it is not only Christian

---

[98]*Brief Outline*, § 203, n. 152.

[99]*Brief Outline*, § 203.

[100]See *Christian Faith*, §§ 15, 19, 27, 154.

consciousness (the first meaning of inner) that is fixed, but also certain modes of religious discourse and practice (the second meaning of inner).

Heterodoxy for Schleiermacher consists in "every element construed in the inclination to keep the conception of doctrine mobile and to make room for still other modes of apprehension."[101] In the *Glaubenslehre* he observes that "no definition of doctrine even when arrived at with the most perfect community of feeling can be regarded as irreformable and valid for all time."[102] Hence, in the grand pedagogical scheme of things, heterodoxy serves a useful purpose. Insofar as reflection on the inner ecclesial consciousness can provide new insight, outer language must be reformable. Moreover, inner Christian discourse and action must be stable and yet mobile in relation to outer cultural currents. Since any manifestation of the Church could be shown to be impure or an imperfection, there is a need for the creative drive toward greater insight and a better understanding of the Church's faith. Schleiermacher offers a benign interpretation of heterodoxy, which is surely uncommon, but he does not deny its potentially harmful character, as we will see when he discusses false heterodoxy and false orthodoxy in terms of heresy.

Both orthodoxy and heterodoxy "are equally important, both in relation to the historical course of Christianity in general and in relation to every significant moment as such within its history."[103]

---

[101]*Brief Outline*, § 203.

[102]*Christian Faith*, § 154, p. 690.

[103]*Brief Outline*, § 204. John Thiel suggests that valid doctrine for Schleiermacher is an ideal state which is only approximated in the real situation of theology through this dialectical tension between the fixed and the moving elements. This contextualizes the important role of the theologian in the process of doctrinal development for Schleiermacher, but it is unable to explain his conviction that any doctrinal formulation is only valid if the Church accepts it and acknowledges it. Thiel rightly emphasizes the role of creativity and imagination in Schleiermacher's (and Drey's) theology, but I think it is preferable to present Schleiermacher's model of the

They are both important because there are fixed and moving elements within Christianity. The tension between orthodoxy and heterodoxy as a tension between fixed and moving elements is the context for the attempts by Church leaders and theologians to articulate the *Glaubensweise* of the Church for their own epoch. In this process church leaders and theologians can serve a "conservative function" within the Church. Theology aids in this "by showing in how many ways and up to what point the principle of the present period has developed itself on all sides and how the germs of improved formulations still to come relate to this principle."[104] At the same time, Schleiermacher believed it is incumbent upon creative individuals to "open the way for a future course."[105] Although the conservative and creative elements within the church are a further manifestation of the productive tension between orthodoxy and heterodoxy and between fixed and moving elements, it must be underscored that for Schleiermacher, any individual theologian's position remains just that--an individual's

---

theologian as an organic leader in service to the community, rather than as a creative individual standing in heroic proportion. Or to put in Thiel's own terms, the creative genius and the hero are recognized as such insofar as they tap into the mind and spirit of the community. Cf. Thiel, "Orthodoxy and Heterodoxy in Schleiermacher's Theological Encyclopedia: Doctrinal Development and Theological Creativity," *Heythrop Journal* 25 (1984): 142-157, esp. 147; "Theological Responsibility: Beyond the Classical Paradigm," *Theological Studies* 47 (1986): 573-598, esp. 582; *Imagination and Authority*.

[104]*Brief Outline*, § 198.

[105]*Brief Outline*, § 199. Schleiermacher insists upon the primacy of the individual conscience in matters of faith. Hence we read: "No one can be bound to acknowledge the contents of such [doctrinal] presentations of Christian truth except insofar as they are the expression of his own religious consciousness, or commend themselves to him by their scriptural character. On the other hand, the revision of the Church's public doctrine is a task in which every individual is bound to take a share, testing the established ideas and propositions in the measure of his power and the helps at his command; he has rights in this matter, in the exercise of which he must be left free." *Christian Faith*, § 154, p. 690.

position--unless it is representative of the Church's faith and accepted by the Church.[106]

Besides the generative and worthwhile relationship between orthodoxy and heterodoxy, Schleiermacher finds destructive extremes that are properly called false heterodoxy and false orthodoxy. False orthodoxy promotes dogmatic antiquarianism by embracing the fixed statements of the Church without fully acknowledging their historical character. It attempts to "retain in dogmatic treatment what is already entirely antiquated in the public pronouncements of the Church and does not exercise in its scientific expression any definite influence upon other points of doctrine."[107]

False heterodoxy, on the other hand, is at work when Christianity assimilates to cultural changes indiscriminately. In doctrinal matters a false heterodoxy stridently protests "against formulations which have well grounded support in pronouncements of the Church and the scientific expression of which does not create confusion regarding their relation to other points of Christian doctrine."[108] In this way, false heterodoxy embraces the mobile element without recognizing the stability and normativity of authentic ecclesial statements.

Those doctrinal formulae that are contrary to the essence of Christianity, i.e., contrary to the Christian *Glaubensweise*, are heretical. Are both false orthodoxy and false heterodoxy heretical for Schleiermacher? His recognition that heterodoxy rightly fostered the historically-changing reception of faith does not mean that anything goes. Heterodoxy is conceptually distinct from heresy.

---

[106]Doctrinal "error is retrained by two forces." If it is the individual who has erred, "it is restrained by the influence of public thought;" whereas if it is a group of believers, "it is restrained by the influence of men of spiritual distinction, spreading clear views ever more widely" (*Christian Faith*, § 155, p. 691). This analysis of group and individual error and correction corresponds with his treatment of the Church's purifying action in *Die christliche Sitte*, 109-133.

[107]*Brief Outline*, § 205.

[108]*Brief Outline*, § 206.

Heresy is an error or a deviation from orthodoxy which conflicts with the definition of Christianity's essence. Although this essence remains unchanged within the consciousness of the Church, the determination of this essence by the Church can vary. Concomitantly, so can the assessment of heresies.[109] Strictly speaking, it is only false heterodoxy that corresponds with heresy; heresy occurs when "an extraneous element [has] become organized within the Church."[110] Alternately, false orthodoxy may not contradict the essence of Christianity, but may not aid in its expression today. It seems logical, even though Schleiermacher does not make the claim, that if something we thought to be orthodox was judged false because it contradicted the essence of Christianity, it would be judged heretical and belatedly recognized as a false heterodoxy.

Either of the destructive tendencies of orthodoxy or heterodoxy when instantiated in communal historical forms must be diagnosed as disease and criticized. Schleiermacher discusses the source of disease in terms of the inner and outer axis: "When a historical organism appears diseased this may be based partly on a recession of vitality, partly on the fact that extraneous factors have entered in and have become organized within it for their own sake."[111] Disease is possible when the inner realm of the Church has become stagnant or fanatical, or when outer elements--foreign modes of dis-

---

[109]In his introduction to the history of the Christian Church he argued that viewed historically one person's heretic could be another person's helpful innovator. "From a historical point of view . . . we must say that in a universal process of development it is natural that someone who was holding a different opinion that was still reconcilable with Christianity could be considered a heretic by someone else" (*Geschichte der christlichen Kirche*, 23). The preference or intolerance for the heretics by the historian must be evaluated by the dogmatician in his or her endeavor to articulate the essence of Christianity. Also see *Christian Faith*, § 21, p. 97.

[110]*Brief Outline*, § 58; see also §§ 61, 62 and *Christian Faith*, § 21.

[111]*Brief Outline*, § 54.

course and action--become organized within the Church partly in doctrine as heresy, and partly in polity, as schism."[112]

Schleiermacher proposes a truly dynamic vision of the Church that affirms its identity and continuity on the one hand, and the creative and destructive forces and tensions associated with the historical existence of the Church on the other. He locates the seat of ecclesial identity, continuity, and ultimately orthodoxy in the inner realm, but here "inner" does not always mean only ecclesial consciousness or contemporary experience. Inner ecclesial identity is informed by discourse and practice in the inner life of the Church and this identity unfolds in relation to the changing world. Thus Church and theologians are challenged to embrace what is true in the canon of the Scriptures and in the creedal confessions, while recognizing the need for new articulations--reformulations--of the faith of the Church at the present time. It may be necessary at times to criticize certain Scriptural and ecclesial formulations in light of the experience of the Church, but this is not because these articulations of faith are irrelevant; instead it is because they only approximate the faith of the Church.

As we shall discover more fully in the chapters that follow, Schleiermacher did not reject the authority of confessions, nor that of the Scriptures in favor of the individual's or the group's modern experience, or the authority of some alien method. He concurred with the classic Reformers that the Scriptures play a purifying and reforming role in the Church. Yet he also sought to provide a theological basis for the criticism of doctrines and of Scriptural propositions which was in keeping with his openness to that which is distinctive about contemporary ecclesial consciousness and to the external sources of doctrinal development. Schleiermacher in this respect was pioneering and prospective; he voiced the legitimate questions and concerns raised by the philosophy of the

---

[112]*Brief Outline*, § 58; § 59 states that the concepts employed here can "be established only by that critical method which is here predominant throughout", which stands in contrast to a strictly empirical or speculative method. See § 32, n. 1.

Enlightenment without giving science or human experience the only or the final word.

Drey followed Schleiermacher's treatment of fixed and moving elements in relation to orthodoxy up to a point. Drey contends that the ecclesial *Überlieferung* is living and not dead because it is composed of fixed and moving elements.[113] The fixed element is found for Drey within the confessions of faith and morals. Some concepts were originally developed (in other words, mature from the beginning) or they have become developed and are now explicitly articulated dogmas and accordingly fixed. However, there may also be implicit dogmas whose concepts require further development before the Church will "close" matters and declare it an explicit dogma.[114] "In Christian doctrine, dogma is distinguished from opinion. . . , the essential from the nonessential, . . . its fixed element [from] . . . its mobile element."[115] The moving elements are theological opinions or the positions of theological schools. If they are not generally recognized in the Church through official pronouncement, they remain the position of an individual or a school, having not developed enough or adequately to be considered the truth of the Christian faith.[116] Drey observes that "not every development or formation of doctrine, be it mediated by historical

---

[113]*Kurze Einleitung*, § 256.

[114]*Kurze Einleitung*, § 257.

[115]*Kurze Einleitung*, § 273.

[116]I think that in principle Schleiermacher could agree with this formulation, even though he would reject the specifically Catholic teaching office it presupposes. As we have seen with Schleiermacher, the role of the individual as apparently heterodox is remedial and reforming. The theologian's presentation of doctrine must be accepted as the authentic articulation of the faith by the community in order for it to become truly orthodox. This is clearly in keeping with the spirit if not the letter of what Drey presents as the relationship of theological opinions to orthodox statements of faith. Individual opinions may appear heterodox but when accepted by the Church at large and enunciated by the official representatives become the fixed and orthodox.

reflection on the Bible or mediated by speculation through ideas, is in the spirit of Christianity; the individual or individuals through which each modification of doctrines has been initiated in the first place can err."[117] Individuals are often inspired by advances in the sciences. "Science always provides new stimuli for the development of Christian doctrines, and leads the mobile element of those doctrines to their completion."[118] What is mobile and developing is a facet of the doctrine as an inner element, but outer sources do inspire doctrinal development.

Drey concludes that orthodoxy strives "to keep the completed element in doctrines, and to construe the mobile element in the spirit of and in agreement with each doctrine." Orthodoxy does not rule out further movement and development of doctrines, even while it affirms the elements already fixed. On the other hand, "heterodoxy is the endeavor to make the fixed mobile, or to construe the mobile in opposition with that [fixed doctrine]."[119] Heterodoxy rejects the closed character of dogmas by attempting to make them still mobile, or by polarizing doctrinal movement from doctrinal fixity. Drey includes in his use of the term "heterodoxy" what Schleiermacher had treated under heterodoxy and false heterodoxy; in so doing, Drey does not provide the term heterodoxy with a benign meaning as is found in Schleiermacher's treatment.

Drey recognized in Catholic thought, as Schleiermacher had in Protestant theology, a false orthodoxy, or in Drey's term, a hyperorthodoxy. He concurred with Schleiermacher that there is a theologically legitimate need for criticism of a lifeless orthodoxy. Drey thereby recognizes with the classic Protestant Reformers and Enlightenment thinkers the need for criticism of theological traditions. Such criticism is based for Drey neither on the need to return to the purity of the Gospel, nor in a rationalistic rejection of faith and revelation. Instead, theological criticism arises from the

---

[117] *Kurze Einleitung*, § 193.

[118] *Kurze Einleitung*, § 259.

[119] *Kurze Einleitung*, § 260.

need to clarify the essence of Christianity and to present it persuasively for the present age. By contrast, hyperorthodoxy exists when one "eliminates all mobility of doctrines, by denying it generally or by elevating opinions to dogmatic status."[120] Discussing the polemical task of theology, Drey states that "[t]he human person can depart from the truth either through apostasy (*Abfall*) from it, or through lagging behind (*Zurückbleiben hinter*) it."[121] It is the latter claim which is noteworthy and it is one on which Drey elaborates: "Lagging behind the truth is inertia (*Trägheit*);" it is the result of "the extinguished activity" of the religious principle or it is a "corruption" in its constant development.[122] Such a failure to develop is a charge Drey employs against Protestants, who have chosen the dead letter and not the living Word in the Church. But hyperorthodoxy and lagging behind the truth also remain problems within Catholicism. Drey thereby admits what Catholics have been slow to acknowledge: there are times when inertia and intransigence within Catholicism and when moribund and corrupt doctrines should be criticized, and that the need for further doctrinal changes be acknowledged.

Orthodoxy for Drey requires affirming the fixed or closed elements of doctrines as dogmas, while remaining open to their further conceptual development. He maintains that the fixed elements are found in the orthodox confessions of the Church's faith and morals, its articulation of the canon of Scriptures, and in the specification of the seven sacraments. Drey distinguishes regions within dogmatic, moral, and sacramental theology that correspond to the distinction between fixed and moving elements. In dogmatic theology the fixed element is spoken of as symbolic and the mobile element as scholastic; in moral theology the fixed is mysticism and the mobile is casuistry; in sacramental theology the fixed is pious emotion in relation to the mystery of the sacrament

---

[120]*Kurze Einleitung*, § 260.

[121]*Kurze Einleitung*, § 240; also see §§ 245-246.

[122]*Kurze Einleitung*, §§ 240, 245.

and the mobile element is the expressions or signs of the sacrament called rite or ceremony.[123]

Drey's theology offers a dynamic understanding of the relationship between the historically mobile character of theology and doctrine and the fixed and essential elements of Catholic Christianity. It is a model of theology and doctrinal development that explicitly incorporates a central role for the hierarchical authority of the Church as guarantor of the truth of the Catholic tradition and as promoter and guardian of the process of handing on the doctrinal tradition. According to its institution and mission, the Christian Church has the authority to establish its essential elements. In Drey's words,

> the theory of the constitution of the Christian Church has therefore to determine how the symbol is to be preserved in its original essence, how it is to be further developed according to the needs of the times and conditions and more closely determined and to that extent be changed; it has to determine through which institution it is to be considered as the agreement of all and--next to the free subjective interpretation--the ecclesially authentic interpretation can be secured at the same time.[124]

Schleiermacher's and Drey's positions on orthodoxy represent a classic difference Protestants and Catholics. As we shall clarify in subsequent chapters, in his description and defense of doctrinal development, Schleiermacher seeks to affirm and qualify the Protestant *sola scriptura* principle. This effort contributed to a new

---

[123]*Kurze Einleitung*, §§ 263, 264-67, 273-4.

[124]*Kurze Einleitung*, § 291. This teaching or prophetic responsibility of the Church hierarchy's is combined with a sacramental or priestly task and a governing or kingly task. The second pertains to the confirmation of the essential sacramental character of its cult, while determining the accidental forms of the liturgy through rite and ceremony, so that "the free subjective movement of the heart is not hindered." The third aspect of the ecclesial hierarchy concerns "the constitutional form of Church government itself or the hierarchy." *Kurze Einleitung*, §§ 292-293.

Protestant vision, a reformulation of the Reformation heritage of *sola scriptura* in light of a new narrative of Christianity. But it is equally important that Schleiermacher's position on the nature of dogmatic formulations be understood as an attempt to be consistent with the traditional Protestant conviction that dogmas are not immutable and free from error. For him, the Scriptures, confessional statements, and creative theology all have a role in informing Christian consciousness, but each must be evaluated in light of the faith of the Church, which in turn can call forth doctrinal changes that are in some ways continuous and in some ways discontinuous. Schleiermacher's openness to both doctrinal continuity and discontinuity is theologically justified by his theology of history in its manifold elements. Doctrines as public confessional statements are historically conditioned and authoritative, but this authority is based on its authentic presentation of the faith of the Church. Because of the power of the Holy Spirit in the Church one can affirm this community's indefectability, but not its infallibility on concrete matters of faith. The theologian, the Church leader, and every Christian must be active in the affirmation and reformulation of the living faith within the modern world.

Drey's theology provides a classic Catholic defense of the authoritative weight of confessional statements as fixed, immutable, and continuous. At the same time, he is an early representative of a dominant and respected approach to doctrinal development within modern Catholic theology, associated with the names of Johann Adam Möhler and John Cardinal Newman, with Josef Geiselmann and Karl Rahner. Drey's approach emphasizes doctrinal identity and developmental continuity within the Catholic confessional tradition, as well as within the traditions associated with the sacraments, morals, and disciplinary matters, even as it recognizes the demands of the changing conditions and impulses which influence the Church's understanding of faith. Drey acknowledges the threat of ecclesial corruption, the need for doctrinal criticism, revision, and reform, but he does not consider whether there could be doctrinal changes in dogmatic formulas that would be either discontinuous, or that would offer some continuity-in-discontinuity.

Drey's model of doctrinal development allows the discovery and affirmation of complementary doctrinal insights, but the prospect of contrasting insights and doctrines is not considered. Drey is like many modern Catholic theologians, for whom the possibility of doctrinal discontinuity is either not recognized or explicitly rejected.

Drey represents a classic modern Catholic approach to doctrinal development not only in denying doctrinal discontinuity, but also because he ultimately rejects the Protestant and Enlightenment criticisms of the Catholic tradition. Drey's alternative is based on the contention that orthodoxy incorporates the fixed and the mobile. A dogmatic judgment of the Church is closed and therefore it may not be criticized directly, but it could be insufficiently developed. A dogmatic formula is true, but it may be incomplete. Drey's comments on hyperorthodoxy and on dogmatic inertia establish the need for doctrinal criticism and development, just as his comments on heterodoxy preclude any acknowledgement of doctrinal discontinuity and confirm his convictions about the teaching mission of the Church's hierarchy.

Even though Drey sounded many traditional Catholic motifs when discussing the nature of doctrine, his formulation on doctrinal criticism and development was generations ahead of its time. It was not until the Second Vatican Council that the official teaching office of the Church publicly declared that doctrinal development was a constitutive dimension of divine revelation in the Catholic faith. And just as doctrinal development was officially accepted at this Council, some theologians were suggesting that a developmental model did not adequately account for doctrinal pluralism, and a few others argued after the Council that the official documents failed to provide a theological justification for the criticism of doctrines and doctrinal discontinuity.[125] Doctrinal criticism, discontinuity, and pluralism have become the flashpoints in the later part of twentieth century Catholic theology. This volatile set of issues is fueled on the one hand, by concerns about

---

[125]See Bradford E. Hinze, "Narrative Contexts, Doctrinal Reform," *Theological Studies* 51 (1990):417-433.

ecclesial responsibility and honesty in exploring areas of needed change in doctrine, and on the other, by the threat of radical doctrinal relativism and secularization. Drey's theology represents a still tenable approach for modern Catholic theology on the issue of doctrinal orthodoxy and development, even though distinctive issues and problems have been raised during the twentieth century that Drey's theology neither explicitly addresses nor resolves.

Now that we have examined the ways Schleiermacher and Drey configure history and how these narrative patterns influence their understanding of the historical dynamics of heterodoxy, orthodoxy, and hyperorthodoxy, we can turn to this question: What is the specific role of theology in the process of doctrinal development and reform?

CHAPTER III

FROM NARRATIVE TO SYSTEM: THE THEOLOGICAL TASKS

What are the responsibilities of the theologian in the process of doctrinal development? What duties are incumbent upon the theologian in relation to fixed and mobile elements in doctrines? Schleiermacher and Drey address these questions in their respective statements about the nature of theology. Put simply, the theologian develops doctrines by faithfully interpreting, critically evaluating, and scientifically presenting the faith of the Christian community. This means that for Schleiermacher and Drey a theologian is an interpreter, a critic, a systematician, and also in each of these tasks the theologian serves as an organic leader in the community. The interpretive and communal tasks of theology are deemed constitutive of all branches of theology, the critical role of theology is found most noticeably in philosophical or fundamental theology, and the systematic role in dogmatic theology.

Schleiermacher's and Drey's theologies of history provide the narrative frameworks for their theologies and the theological justification for doctrinal development. They believed that the theologian must be faithful to the narrative plot that emerges from the idea of the kingdom of God. Theology is inseparable from this narrative structure of the revelation of the kingdom of God, which has its origins in the New Testament and is organically unfolding in the Church and the world. The idea of the kingdom of God and the narrative structure it yields provide Schleiermacher and Drey with a web of beliefs for their theology, which is drawn from and corroborated by the primary language of faith in biblical, creedal, and liturgical forms.[1]

However, theology for Schleiermacher and Drey is neither solely nor primarily a narrative representation of the scriptural, creedal, and liturgical testimony of faith. The narrative dimensions of the idea of the kingdom of God provide a normative interpretation of the historical experience of the Christian community, but not its sole or final articulation. Doctrines can and must further develop in accordance with the organic and pedagogical dynamics at work in the dramatic unfolding of the kingdom of God. This doctrinal development is requisite for the historical mediation of salvation. According to Schleiermacher and Drey, it is not sufficient for theology to remain within the confines of the narrative discourse that emerges from the idea of the kingdom of God.

The reason that repeating the narrative of the primary language of faith is inadequate for theology becomes initially intelligible when we stand back and view the architectonic of these two thinkers' respective theological encyclopedias. Their views of the divisions and unity of theology provide the appropriate context for examining how the interpretative, critical, systematic, and communal responsibilities of theology both relate to the narrative of the kingdom and take us beyond it in the process of doctrinal criticism, reform, and development.

Schleiermacher, as is commonly known, envisioned theology as a science governed by the principles of ethics--"the science of the principles of history."[2] Ethics includes speculative knowledge

---

[1]For the use of the term "web of beliefs" in theology, see Ronald Thiemann, *Revelation and Theology* (Notre Dame: Notre Dame University Press, 1985), 71-91.

[2]*Brief Outline*, § 29. cf. *The Christian Faith*, § 2. *Dialektik* provides a formal theory of science that divides the real sciences into physics or the science of nature, and ethics as the science of reason and history. In Birkner's words, dialectic offers a "discussion of the essence and the transcendental presuppositions of knowledge (*Wissen*)." In contrast to Fichte,

through concepts and an empirical knowledge of what is given in reality through the study of history. In addition to these speculative and empirical branches of knowledge, there exist, under the aegis of ethics, various mixed sciences that combine speculative concepts and empirical judgments for critical cognitive purposes or for technical practical purposes.[3]

Theology is a positive science, along with medicine and law. The diverse scientific elements within these endeavors are positive because they are not united through a deduction from some idea of science or knowledge, but "because they are requisite for carrying out a practical task."[4] Philosophical theology is a mixed science that combines speculative concepts and empirical knowledge for the purpose of a critical apprehension of the essence or idea of Christianity within history.[5] Historical theology is empirical and seeks to describe diverse periods in the history of Christianity.[6] Practical theology is a mixed science of a technical kind, because it combines the speculative and the empirical viewpoints in the service of a practical task.[7]

Hegel, and Schelling, Schleiermacher's dialectic does not proceed from above to those below, but its movement of thought is from below to above. See *Schleiermachers Christliche Sittenlehre* (Berlin: Verlag Alfred Töpelmann, 1964), 31, 30-64; H. Süskind, *Der Einfluß Schellings auf die Entwicklung von Schleiermachers System*, 49-56.

[3]Philosophy in this schema is field-encompassing for it develops the formal theory of science (dialectics) as well as provides the speculative aspects of physics and ethics. Under ethics as a mixed (speculative and empirical) endeavor, on the side of the critical enterprise there is generated a philosophy of history, a political philosophy, and a philosophy of religion, and on the technical side is developed hermeneutics and pedagogics.

[4]*Brief Outline*, § 1. See also *Gelegentliche Gedanken über Universitäten in deutschen Sinn. Sämmtliche Werke*, division 4, vol. 4, esp. 579.

[5]*Brief Outline*, § 32.

[6]*Brief Outline*, §§ 27-28.

[7]*Brief Outline*, §§ 257, 258.

The entire theological enterprise coalesces to determine and foster a "determinate mode of faith (*Glaubensweise*), that is, a determinate manner of being conscious of God."[8] This is accomplished by interrelating empirical, speculative, and practical modes of knowledge in the pursuit of theology's work.[9] This work is empirical insofar as it describes the positive, communal consciousness of the Church in its manifestations. Theology is never solely speculative, but through the mixed science of philosophical theology, the historical manifestations of the idea or essence of Christianity are clarified and evaluated.[10] Theology is practical since it shapes the nature of ecclesial ministry and fosters technical skills in light of the content of Christianity. The diverse branches of theology must work together: philosophical theology, as apologetics and polemics, work in conjunction with historical theology to determine the continuity and discontinuity of the essence of Christianity throughout history. Historical theology would be mere chronicle without the ideas of the kingdom of God, redemption, and the essence of the Church, ideas which are clarified by philosophical theology. Historical theology is subdivided into exegesis, church history, and dogmatic theology. These historical enterprises are to describe, examine, and clarify the "*bestimmte Glaubensweise*" of the Church as it is manifested in

---

[8]*Brief Outline*, § 1.

[9]As stated in the *Brief Outline*: "Since historical theology attempts to exhibit every point of time in its true relation to the idea of Christianity, it follows that it is at once not only the foundation of practical theology but also the verification of philosophical theology. . . . Accordingly, historical theology is the actual corpus of theological study, which corpus is connected with science, as such, by means of philosophical theology and with the active Christian life by means of practical theology" (§§ 27-28).

[10]As we shall find, dogmatics for Schleiermacher is considered an empirical-descriptive enterprise. However, it includes the scientific task--which he does not call speculative--according to which the distinctive terms and relationships of the description of the Christian faith are ordered and clarified.

different periods of history. Practical theology provides the teleological unity of the whole enterprise. Ecclesial service is not simply technical know-how, but rather must be the consistent expression of the essence or idea of Christianity, which provides the material unity of the entire theological encyclopedia.

The theological encyclopedia of Johann Sebastian Drey is animated by a similar interplay between empirical, speculative, and practical interests. Drey's architectonic, however, is noticeably different from Schleiermacher's. It is divided into historical propaedeutic, scientific theology, and practical theology.[11] Historical propaedeutic is empirically directed toward the origins and development of Christianity. Employing an organic construction, historical theology interprets the facts of history in relation to the guiding ideas. Practical theology is oriented by the practical interest associated with Christian ministry. Scientific theology constructs the idea or essence of Christianity within fundamental theology and dogmatic theology.

Drey acknowledges his debt to Schleiermacher's understanding of ethics when he discusses practical theology[12] and also when he defends the practical interest that guides all of theology, which justifies its status as a positive science. In addition, Schleiermacher and Drey both accentuate the importance of historical theology and work with similar principles of interpreting history. However, Drey

---

[11]*Kurze Einleitung*, § 77.

[12]*Kurze Einleitung*: "Since the Church is an ethical state, a kingdom of God, and Church government aims on a grand scale and Church service on a small scale at presenting such [an ethical state and kingdom of God] in its appearance; and if one gives--with Schleiermacher--the name 'ethics' to the universal science of principles, which describes how necessary ideas residing in the nature of the human person develop in the course of history, how they form communities and customs, then the Church leader has to know especially these principles, and insofar as his actions in Church governing are not to be acquired blindly and unconsciously, but should rather also be built on scientific principles, he must have abstracted out of them his theory of Church government and politics" (§ 383).

does not follow Schleiermacher in incorporating dogmatics in the theological system under the aegis of historical theology. Drey's presentation of the scientific nature of fundamental or philosophical theology and dogmatics in terms of a speculative construction has often been judged fundamentally different from Schleiermacher's approach.[13] This contention demands closer scrutiny.

It is usually the case that Drey's conception of theology as a scientific construction is placed in close proximity to Schelling's *Vorlesungen über die Methode des akademischen Studiums*, and any relation to Schleiermacher's *Kurze Darstellung* is minimized. There are solid reasons for exploring Drey's relation to Schelling's early philosophy: Drey agrees with Schelling that construction entails

---

[13]Josef Geiselmann initiated this judgment: "Certainly Drey was influenced by Schleiermacher in the determination of dogmatics . . . [and] fundamental theology. However, this fact is only of peripheral significance." *Die Katholische Tübinger Schule* (Freiburg: Herder, 1964), 26, n. 41; see also Josef Rief *Reich Gottes und Gesellschaft nach Johann Sebastian Drey und Johann Baptist Hirscher* (Paderborn: Ferdinand Schöningh, 1965), 80-82; Franz Schupp, *Die Evidenz der Geschichte: Theologie als Wissenschaft*, esp. 125-144. Schupp contends that "Both [Drey und Schleiermacher] recognize in Schelling's *Vorlesungen* [*über die Methode des akademischen Studiums*] the concept of a strong science developed there. However, Schleiermacher is of the opinion that it could not be used in dogmatics, for such a deduction out of the idea of the absolute is impossible in it. With that, a presentation of dogmatics in the form of a pure science is out of the question, and so it appears properly placed for him also under the positive sciences. From this arises for Drey the task that is indicated by Schelling as the essential element in the study of theology, namely *to unite the speculative and the historical construction*, which for Drey means that the same material that is first *discovered* through historical study, is here *brought into a system* through scientific construction. The concept of the construction of the system circumscribes the entire program of dogmatics as a science" (134). Fehr says that "[l]ike Schleiermacher, Drey locates th[e] original sense of God as a feeling arising in the *Gemüt*, "the deepest ground of the soul." At the same time, he differs from Schleiermacher in maintaining that the feeling is based on an objective reality: the actual rootedness of all things in God" (*The Dogmatics of Drey*, 49).

finding necessity in the apparent contingencies of history from a "higher viewpoint"; construction enables him to acknowledge real contact with and knowledge of the noumenal realm through the phenomenal realm by means of an intellectual intuition; and he holds that the Idea unfolds in nature and spirit, and in the ideal and real. Drey's dependence upon Schelling, which was initially investigated by Josef Geiselmann and further explored by Josef Rief, Franz Schupp, Wolfgang Ruf, and Wayne Fehr, is beyond dispute. But a case can be made that Drey's distinctive position stands closer to Schleiermacher's than has been usually recognized.[14]

It is helpful to recall that for Schelling, the different divisions of human knowledge share in a primal knowledge (*Urwissen*) which is found in God. God is the Absolute who unites the ideal and the real in a primal knowing.[15] Human creatures share in this primal knowing, but because of finitude human knowing is fragmentary and partial. The ideal and the real, thought and being are never truly and fully united for the human person. Thus, what is perfectly united in the Absolute--eternal primal knowing--the human species divides and distinguishes. Philosophy as the science of ideas grasps the ideal content of the Absolute's eternal knowing, but it does not grasp the unity of the ideal and the real with anything close to perfection. In contrast to the ideal science of philosophy stand the real sciences, which are positive sciences since they serve the state. The real sciences are divided into theology, the highest real science, which concerns "the absolute point of indifference in which the

---

[14]Robert Stalder explored a variety of the similarities between Schleiermacher's and Drey's theologies, see *Grunlinien der Theologie Scheiermachers I. Zur Fundamentaltheologie* (Wiesbaden: Franz Steiner Verlag, 1969), 82-127. Recently Abraham Kustermann has offer a nuanced corrective to Geiselmann's underestimation of Schleiermacher's influence on Drey's theology and to what he judges as Stalder's overemphasis on Schleiermacher's influence, see *Die Apologetik Johann Sebastian Dreys*, 43, 74, 181-199. Also see the work by Nico Schreurs and John Thiel.

[15]See Schelling, *On University Studies*, 1-50 and Fehr, *The Dogmatics of Drey*, 73-105.

ideal and the real worlds are apprehended as one;" the natural sciences, which examine "the real aspect of the absolute;" and the science of history in the broadest sense, which treats the "ideal aspect of the absolute."[16] These real sciences aim at a synthesis of the historical and the philosophical ways of knowing. In particular, theology for Schelling strives after a "higher viewpoint," attempting through an intellectual intuition to find the infinite in the finite, the necessary in the accidental, and the providential in what appears as fate. Objectivity for Schelling is the intuition of the whole through the idea which is shared by and determines the communal spirit.[17]

A comprehensive analysis of Schleiermacher's philosophical position in relation to Schelling's is beyond the purview of this study.[18] However, it must be pointed out that Schleiermacher's position shares certain characteristics with Schelling's.[19]

---

[16]Schelling, *On University Studies*, 78.

[17]See Schelling, *On University Studies*,, 67-69. See Gerald McCool's helpful summary of research on Drey and Schelling, *Catholic Theology in the Nineteenth Century* (New York: The Seabury Press, 1977), 67-81.

[18]This would require a comparison of Schleiermacher's *Dialektik* and *Ethik* in relation to Schelling's early philosophy of identity as enunciated in *System of Transcendental Idealism* and *On University Studies*. Schleiermacher refers to these two books by Schelling in letters and diaries written between 1800 and 1804 as well as to *On the World Soul* and *Bruno*. F. C. Baur, K. G. Bretschneider, and H. G. Tzschirner alleged that Schleiermacher was dependent upon Schelling's philosophy, see Schleiermacher's *On the Glaubenslehre: Two Letters to Dr. Lücke* (trans. by J. Duke and F. Fiorenza) AAR Texts and Translations 3 (Chico, CA: Scholars Press, 1981), 48, 99-100, n. 14. Also see Süskind, *Der Einfluß Schellings*, G. Mann, *Das Verhältnis der Schleiermacherschen Dialektik zur Schellings Philosophie* (Stuttgart, 1914), and Richard Brandt, *The Philosophy of Schleiermacher* (New York: Harper and Brothers, 1941). Manfred Frank suggests that Schleiermacher's position should be investigated in relation to the Schelling's later philosophy, in *Das individuelle Allgemeine*, p. 104, n. 60.

[19]For the history of reception of Schleiermacher's philosophy, see Gunter Scholtz, *Die Philosophie Schleiermachers* (Darmstadt: Wissenschaftliche Buchgesellschaft, 1984).

Schleiermacher agreed with the early writings of Schelling about the need for combining speculative and empirical modes of knowledge in university studies and in theology, but they disagreed on the nature of this synthetic unity. Schleiermacher, also like Schelling, recognized an intuition of the whole through the idea (or essence) which is shared by and informs the community and animates this communal spirit. Unlike Schelling, however, Schleiermacher's intuition does not yield a *Wissenschaft* of a speculative nature, but a knowledge which is both inductive and affective.[20] A further divergence from Schelling's position is no less significant. Schleiermacher did not seek to deduce ethics or theology from a primal knowing. The entire enterprise of a transcendental deduction was something Schleiermacher rejected in favor of an approach which emphasized induction and practical, tentative judgments, rather than the deductive and necessary paths traversed by Fichte, the early Schelling, and Hegel in their quest for certainty or absolute knowing.[21]

In comparing Drey's understanding of the nature of theology with Schelling's and Schleiermacher's programs, two points have often been overlooked by those who wish to show Drey's connection with Schelling. First, Schleiermacher's position on the organic

---

[20]On the problem of "Anshauung," see and Van A. Harvey, "On the New Edition of Schleiermacher's *Addresses On Religion*," *Journal of the American Academy of Religion*, 52 (1972): 488-512; Brandt, *The Philosophy of Schleiermacher*, 95-144, and Andreas Arndt, "Introduction," *Dialektik (1811)* (Hamburg: Felix Meiner Verlag, 1986), xxxii-xxxv. Brandt states that "what Schleiermacher called the 'intuition' of or 'sense' for the whole is strikingly similar to what Schelling seems to have meant by the phrase 'intellectual intuition.' Both men referred by this word to the becoming aware of the interrelationship of finite objects in the Infinite, in some way or other" (154).

[21]See Schleiermacher's review of Schelling's *Vorlesungen über die Methode*, *Aus Schleiermachers Leben in Briefen*, 4:579-93, especially 581-585. Schleiermacher voices his dissatisfaction with Schelling's idealistic formulation, his deductive method of construction, and his attempt to distinguish between disciplines on the basis of the distinction between the ideal and the real, which for Schleiermacher is only a relative opposition.

interpretation of history and the history of Christianity, which was forged in the context of various conversations going on in post-Kantian German romanticism and idealism, was in part influenced by Schelling's formulation of the interplay between empirical knowledge and speculative concepts. This means that Drey and Schleiermacher have a common source of influence in Schelling, although they stand in different relations to him. Secondly, while Drey's understanding of fundamental theology as a scientific "construction" shows the stamp of Schelling's philosophy, it also echoes Schleiermacher's formulation in the first edition of the *Kurze Darstellung*: philosophical theology attempts a "construction" of the essence of Christianity.[22] Even Drey's professed departure from Schleiermacher's understanding of apologetics need not be construed as a total rejection of Schleiermacher's position. The argument will be advanced here that on certain, not all, issues Drey's rejection of Schleiermacher's position is a rejection of one interpretation of Schleiermacher's position, albeit an all-too-common one, but not the only one. In turn I will suggest that despite various important differences, Drey's position on the nature of apologetics and dogmatics remains structurally similar to the position advanced by Schleiermacher, and that this commonality rests in large measure on their organic and pedagogical

---

[22]In the first edition of the *Kurze Darstellung* we read: "While philosophical theology presupposes the material of historical theology, it in turn provides the grounds for the judgment concerning each particular [historical perspective on Christianity] and thus concerning the overall historical perspective (*Anschauung*) on Christianity. . . . The philosophical part of theology and the practical part stand together over against the historical part, since they are immediately directed toward practical matters, whereas it [i.e., historical] is directed only towards observation. They stand over against each other in that through the philosophical part the object of the practical part is first established and in that the philosophical part fastens upon the most elevated sort of scientific construction (*die höchste wissenschaftliche Konstruktion*) while the practical part comprises the most particular details in its role as technology" (*Brief Outline*, §§ 65-66, nn. 32, 33, translation annotated; also see § 44, n. 13)

interpretations of the drama of the kingdom of God and on the implications for theology that derive from them.

The Hermeneutic Task

The previous chapters have explored how both theologians understand Christian theology as a hermeneutic enterprise, which seeks to interpret faithfully the multifaceted essence of Christianity as it develops throughout history. Since Christianity is a positive religion, the concrete historical and communal character of this religion must be understood in its origins and development. Consequently, historical theology as a hermeneutic undertaking provides the backbone for Christian theological discourse insofar as it interprets the experience, discourse, and action of the Christian community over time. It is through historical theology that one comes to understand the inner and outer dynamic at work in doctrinal development. It is through historical theology that one grasps the tensions and interplay between fixed and moving elements within Christianity, and among orthodox, heterodox, and hyperorthodox individuals, movements, and traditions.

Schleiermacher and Drey describe the hermeneutical character of historical theology with some precision. Leaving their differences aside for the moment, these theologians agree that the technical and grammatical tasks of interpretation situate a text and an author in a linguistic heritage and historical setting, and strive to understanding this text in terms of the original creative act of the author in relation to this linguistic environment. In historical theology, these operations are most clearly seen in the exegesis of the Scriptures. More broadly, however, historical theology must interpret the traditioning process at work in the history of Christianity by attaining a historical knowledge of the *Glaubensweise* (in Schleiermacher's word) and the *Überlieferung* (for Drey) of the Church. This requires an appreciation of the interplay between the technical and the grammatical; between the Church's consciousness, discourse, and action in relation to the discourse and action in the culture at large; between fixed and moving elements; between the inner and outer elements influencing the life and doctrine of the Christian community. By appreciating these complex dynamisms, the subject matter of this history is understood and passed on by the community. Exegetical and interpretative techniques are employed in this process of interpretation, but these must never hinder the attempt to render faithfully what is distinctive about this history. There is no separation between truth and method for either figure.[23]

Historical theology and interpretation are given an unprecedented place within theology by these two thinkers. As we have already seen, Schleiermacher and Drey believed that an empirical, chronicle approach to history was inadequate for understanding history in general, and could not adequately serve the hermeneutic purposes of theology. An organic construal of history was needed that would provide a plot that would show the individual parts in relation to the whole. Primitive Christianity remains normative in their theologies, but not static. *Urchristentum* is but the beginning of the Church's doctrinal legacy, which serves

---

[23]The choices Gadamer offers (1) between truth and method, and (2) between Hegel's principle of historical mediation of the truth of tradition and Schleiermacher's attempt to reconstruct through a psychological method the genesis of texts, are problematic. His study gives insufficient attention to Schleiermacher's treatments of the grammatical side of hermeneutics and of the nature of historical theology insofar as it illustrates his hermeneutical method. This is required in order to give a fairer assessment of Schleiermacher's position on the linguistic and communal character operative in the mediation of the truth of traditions. Gadamer's insight into the history of effects of a given work is not prefigured in Schleiermacher's writings, but neither should it be viewed as antithetical to Schleiermacher's own dialogical paradigm. Cf. Hans Georg Gadamer, *Truth and Method*, 166-169, 184-197, 300-307.

the historical mission of mediating the redemptive and regenerating power of Christ in the world.[24]

By establishing historical theology as an essential theological enterprise concerned with the whole of Christian history, Schleiermacher and Drey place normative texts (the Bible, creeds, and liturgies) and practices (moral, cultic, and administrative) within the ongoing history of communal experience. Fundamental and systematic theology, in their judgment, could no longer begin with propositions from the Bible or creeds separated from the historical faith of the community. Their views of historical theology contribute to a genuinely historical understanding of the Christian tradition and provide a clear alternative to a static, classicist vision of theology, which emphasizes the obedient reception and repetition of biblical and creedal formulas. Historical theology for them is, as we shall see, intrinsically related to their scientific (or constructive) theology. It is this combination of historical and scientific enterprises that engenders a mediating model of theology that reflects upon authoritative religious texts and practices within constantly changing communal contexts and intellectual horizons.

The Task of Fundamental Theology

Besides faithfully interpreting the traditions of the Christian Church in texts and practices, theology must also determine and clearly articulate the essence of Christianity as a positive religion and, on the basis of this essence, criticize deviations. Schleiermach-

---

[24]Schleiermacher and Drey affirm the normative character of *Urchristentum* and find in the original revelation more than the prototype for Christian faith and action. At the same time, their development models permit new and creative insights into the Christian heritage. Cf. Robert L. Wilken, *The Myth of Christian Beginnings* (Garden City, New York: Anchor Books, 1972), and Elizabeth Schüssler Fiorenza, "The Will to Choose or Reject," in *Feminist Interpretation of the Scriptures* (Philadelphia: The Westminster Press, 1985), 125-136.

er argued in his *Kurze Darstellung* that this was the task of philosophical theology. So conceived, philosophical theology does not offer arguments for the existence of God, does not present the attributes of God which are known through creation, and does not construct a moral religion of reason apart from revelation. With these alternatives in mind, philosophical theology is probably a misnomer since it implies a discipline that rationally constructs the existence and nature of God, or what Christianity should be, prescinding from the historically determined character of this faith. For Schleiermacher, on the contrary, philosophical theology is inseparably related to historical theology: the essence of Christianity can only be discerned within the history of Christian ecclesial traditions. The task of philosophical theology is to critically ascertain and clarify the essence of Christianity as it is manifested within history.

Schleiermacher spoke of the theological task of criticism under the rubric of philosophical theology. Philosophical theology is a critical discipline because it seeks to examine empirical material of the history of Christianity from the point of view of speculative concepts.[25] Apologetics and polemics are subspecies of philosophical theology. Apologetics investigates "the distinctive nature of Christianity, and likewise of Protestantism," in order to examine the "conviction of the mode of faith propagated within a particular Church community" because the "vitality of the fellowship" is based on the communication of this conviction by the Church leadership.[26] Polemics aims to bring diseased deviations of the distinctive essence of Christianity and Protestantism to light.[27] Apologetics is directed outward because it seeks to articulate the distinctiveness of Christianity in order to "ward off [external] hostility toward the community," whereas polemics aims

[25]*Brief Outline*, §§ 32, 35-37.

[26]*Brief Outline*, § 39.

[27]*Brief Outline*, § 40.

to address inwardly disputed issues concerning the identity of Christian faith.[28]

Although Schleiermacher never entitled any of his writings "apologetics," he addresses apologetic issues in *Über die Religion* and in the introduction to the *Glaubenslehre*. In these he wrote of the nature of religion and the variety of religious communities, and he sought to articulate the distinctive essence of Christianity. In the strict sense, it is this latter move--defining the essence of Christianity--which constitutes the apologetic task, but for Schleiermacher apologetics always presupposes the first two steps.[29] He willingly admits that philosophical theology as an apologetic enterprise (in his sense) was not an adequately developed discipline.[30]

For Schleiermacher philosophical theology commences "from above" Christianity. This is not intended as a speculative or idealist starting point that begins in the realm of thought. Rather it is meant in "a logical sense" since it begins with "the general concept of a religious community or fellowship of faith" and from that examines the variety of historical manifestations of religious

---

[28]*Brief Outline*, §§ 39-40.

[29]Schleiermacher's introduction to the first edition of the *Glaubenslehre* received intense criticism. In the second edition, he sought to avoid the appearance of a speculative foundation for dogmatics being established in the introduction by clarifying the various claims of his introduction. He contends that his statements on the nature of religion and religious communities were borrowed from ethics, his statements on the diversity of religious communions were borrowed from the philosophy of religion, and his discussion of the essence of Christianity was derived from apologetics. None of these constituted dogmatics proper, nor did they determine the content of dogmatics. See *On the Glaubenslehre: Two Letters to Dr. Lücke*, translation and introduction by James Duke and Francis Fiorenza, (Chico California: Scholars Press, 1981), 5, 56-59, 76-80. The connection of apologetics with the philosophy of religion and with ethics is treated in the second edition of *Brief Outline*, §§ 22-24, 29.

[30]*Brief Outline*, § 29.

communities.[31] Philosophical theology is a critical enterprise because it judges the empirical history of Christianity (and positive religions) in relation to the conceptual (i.e., speculative) determination of the idea of Christianity as one specific positive religion. It is because Schleiermacher's philosophical theology is a critical enterprise, and neither solely empirical nor solely speculative, that his view of Christianity "from above" issues forth in apologetics as a critical determination of the essence of Christianity and in polemics as the criticism of deviations from this essence.

In the introduction to the *Glaubenslehre*, Schleiermacher articulates the essence of Christianity as determined by apologetics: "Christianity is a monotheistic faith, belonging to the teleological type of religion, and is essentially distinguished from other such faiths by the fact that in it everything is related to the redemption accomplished by Jesus of Nazareth."[32] This definition is the culmination of a lengthy argument about the nature of the Christian religions in relation to other polytheistic, monotheistic, aesthetic, and teleological types of religion. It is the combination of soteriology and christology that identifies the distinctive character of the Christian religion.

This critical discrimination of the essence of Christianity, is a historically-informed judgment concerning the precise nature of Christianity as Schleiermacher finds it instantiated in different, concrete ways throughout history. This historical judgment of what is unchanging and essential in Christianity provides the subject matter of philosophical theology. But it is equally important to understand that Schleiermacher's dogmatics offers a concrete determination of the essence of Christianity as it exists in his own time, not *from above* the various historical forms, but *from within*

[31] *Brief Outline*, § 33; cf. *Der christliche Glaube* (first edition), § 6.
[32] *Christian Faith*, § 11, p. 52.

the Christian community in its present situation.[33] In the second *Letter to Lücke*, Schleiermacher explains:

> The *Glaubenslehre* should not be construed as though its chief task were to receive and hand on in a continuous tradition as much of the previous material as possible. Instead, in times such as these our primary concern should be to take into account what appears to me to be the inevitable and immediate future. To be sure, we ought not to sacrifice or even obscure anything essential to evangelical Christianity. But we must in good time rid ourselves of everything that is obviously only secondary and based on presuppositions that are no longer valid, so that we might avoid becoming ensnared in useless controversies that might lead many easily to give up hope of ever grasping what is essential.[34]

Dogmatic theology cannot reject what philosophical theology has critically determined to be essential, rather dogmatics seeks to present the essential with more specificity by describing the ecclesial consciousness in its present state. Thus, the essence of Christianity is the subject matter of both philosophical and dogmatic theology: philosophical theology determines this subject matter as found in its various historical forms; dogmatics describes this essence as it exists in the present historical period.

Drey initially agreed with Schleiermacher's formal articulation of the nature of philosophical theology as he found it in the first edition of the *Kurze Darstellung*. In language close to Schleiermacher's description of philosophical theology, Drey's *Kurze Einleitung* describes a distinct branch of theology, fundamental theology, as that discipline responsible for defining the essence of Christianity and opposing contrasting religious and communal ideas.[35]

---

[33]See this distinction in the first edition of *Brief Outline*, § 252, n. 205.

[34]*On the Glaubenslehre*, 67.

[35]Rather than calling the genus of apologetics and polemics philosophical theology, Drey refers to it as *Grundlegung*, which is further contrasted with the *specielle Wissenschaft* that includes the "System of Christian Doctrines," and the "System of the Church."

Drey's presentation of the nature of apologetics in the *Kurze Einleitung* resembles the basic description found in the first edition of the *Kurze Darstellung*: apologetics determines the essence of the Christian religion.[36] Most importantly, Drey and Schleiermacher agree that the "highest scientific construction" within apologetics entails ascertaining the essence of Christianity through an intuition of this essence within history.[37] Thus philosophical theology is a discipline that mediates between speculative concepts and the empirically, historically given, in order to critically determine the essence of Christianity.[38] For both authors, the role of apologetics is to articulate the essence, examine it in its historical manifestations, and to ask the critical question: has it been adequately maintained and continued throughout the traditioning process?

Drey also echoes Schleiermacher when he writes of the critical task of polemics within fundamental theology, even though he does not use Schleiermacher's terms for the diseased state (*Krankheitszustand*) of the ecclesial body. The two concur on the critical role of the discipline in challenging schismatic and heretical distortions of the essence.[39]

While Drey formally agrees with Schleiermacher on the nature of apologetics and polemics in the *Kurze Einleitung*, there are a number of noteworthy discrepancies. First, Drey never describes fundamental theology as a critical discipline distinct from a

---

[36]See *Kurze Einleitung*, §§ 72, 221-247.

[37]*Kurze Einleitung*, §§ 229-230. *Brief Outline*, § 65, n. 32. Terrence Tice is justified in translating *Anschauung* as perspective, but for Drey, with his knowledge of Schelling's philosophy, the term could easily connote intuition.

[38]*Kurze Einleitung*, §§ 223, 226.

[39]Compare *Kurze Einleitung*, §§ 246 and 240 with *Brief Outline*, § 56, n. 25 and § 57, n. 26. Both theologians discuss hyperorthodoxy or extreme orthodoxy when examining dogmatic theology, but neither mentions this problem when they treat the nature of polemics. However, in principle, the criticism of hyperorthodoxy could be included in polemics insofar as it is seen to violate the essence of Christianity.

speculative or empirical discipline in the way that Schleiermacher did.[40] Drey expresses agreement with Schleiermacher's definition of ethics as the science of the principles of history,[41] and he posits the importance of historical (empirical) and rational (speculative) modes of knowledge in fundamental theology. But Drey speaks of fundamental theology as a science, which unites the empirical and the speculative through a philosophical construction from the idea or essence of Christianity. It seems accurate to say that for Drey the formation of the concept of the essence of Christianity is obtained through a rational intuition, which is confirmed in history, whereas for Schleiermacher the formation of the concept of the essence is through a critical judgment deriving from history.[42] Neither separates the conceptual and the historical in their discrimination of the essence, but the way they come to determine this essence appears different. If there is a difference here between Drey and Schleiermacher, as I think there is, it is a subtle and important one that is rooted in Drey's agreement with Schelling's early philosophy, and Schleiermacher's nuanced disagreement.

A second and related difference is that for Drey apologetics defends the necessity of Christianity as divinely posited and not accidental or contingent.[43] Now it must be acknowledged that Schleiermacher writes of the necessity of Christianity in the first edition of the *Kurze Darstellung*, but only once. When discussing the problem of indifferentism in the Church in relation to the task of polemics, he said that "(i)f Christianity is thought to have a necessary existence (*eine notwendige Existenz*), then that [alternative] version of Christianity must be shown to be a diseased condition."[44]

---

[40]This is more clearly sated in the second edition of the *Brief Outline*, § 32, but it is implied in the first edition in § 32, n. 1, and § 37, n. 6.

[41]*Kurze Einleitung*, § 383.

[42]*Kurze Einleitung*, §§ 223, 230.

[43]*Kurze Einleitung*, § 234. cf. Stalder, *Grundlinien der Theologie*, 101.

[44]*Brief Outline*, § 56, n. 25. Schleiermacher also argues in the first and the second editions of the *Kurze Darstellung* that "in ethics it must be possible to show that the founding and existence of such associations [based on

Drey may have judged that Schleiermacher's early position was in this respect consistent with his own. However, Schleiermacher did not describe apologetics in terms of defending the necessity of the Christian religion, and the above formulation is dropped in the second edition of the *Kurze Darstellung*. The distinction between accidental and necessary is, of course, a prominent feature in Schelling's philosophy of identity.

A third difference is that Drey speaks about the essence of Christianity in terms of the idea of the kingdom of God. Schleiermacher did not define the essence in the *Kurze Darstellung*, but in the introduction to the *Glaubenslehre* it was identified in terms of "redemption accomplished by Jesus of Nazareth."[45] In Drey's later writings he would speak of the *Gottmensch* and the Incarnation as the *Grundidee* of Christianity. By contrast, whenever Schleiermacher spoke about soteriology in relation to christology, whether in the introduction or within the body of dogmatics, he deployed the image of the kingdom of God to clarify what is distinctive about Christianity. Thus, in the strict sense, there is a difference between their articulations of the essence of Christianity. Yet in practice, for both, the idea of the kingdom of God as determined within Christianity describes that which is essential for Christianity. A christological title, or a christological affirmation inseparably bound to a soteriological claim, provides a shorthand way of defining this essence.[46]

A fourth and final difference is that for Drey apologetics articulates the essence of the Christian religion on the ideal side in

---

religious piety] comprise a necessary element in the development of humanity" (§ 22, n. 31). To argue for the necessity of religion, which is always communal for him, is not the same as seeking to demonstrate the necessity of various aspects of Christianity. Thus he says, "[w]e entirely renounce all attempt to prove the truth or necessity of Christianity. . ." (*Christian Faith* § 11, p. 60).

[45]*Christian Faith*, § 11, p. 52.

[46]Cf. Kustermann, *Die Apologetik Johann Sebastian Dreys*, 198, 314, n. 15.

terms of the idea of the kingdom of God, and it expresses the essence of the Church, which is the real side, that it, the historical embodiment, of the kingdom of God.[47] This distinction between the ideal and the real reflects a central distinction in Schelling's *Vorlesungen über die Methode.* But note also the following statement made by Schleiermacher in the first edition of the *Kurze Darstellung*: "Since the proper nature (*Wesen*) of a particular form of religion is expressed most discernably in its dogmas [or teachings], on the ideal side, and on the real side in its polity (*Verfassung*), it must be shown, if the inner consistency of Christianity is to be represented, how that same essence is expressed in both."[48] This is the only use of the ideal and real distinction in the first edition of the *Kurze Darstellung* and it drops out in the second edition. On the other hand, this distinction between ideal and real remains important for Drey's theology.

We can conclude from these four issues that Drey could easily perceive that his own position on apologetics mirrored Schleiermacher's. However, when viewed in light of the second edition of the *Kurze Darstellung* and from the discussions in the *Glaubenslehre*, differences come to light that were accentuated and compounded in their later writings, but that were in evidence from the beginning. These differences in no way challenge the basic agreement between Schleiermacher and Drey on the overall design and purpose of the discipline of fundamental theology, but they offer important indications of differences that will subsequently increase.

In the first volume of Drey's three volume *Apologetik*, which appeared in 1838, he confesses that in his earlier formulations he had agreed with Schleiermacher. "I found acceptable for a time the same construction [of apologetics] given by Schleiermacher, and

---

[47]*Kurze Einleitung*, §§ 71, 222; for the essence of the Christian doctrines, see §§ 230-232; and for the essence of the Christian Church, see §§ 233-236.

[48]*Brief Outline*, § 49, n. 19; also see § 44, n. 13 where Schleiermacher states that apologetics must "demonstrate the essence of Christianity, basing itself on a general determination of that in terms of which the distinctive nature of a particular Church and form of religion is to be identified."

according to this the outline of apologetics was designed in my *Introduction to the Study of Theology*."[49] However with this new publication Drey believes himself to be breaking away from Schleiermacher's plan. Let us quote him at length to set forth his reasoning:

> However I later became convinced that Schleiermacher's construction of apologetics stands in the closest connection with his construction of dogmatics. For since he assigns to the latter the task of presenting the doctrine of the Christian Church which is valid for a particular time,[50]--thus, the variable and therefore not the essential in the content of Christianity--it was necessary, if something in this content is essential, to include it in another discipline, and here he looks to apologetics. However, disregarding all of this entirely, since then it has been demonstrated from different sides and in different ways that nothing of Christian doctrine can revert to the system of apologetics, insofar as it [apologetics] wants to be a special theological discipline. Thus the essence of Christianity, which apologetics has to present, can be only the essence of its origin and proper definition, or it can be only the *basic character of its entire manifestation*, which is here to be determined and justified. From this point of view, after long reflection and, as will become clear from this work, not without careful comparison and testing of the other views, I have defined and executed the task of apologetics. And only if it is grasped from this point of view, can it serve, according to my convictions, as foundation for the system of Christian theology, and make the same claim on a particular place. For besides, it [apologetics] would always have to borrow its principles and its subject matter from the

---

[49]*Apologetik*, 1:iv. Drey refers to his *Kurze Einleitung*, §§ 230ff, where he treats the nature of apologetics.

[50]Drey is quoting verbatim the 1820-1821 edition of Schleiermacher's *Der christliche Glaube*, § 1. In the revised second 1830 edition, Schleiermacher keeps this proposition as § 19 with the change of "gegebenen" for "bestimmen" (Zeit).

individual organic disciplines, only as an aggregate of the different apologies for Christianity.[51]

Drey no longer agrees with Schleiermacher's conception of apologetics and its interrelationship with dogmatics. Relying on Schleiermacher's definition of dogmatic theology, he contends that for Schleiermacher the variable rather than the essential is the proper subject matter of the dogmatics. Drey suggests, and he is not the last to do so, that Schleiermacher's dogmatics presents a cultural Christianity, swayed by the variable fads of a particular time. Schleiermacher's definition of dogmatic theology may lend support to Drey's interpretation by suggesting that he is primarily concerned with doctrines valid in the present time. However, Drey's interpretation fails to recognize that the essence of Christianity is for Schleiermacher the subject matter of both philosophical theology and dogmatic theology.[52]

In Drey's new formulation, the aim of apologetics is to determine rightly and justify the divine positivity or basic character of Christianity in its entirety. Dogmatics, on the other hand, constructs a system which specifies the doctrinal content of the essence of Christianity rather than attempt to prove its divine origin.

---

[51] *Apologetik*, 1:iv-v, emphasis Drey's.

[52] Read the comment of Stephen Sykes on Schleiermacher's dogmatics: "When we come . . . to the proper subject matter of dogmatic theology, the concept of the essence of Christianity disappears from the scene. Contrary to what one might expect, the content of dogmatics is not said, in the *Brief Outline*, to consist in the elaboration and explanation of all that is implicit in the formulated essence." *The Identity of Christianity* (Philadelphia: Fortress Press, 1984), 97. Sykes argues, like Drey, that Schleiermacher was concerned with the faith of the Church at the present time, but unlike Drey, Sykes correctly recognizes that for Schleiermacher the essence of Christianity was the subject matter of dogmatics and there was no need to belabor the obvious (97-98).

Apologetics properly conceived is "for the purpose of the scientific knowledge of the whole of Christianity and its positive basic character as the perfect revelation, on which rests everything and with which everything is given: truth, salvation, holiness, and blessedness."[53] Apologetics does not hinder the dogmatic task of providing a scientific presentation of the essence of Catholic Christianity in its details; it serves it by setting forth the basic character of the Catholic Christian faith and demonstrating the divinely ordained status of each of its components.

Why did Drey develop an alternative to Schleiermacher's apologetic method? Apparently Drey believed his own conception of apologetics would safeguard the enterprise from the kinds of criticisms that Schleiermacher's introduction to the *Glaubenslehre* received.[54] The principal complaint raised, which is reflected in Drey's own position, is that in Schleiermacher's introduction he had philosophically determined the essence of Christianity outside of dogmatics proper, and had thereby philosophically constructed and predetermined what his conclusions would be in his dogmatic treatments.[55] Thus, Drey's approach enables dogmatic theology to present the essence of the doctrinal system of the Church for a

---

[53]*Apologetik*, 1:18.

[54]For criticisms of Schleiermacher's *Der christliche Glaube*, and his response, see *On the Glaubenslehre*, 2-6.

[55]Fehr tells us that Drey in his lectures on dogmatics argues that Schleiermacher, Zimmer (following Schelling), and Marheineke (following Hegel) were guilty of transforming Christianity into philosophy. On the other hand Drey believed that the Fathers and certain scholastics transformed philosophy into Christianity. Drey sought to affirm the historical and the scientific character of Christianity and so to integrate philosophy and Christianity. See Fehr, *The Dogmatics of Drey*, 154-155. In the preface to the second slightly revised edition of the first volume of *Die Apologetik* (1944), Drey describes Schleiermacher as "the newest and latest phase" of rationalism or of "the kind of System, which recognizes no other revelation of God except the primitive one already contained in reason" (xx). He then mentions Schleiermacher's treatment of miracles and inspiration, issues we will examine later.

particular time. Drey drops Schleiermacher's language of "the essence of Christianity" altogether within apologetics, presumably to distinguish his position from Schleiermacher's. Instead, Drey states that apologetics demonstrates the divine positivity of Catholic Christianity by showing the divine origin of the basic characteristics of religion, Christianity, and the Catholic Church.

Drey's departure from Schleiermacher's approach to apologetics was elaborated in his *Apologetik*. But was it a genuine departure? Let us review the grand threefold schema of his apologetics in order to answer this question. First, Apologetics provides a general, "purely scientific," and not critical, treatment of religion and revelation in their common characteristics.[56] He does not seek a construction of the essence of Christianity, but rather he strives to prove the divine origins of the content of Christianity, its revelatory character, and its salvific import.[57] Accordingly, the first volume of Drey's *Apologetik* examines basic characteristics of religion: the immediate and mediated revelation of God in human consciousness,

---

[56]*Apologetik*, 1:18. Drey states that "apologetics of Christianity can only be conducted out of the principles of philosophy of religion and the history of religion." This still echoes Schleiermacher. But not so when he speaks about apologetics as a philosophy of revelation that considers the idea of revelation and examines the content and embodiment of the idea of revelation in Christianity (1:6). This is contrary to the critical role of apologetics in relation to empirical knowledge of historical forms of Christianity in Schleiermacher's model. Thus Drey also says, "(t)he idea itself . . . is the eternal; it is that which realizes itself in the factual and the temporal, which is in itself the one and the same; in the manifestation, however, it forms itself in multiple ways; it can for that reason be conceived and judged only from within itself. For that very reason the idea of revelation is indeed also Christian, because Christianity also is an act of revelation, a peculiar realization of the idea. . . "(7).

[57]*Apologetik*, 1: vi, 24. Kustermann suggests that the method of construction drops out of Drey's later works. See Kustermann, *Die Apologetik*, 256.

or what could be described as the transcendental and the categorical nature of revelation.[58]

Second, apologetics develops a more concrete analysis of revelation in natural and historical world religions (Eastern, Western, and, then, an extended treatment of Judaism), in comparison with the nature of Christianity as a positive and historical religion (culminating in a defense of the resurrection of Jesus Christ).[59] In his second volume, Drey examines "Religion in its historical development," in family, national, and historical expressions. He investigates how religion has manifested itself in nature and history;[60] the "heathen" creation and nature religions, and Eastern and ancient Western religions; the development of the true religion through the continuing revelation in Judaism;[61] and finally the revelation of God through Christ.[62] This portion, devoted to "the fullness of revelation through Christ," does not leave us with a proposition briefly encapsulating the "essence of Christianity" as Schleiermacher's introduction to the *Glaubenslehre* does. But the basic characteristics (or essence) of Christianity developed in these sections establish the distinctive plan of redemption fulfilled in Christ in contrast to Judaism and nature religions. Moreover, the basic depiction of Christianity is not profoundly different from Schleiermacher's essence of Christianity as he describes it in the *Glaubenslehre*: the personality, teaching, and work of Jesus Christ are the source of Christian redemption and they indicate its uniqueness in comparison with Judaism and nature-based religions. Drey distinguishes his position from that of Schleiermacher's in terms of what constitutes a legitimate argument in apologetics and in christology, both of which we will comment on

---

[58]*Apologetik*, 1:309-317.

[59]*Apologetik*, 1:25.

[60]*Apologetik*, 2:64-74.

[61]See *Apologetik*, 2:162-169, 174-190.

[62]*Apologetik*, 2:199-363.

in due course, but not in terms of the task of determining the basic characteristics of Christianity.

Third, apologetics argues for the revealed nature of the Catholic Church. In the third and final volume of *Apologetik*, Drey defends the basic characteristics of the Catholic Church as divinely inspired and protected by its hierarchical structure, priesthood, and constitution.[63]

Apologetics for Drey treats the revelation of God and the human reception of this revelation. Drey utilizes various kinds of proofs and criteria in demonstrating the divine character of revelation.[64] Since revelation announces a person as envoy, the proof of this revelation rests partially upon this person, first, through his distinctive personality--the person's knowledge, moral character, and intended plan, and second, through the deeds and events of his life.[65] In the former, the divine nature of revelation becomes evident by showing the fitting character of this person.[66] The latter deeds and events provide outer criteria for judging revelation; in Christianity, miracles (including the miracle of the resurrection) and prophecy are outer historical criteria.[67] Third, and "partially above these [outer criteria]" there are inner criteria based on the content of revelation.[68] Drey posits several inner criteria for demonstrating the divine positivity of revelation. These are contrasted and united with the outer historical criterion for revelation (e.g., miracles and prophecies).[69] There are inner criteria based on the material content of the revealed teachings, but all are based on the main criterion of conformity with human reason. There are also inner criteria based on the formal

---

[63]*Apologetik*, 1:26.

[64]See *Apologetik*, 1:324-379. These criteria will be examined again in Chapter IV.

[65]*Apologetik*, 1:331.

[66]See *Apologetik*, 1:331-332, 334-344.

[67]See *Apologetik*, 1:344-363.

[68]*Apologetik*, 1:332, 363-380, especially 367-374.

[69]*Apologetik*, 1:374-380.

presentation of this content. The positive material criteria are: the rational truth of the teachings of revelation; the moral holiness of these teachings; and, the human purposes and needs addressed by these teachings. The formal criteria are: the sacred dignity of the presentation; and, the fact that the comprehensibility and obscurity of the presentation must adhere to the addressee and not only to the subject matter--discourse must be addressed to the heart (*Gemüt*). Drey adds a further criterion based solely on the conformity of the teachings with the needs of heart, specifically with pious feelings as they inspire holiness, moral behavior, and reverence for the beautiful. This criterion is identified with what previous theologians called the inner "testimony of the Holy Spirit." This inner self experience cannot be treated among the proper proofs of revelation, which are based on something objective or at least communicable, i.e., the criteria from the proper content or the criteria from the form of the revealed teaching. On the basis of these criteria a divine revelation can be denied, affirmed, or acknowledged as a probability.

Does the later apologetics of Drey differ from Schleiermacher's? The most important difference, in Drey's estimation, concerns the relationship between apologetics and dogmatics.[70] Drey believes that Schleiermacher treats the variable elements and not the essence of Christianity in dogmatics; in this case, apologetics establishes the essence outside of dogmatics. Drey seeks to distinguish his position by stating that apologetics demonstrates the divine positivity of the basic characteristics of religion, Christianity, and the Catholic Church. The basic characteristics of Christianity are not constructed or critically determined, rather they are provided by the fact of revelation. A final difference, which we shall return to

---

[70]It seems quite plausible that when Drey read the first edition of the *Glaubenslehre*, serious questions arose in his own mind about Schleiermacher's (and his own) understanding of the nature of apologetics. See Kustermann, *Die Apologetik Johann Sebastian Dreys*, 187-199; and, Nico Schruers, "Johann Sebastian Drey und Friedrich Schleiermacher. Ein Forschungsbericht," (unpublished essay), 6.

shortly, concerns Schleiermacher's rejection of external proofs from miracles and prophecies for the Christian religion.

Still, without minimizing Drey's own reservations and criticisms, the broad outlines of his apologetics remain consistent with Schleiermacher's expressed position. Within Schleiermacher's framework, the very first part of Drey's *Apologetik* on the nature of revelation would be borrowed from ethics as the knowledge of history and reason.[71] Second, the differentiation of the stages in the history of religions culminating in the Christian religion would be for Schleiermacher a task done by a philosophy of religion, "a discipline which by its reference to the idea of 'church,' relates to ethics in a similar fashion as another which refers to the idea of 'state' and still another refers to the idea of 'art.'"[72] Schleiermacher contends that distinguishing between natural religion and positive religions is a task for the philosophy of religion, but these concepts remain valid for the apologetics of every religious community.[73] Third, after Drey describes the basic character of the manifestation of Christianity, he goes on to argue for the specific, historical character of Catholic revelation as the foundation for the Catholic Church. Although the first edition of Schleiermacher's *Kurze Darstellung* indicated that apologetics should distinguish not only forms of religion, but also distinct churches, in his later work any suggestion of an ecclesial apologetic is incorporated into the Christian form of religion and is also taken up within dogmatics proper.[74]

---

[71]See *Kurze Einleitung*, § 383, *Brief Outline*, § 35, n. 4; and *Christian Faith*, §§ 3-6.

[72]*Brief Outline*, § 23.

[73]*Brief Outline*, § 43; See also *Christian Faith*, §§ 7-10.

[74]In the first edition Schleiermacher distinguishes the idea of religion and of the Church and of the historical forms of religion and churches, whereas in the second edition this distinction is not employed. Religion is always communal for Schleiermacher, and apologetics in his later writings does not need to offer a separate defense of the ecclesial character of Christianity. See *Brief Outline*, § 32, n. 1, and § 33 and *Christian Faith*, §§ 23-24.

If apologetics establishes the essence of Christianity, which Schleiermacher at one point claims as its basic task, then Drey has broadened the notion of apologetics to encompass what Schleiermacher would have included under the designation "Ethics," and philosophy of religion. But, like Drey, Schleiermacher believed that a discussion of the nature of religion and the diverse types of religious communities should be included within apologetics.

An important question remains: What is the difference between Schleiermacher's "essence" of Christianity and Drey's "basic characteristics"? The later Drey believed that by reserving the task of deducing the essence of Christianity in terms of specific doctrines for dogmatics, he had secured the integrity of dogmatics against the accusation that apologetics or some external philosophy had established its content. So for Drey, apologetics demonstrates the basic characteristics of Christianity, while dogmatics scientifically formulates the specific doctrines of Christian faith. Even though Schleiermacher's language is different--apologetics determines the essence and dogmatics describes the current consciousness of the Church, a parallel can be detected. Apologetics, for Schleiermacher, in its attempt to present what is essential or most basic, makes a critical, concrete judgment about the essence of Christianity drawn from and abstracting from Christian history, which includes the current state of the Church, the domain of dogmatics. Dogmatic theology formulates the individual doctrines of the Christian faith with more specificity and is concerned with the adequacy of the presentation for the present time. Would Drey disagree? In fact, the essence of Christianity is the subject matter of both apologetics and dogmatics for Drey and Schleiermacher, Drey's interpretation of Schleiermacher's position notwithstanding.

What does distinguish apologetics and dogmatics for them is not the essence of Christianity--which provides the subject matter for both disciplines, but the mode of arguments or the methods that are deemed appropriate for these distinctive enterprises. As we have seen, Schleiermacher employed a critical method within apologetics, combining speculative and empirical kinds of knowledge. The aim was to establish the essence from amidst the various manifestations of Christianity. This essence, which must be constantly open to revision, provides a basis for criticizing deviant manifestations within Christianity and for communicating the conviction of the truth of the mode of faith promulgated within the Christian community.[75] Drey's method for apologetics combines speculative and empirical kinds of knowledge, but the aim of establishing the essence or basic characteristic of Christianity is to prove or demonstrate the divine positivity of Christianity and specifically Catholic Christianity.

It seems that during the 19 years after his *Kurze Einleitung* appeared, Drey tempered the critical nature of fundamental theology as he originally understood it, in favor of a rational defense of the positively-determined characteristics of Christianity. It is not that apologetics no longer serves any critical purpose. The later Drey still believes that apologetics must criticize lifeless manifestations of Christianity and the Catholic Church and must criticize suprarationalism as well as rationalism; perhaps this is quite enough for the affirmation and development of doctrine. However, Drey no longer writes of the problems of hyperorthodoxy and doctrinal inertia, there is no more mention of the imbalances evident in some scholastic thinkers;[76] instead, the theological critique offered by fundamental theology targets predominantly the innovative, without discussing those positions that are lagging behind, have inertia, or are decaying. Schleiermacher differs from the later Drey in that for Schleiermacher the essence continues to serve as the basis for criticizing not only heresies and schisms, but also the extremes of orthodoxy. This critical character in Schleiermacher's philosophical theology serves as a guardian for orthodoxy, but it also serves as a strong impetus for the development and reform of doctrine.

---

[75]*Brief Outline*, §§ 37, 39.

[76]Cf. "Revision," 87-89, 93.

The Scientific Task of Dogmatic Theology

Dogmatic theology contributes to doctrinal development by seeking to present the Christian faith in a way consistent with the contemporary life of the Church and responsive to contemporary currents of thought and practice. There is a creative and constructive character to dogmatics, which needs to be emphasized when we speak about doctrinal development, but there is also a matter of fidelity and honesty involved--fidelity to the essence of Christianity as the very substance of faith, and honesty in interpreting the entire history of Christianity, especially in interpreting the ecclesial situation in the present.

These tasks and commitments characterize Schleiermacher's and Drey's theological encyclopedia, but they coalesce in their presentations of the scientific task of dogmatic theology. It is on the basis of these characteristics that a subsequent generation identified these theologians as pioneers in fashioning a "mediating" method in theology: one that mediates between the Christian tradition and the modern world.[77] Mediating between the Christian tradition and the modern world requires being responsive to the inner and outer dynamics of doctrinal development as they pertain to the task of dogmatic theology. Accordingly, Schleiermacher and Drey, as we will seek to show, employ a method in dogmatic theology which, on the one hand, strives to present the

---

[77]The term "mediating theology" was coined in the journal *Theologische Studien und Kritiken*, which was founded in 1828 and associated with the heirs of Schleiermacher and Hegel. For the Protestant history of the appellation, see Ragner Holte, *Vermittlungstheologie* (Uppsala: Almqvist & Wiksell, 1965), Emanuel Hirsch, *Geschichte der neuern evagelischen Theologie* (Münster: Antiquariat Th. Stendergoff, 1984), 5:364-430, and, Claude Welch, *Protestant Thought in the Nineteenth Century* (New Haven: Yale University Press, 1972), 1:269. The Catholic Drey is not included in these histories of Protestant theology, but he properly belongs in this category. See Francis Schüssler Fiorenza, *Foundational Theology* (New York: Crossroad, 1984), 249-284.

Christians doctrines in a way that is coherent with the experience or consciousness of the Church (the first meaning of inner) and coherent with the linguistic heritage that has expressed and shaped the experience of the Church (the first meaning of outer). Their dogmatic method strives, on the other hand, to formulate the doctrines (the second meaning of inner) in a way responsive to modern thought, that is, the state of science and philosophy in the present age (the second meaning of outer). Their approaches to dogmatic theology reformulate the classical understanding of theology and by so doing pave the way for the correlation methods developed by Paul Tillich, Karl Rahner and their Protestant and Catholic heirs.[78]

While Drey and Schleiermacher have in common a mediating orientation, their approaches to dogmatics are, nevertheless, significantly different, indeed, one could say, opposite. For Schleiermacher the dogmatic enterprise begins by describing (more accurately interpreting) the pious consciousness of the Christian Church at a given time, and then develops derivative concepts of God and the world. Dogmatic propositions should do three things: (1) refer to descriptions of religious consciousness; (2) cohere with the primary language of faith of the Protestant confessions and the Scriptures, especially the language of the kingdom of God; and (3) be adequate to the contemporary state of science and philosophy.[79] Drey, on the other hand, is speculative in the sense that he begins with the idea of the kingdom of God and deduces the various

---

[78]Cf. Fiorenza, *Foundational*, 276-284.

[79]Schleiermacher emphasizes in the *Glaubenslehre* (e.g., §§ 30-31) that dogmatic propositions must cohere with the descriptions of the consciousness of the Church, and acknowledges that they must be coherent according to the recent state of science. He also insists that all propositions (*Sätze*) must cohere with the Evangelical confessional documents or else the New Testament Scriptures. (§ 27) The image of the kingdom of God is a focal point in Schleiermacher's use of the Scriptures.

doctrines from that idea;[80] these doctrines must cohere with the symbols of the Christian Church; they are confirmed by the mystical and historical experience and reality of the ecclesial community; and the theologian must strive to clarify and develop these doctrines in accordance with the current state of scientific knowledge. Schleiermacher's dogmatic method is descriptive and mediating; Drey's dogmatic procedure is deductive and mediating. Let us examine their logic at work.

For Drey both fundamental theology and dogmatic theology are truly scientific since they provide a philosophical construction out of ideas.[81] Fundamental theology, specifically apologetics, seeks, according to the early Drey, to provide a philosophical construction of the essence of Christianity and of the essence of the Christian church as the ideal and the real sides of the kingdom of God. According to later Drey, apologetics demonstrates the divinely-posited basic characteristics of Christianity and the Catholic Church. Likewise, Drey distinguishes a "system of Christian doctrines," or dogmatic and moral theology, on the one hand and a "system of the Christian church," or a theory of cult and government, on the other.[82] This distinction reflects the difference between the ideal and the real manifestations of the kingdom of God.[83]

---

[80]I use speculative here in contrast with Schleiermacher's descriptive (meaning empirical) approach, because Drey begins, following German idealists, with the realm of ideas. This usage of speculative is not Drey's own as he employs it in contrast to *Symbolik*. We will treat that usage shortly.

[81]For the contrast between philosophical construction and historical construction, see *Kurze Einleitung*, §§ 56, 64-66.

[82]*Kurze Einleitung*, §§ 253-254.

[83]See *Kurze Einleitung*, § 71.

Based on Drey's treatment in the *Kurze Einleitung*,[84] what distinguishes the special science of dogmatics from apologetic theology is that dogmatics deduces all of the individual doctrines of Christianity from the idea of the kingdom of God, whereas apologetics presents the basic characteristics of Catholic Christianity as a religion of redemption made possible through the work of God in Jesus Christ and mediated by the Church.[85] As Drey explains dogmatics, "[t]he task of this part of scientific theology is to present --through the construction of the whole out of its idea [i.e., the idea of the kingdom of God] and by means of systematic consequences-- the doctrine of Christianity in the development which it has received so far and in relation to the Christian confession, whose belief one shares."[86]

Drey proposes a twofold mission for dogmatic theology: to affirm what has been closed or fixed in doctrinal articulations, and to push forward what is still mobile and in need of further development. The first ecclesial interest he calls "*Symbolik*," for it is concerned about dogmatic consistency with confessional statements. The second speculative interest is called "*Scholastik*" and it promotes scientific speculation on doctrines.[87] What has

---

[84]This analysis of Drey's understanding of dogmatic theology is based almost exclusively on his *Kurze Einleitung*. In addition to what he says there, Drey lectured on dogmatics between 1815 and 1834. Three handwritten volumes of these lecture are kept in the Library of the Wilhelmstift in Tübingen. There are four sets of student notes on Drey's dogmatic lectures; a small portion of one set has been published in Geiselmann, *Die Katholische Tübingner Schule*, 210-23. Wayne Fehr's dissertation, *The Birth of the Catholic Tübingen School: The Dogmatics of Johann Sebastian Drey*, offers the first major study of these lectures.

[85]On the idea of the Kingdom of God see *Kurze Einleitung*, §§ 58-60; On the deduction of the individuals from the idea, see §§ 64, 248, 253-255.

[86]*Kurze Einleitung*, § 255.

[87]*Kurze Einleitung*, §§ 262-263. Drey speaks of it as a "speculative interest" in § 51. The dynamic polarity between "Symbolik" and "Scholastik" is analogous to, but not the same as, the united polarity Drey developed

been dogmatically defined by the Church is fixed and unchanging for Drey and dogmatic theology must faithfully adhere to these confessional claims.[88] Yet the theologian also has a calling to push forward the implicit dogmas of the Church which have yet to be declared by advancing theological opinions. The dogmatic mission of scholastic or scientific speculation secures the mediating nature of dogmatic theology: it promotes theological creativity and further development on individual doctrines in light of the present state of scientific knowledge.

> Whatever is not yet completed within Christian doctrines is mobile; since the completion is for the Church the only objectively valid criterion of Christian truth, and the mobile concept lacks this criterion, it is thus called, in this context, opinion; and insofar as disagreement prevails among the scholars within the Church or in the school, it is called, school opinion, [or] theological opinion. Basically it can, however, notwithstanding that disagreement, still be Christian truth, which has only not yet developed to that degree that it could be universally known as such in the Church. For that reason and because it is the destiny of Christian doctrine to unfold increasingly clearly, and the theologian as teacher of his church is called to work for that purpose--opinions are also not merely an accidental, but rather a necessary object of dogmatic-moral inquiries and presentations.
>
> And here the relationship of science to Christian doctrine and to the church manifests itself. Science gives ever new inspirations toward the development of Christian doctrines and leads its mobile element toward its completed state. Hence, it works into the hands of the Church, because the impulse to further development and to a closer determination of the concepts can proceed only from individuals, and before the completion of a concept can occur, the same [i.e., the completion] must be prepared. This is the very

---

between the mystical principle (which does not strictly correspond with *Symbolik*) and the dialectical principle (which is similar to the nature of *Scholastik*) in his essay "Revision," 88.

[88] *Kurze Einleitung*, § 257.

purpose of science in relation to the formation of Christian doctrines.[89]

Theological speculation brought about the beginning of theology; it arose from the symbolic confession of faith, but it never became distinct from it: "the true dogmatic is neither merely symbolic nor merely scholastic, but rather the union of both."[90] Scientific speculation springs from within the empirically-historically revealed faith and strives to ground it.[91] Philosophical construction within apologetics demonstrates the necessity of the divinely posited revelation. Within dogmatics, philosophical construction seeks to "raise to the proper science the empirical-historical knowledge of Christianity, when its content is brought back to an idea and is presented out of this in the proper deduction of the individual."[92] Thus dogmatic theology deduces from the idea of the kingdom of God the diverse doctrinal claims about the nature of God, creation, sin, Christ, redemption, Church, and eschatology.[93] Dogmatic theology seeks to present, clarify, and develop these individual doctrines as the necessary unfolding of the idea of the kingdom of God within history. Thus are these doctrines shown to be necessary for reason, for the "whole" which is the scientific system, and most importantly for salvation.[94] In this process the mobile elements within doctrines move toward the

---

[89]*Kurze Einleitung*, §§ 258-259.

[90]*Kurze Einleitung*, § 263; see § 42 for the rise of theological speculation.

[91]*Kurze Einleitung*, §§ 63, 308.

[92]*Kurze Einleitung*, § 65; also § 316.

[93]See Fehr's discussion of Drey's lectures on dogmatic theology, "Praelectiones Dogmaticae," *The Dogmatics of Drey*, 178-244.

[94]*Kurze Einleitung*, § 309. Each dogmatic subject is deduced from the idea of the kingdom of God, but it is also situated in the narrative pattern of the economy of the kingdom of God. This "drama" of the kingdom of God provides Drey with a narrative coherence, even though he speaks of the identity which follows from the deduction out of the "idea" of the kingdom of God.

completion which marks the fixed elements and theological opinions become embraced by the Church universal.[95]

Each doctrine that is speculatively deduced from the idea of the kingdom of God must also be consistent with the historical and mystical experience of the Church. The ideal must be realized in the concrete. We can speak of a correlation between each doctrine and the historical, mystical experience of the Church. Dogmatic theology errs if it fails to recognize that these ideas are empirically-historically rooted in the reality of the Church.[96] The ideal side of the kingdom of God is confirmed in reality in this historical experience of the Church.

For Schleiermacher, dogmatic theology advances the development of doctrine through a coherent, dialectically precise, and systematic presentation of the "doctrine valid in a Christian Church at a given time."[97] All doctrinal statements (*Glaubensätze*), be they poetic, rhetorical, or didactic, are "accounts of the Christian religious affections set forth in speech" and its connections.[98] Thus, doctrines as expressed in the Scriptures, in preaching, in catechesis, and in dogmatic theology render public the consciousness of the Christian community of faith. Doctrinal statements (*Glaubensätze*) can be poetic, rhetorical, and didactic. But dogmatic propositions (*dogmatische Sätze*) are a specific kind of doctrinal statement: a didactic mode of discourse. Since dogmatic propositions are a species of doctrine, they present religious affections and therefore have an ecclesial character. Since they are didactic, they have a scientific character.[99] By clarifying the ecclesial and scientific characteristics of dogmatic theology, we will come to

---

[95]*Kurze Einleitung*, § 319.

[96]On the historical character of doctrines see *Kurze Einleitung*, §§ 257-261; On the need for mystical consciousness in order to avoid fruitless speculation and unprofitable word-games, see §§ 56, 82, and "Revision," 81; On the ecclesial basis of all theological knowing see *Kurze Einleitung*, § 54.

[97]*Christian Faith*, § 19 (translation amended).

[98]*Christian Faith*, § 15, p. 76, also see § 13, postscript.

[99]*Christian Faith*, § 17; cf. *Brief Outline*, § 177.

understand the role of dogmatic theology in the development of doctrine.

Dogmatic theology renders an interpretation, a description of the current consciousness of the Church. This is an ecclesial characteristic of dogmatic theology, which serves to acknowledge the faith of the Church and honestly assess the need for further doctrinal development. Schleiermacher's understanding of this descriptive task builds on his conception of the relationship between doctrines and religion. Religion is understood as that highest form of consciousness best spoken of as a feeling of absolute dependence, which has God as its immediate "whence."[100] This highest form of human self-consciousness is also *always* joined by lower levels of consciousness. Moreover, the immediate and unchanging nature of religious consciousness is *always* positively determined or shaped by its distinctive outward source in a fixed fact of history and by the precise inward modification of ecclesial consciousness.[101] While apologetics articulates the essential character of the Christian consciousness, dogmatic theology seeks to clarify the nature of this essence by describing how it is concretely manifested in the Christian community at a given time.

Dogmatic theology commences with "the direct description of the religious affections" of a church.[102] Although human self-consciousness, for Schleiermacher, includes consciousness of self, God, and the world, he insists that any statements about God and the world within dogmatics must develop out of descriptive statements about religious consciousness.[103] Such a dogmatic method, Schleiermacher believed, prevents the claims of speculative metaphysics and the sciences from making incursions into the dogmatic domain. At the same time, it recognizes a legitimate role

---

[100]*Christian Faith*, § 4.

[101]*Christian Faith*, § 10.

[102]*Christian Faith*, § 31, p. 127.

[103]*Christian Faith*, §§ 30, 35; also *On the Glaubenslehre*, 70-73.

for free scientific inquiry and speculation within their respective arenas.[104]

The ecclesial value of a doctrinal proposition is judged not only in terms of whether it describes ecclesial consciousness, but whether it is heretical. Does a doctrinal proposition contradict the essence of Christianity? Does it cohere or correlate (*Zusammengehörigkeit*) with the linguistic heritage of Protestant Christianity--the Protestant confessional documents, or if this is lacking, with the New Testament Scriptures?[105] On the basis of this ecclesial dimension, one can rightly say that for Schleiermacher there is a correlation between doctrinal propositions as a description of the religious experience of this current historical community of Christian faith and the linguistic heritage of the Church.

What is often overlooked in this context is the importance of the language of the kingdom of God within Schleiermacher's dogmatics. The language of the kingdom of God provides a biblical narrative setting for his treatment of specific issues and this language often is employed to test the congruity or fidelity of Schleiermacher's dogmatic formulation. After describing the consciousness of the church and offering derivative statements about God and the world, Schleiermacher is compelled to show how his treatment is consistent with a variety of claims about the kingdom of God.[106] As he states most explicitly in his section on the work of Christ,

> When we have . . . developed the subject in our own way, as above, on the basis of our own Christian experience, it is still worthwhile (*so gebührt uns doch*) to preserve a continuity with those original presentations [of the threefold office of priest, prophet, and king], for the first theoretical interpretation of Christianity was based upon a comparison of the new Kingdom of God with the old. And so we

---

[104]*On the Glaubenslehre*, 63-64.

[105]*Christian Faith*, § 27.

[106]*Christian Faith*, § 9, p. 43, §§ 102-105, pp. 439-475, § 113, p. 528. Also see *Die christliche Sitte*, 78-79, 242, 289-290, 324, 450.

> have to show that our conception is in agreement with that which the earlier Christians formed for themselves. . . .[107]

This task is not simply worthwhile or fitting, it as a duty. The image of the kingdom of God is the privileged motif by which Schleiermacher correlates his doctrinal propositions with the Bible.

Besides being judged for their ecclesial character, Schleiermacher contends that doctrinal propositions must also be assessed in terms of their scientific value. But what does scientific mean in this context? For Schleiermacher the question is this: are the doctrines logically precise, consistent with the current state of scientific knowledge, and systematically arranged? Schleiermacher does not adhere to Schelling's or Hegel's understanding of *Wissenschaft*, in which the specific sciences are viewed as the regionalized participation in an absolute and primal *Wissen*. Dogmatic theology as a science is a dialectical enterprise, but dialectical in a specific sense:

> The term 'dialectical' is . . . taken in exactly the ancient sense. The dialectical character of language therefore consists in its being formed in a technically correct manner, that it may be used in all discourse for the communication and correction of the knowledge in question.[108]

Thus dogmatic theology aims at articulating precisely and with clear focus the doctrines of the church, thereby to state completely the essential character of Christianity as it is concretely embodied at the present time.

The use of dialectical discourse within dogmatics is influenced by philosophy, but it does not require adhering to one philosophical system. Logical clarity of expression is aided by attention to the debates and changes going on within the realm of philosophy, "but it is neither necessary nor profitable to know which philosophical

---

[107]*Christian Faith*, § 102, p. 439.

[108]*Christian Faith*, § 28, p. 118.

system a theologian adheres to, so long as his language is correct and self-consistently formed."[109]

The dogmatic theologian strives for logical coherence and clarity when formulating dogmatic propositions. There is no special logic here; expressing religious affections and their connections "follow the same laws of conception and synthesis as regulate all speech."[110] Dogmatics strives for the "highest degree of definiteness," even though dialectical discourse is "a derivative and secondary form."[111] And yet, "the dialectical function is brought to bear on the utterances of the religious self-consciousness and guides the expression of them."[112]

Schleiermacher's emphasis on articulating dogmatic propositions with a logical precision that is consistent with the usage of language in philosophy and science implies the creative and mediating character of dogmatic theology. The theologian cannot merely reiterate the primary language of faith, rather he or she must articulate this faith anew in every generation so that it can be understood and received in each age and so that the Church might clarify this Christian faith with greater precision.

Dogmatic theology is scientific in an additional sense: it must construct a system of doctrine whose doctrinal formulations cohere. The parts of the system are related to one another systematically and so make up the whole. As Schleiermacher confesses, doctrines are not united through a deduction.

> My systematic skill, if I can boast of any in dogmatics, does not depend on principles and deductions. . . . It is quite simply the skill of discovering an organizational plan that can convince the readers that the presentation is complete and can refer them, if not

---

[109]*Christian Faith*, § 28, p. 119. On the dependence of dogmatics on philosophy see *Brief Outline*, § 213, also *On the Glaubenslehre*, 80-83, 85-87.

[110]*Christian Faith*, § 13, postscript.

[111]*Christian Faith*, § 16, p. 79; also § 28, and *Brief Outline*, §§ 209, 213-214.

[112]*Christian Faith*, § 16, p. 81.

> immediately, at least by mediation, from each dogmatic proposition back to the immediate self-consciousness that it represents."[113]

Schleiermacher concludes, "[t]he dialectical character of the language and the systematic arrangement give dogmatics the scientific form which is essential to it." He explains that "the very essence of systematic arrangement [is] that by comprehensive co-ordination and exhaustive subordination each proposition should be brought to a perfectly definite relation with all others." What dogmatic theology finally has is "the fundamental inner fact of Christian piety," for "what [dogmatics] has to arrange consists simply in the different modifications of this fact which emerge, according to its differing relations with the other facts of consciousness," so that they appear as a "complete whole."[114]

We can clarify Schleiermacher's position on the scientific task of dogmatics and its role in doctrinal development by contrasting it with Drey's. For Drey the idea of the kingdom of God constitutes the positive and divinely determined religion of Christianity on the ideal side, which in turn becomes "real" and "objective" in the consciousness of the Church. Dogmatic theology seeks to trace that idea as it unfolds on the ideal side into the individual parts as they make up the whole of the system and as it becomes real in the Church--through mysticism and in structured relationships. Schleiermacher, on the other hand, contends that it is the consciousness of the Church that presents the positive religion of Christianity, and that this consciousness has an enduring framework

---

[113]*On the Glaubenslehre*, 70; also see *Christian Faith*, § 18, p. 87.

[114]*Christian Faith*, § 28, p. 121; see also *On the Glaubenslehre*, 69-70 and *Brief Outline*, §§ 213-214. In *Christian Faith*, § 20-31, Schleiermacher discusses "a rule according to which some (material) will be adopted and others excluded" and "a principle for their arrangment and interconnection." We will examine the rule and the principle in the context of this entire section more carefully in our next chapter when we discuss the criteria for right development and reform.

in terms of the Creeds and the New Testament, and often he focusses on the biblical idea of the kingdom of God.

Drey states that dogmatic propositions must be judged on the basis of *Symbolik*--their coherence with official dogmas of the Church, and *Scholastik*--their systematic development and responsiveness to the state of scientific knowledge at the time. Schleiermacher provides an analogue when he distinguishes the ecclesial value and scientific value of dogmatic propositions.[115] Schleiermacher speaks of the ecclesial as the religious affections, the essence of Christianity, *and* the religious linguistic statements of confessional documents and the Scriptures. With Drey, however, the ecclesial is primarily identified with the Church's officially stated dogmas and derivatively with the Scriptures and the religious experience of the Church. Both maintain that dogmatic theology must promote doctrinal development so as to be responsive to the historical character of faith--for Schleiermacher doctrines are further clarified through dialectical discourse, for Drey doctrines are developed through speculation. They disagree on the relative weight that is given to confessional statements: Drey gives greater weight to dogmatic traditions, for they are "closed"; Schleiermacher gives them weight, but they are not closed and further questions may call for revisions of the previously accepted formulations. This difference will concern us again in the next chapter.

They also disagreed on how dogmatics is organized. Drey states that his dogmatics is united by the deduction of all the specific doctrines from the idea of the kingdom of God,[116] whereas

---

[115]Schleiermacher's treatments of the ecclesial and scientific dimensions of dogmatic propositions are most clearly articulated in *The Christian Faith*, § 17 and in the *Brief Outline*, § 177, in the second editions. But they can also be found in the first editions. See *Der christliche Glaube* (1st ed), §§ 30, 31; *Brief Outline*, § 177, n. 126.

[116]Fehr's work and the selection and commentary in Geiselmann, *Die Katholische Tübinger Schule*, make it apparent that Drey in his lectures on dogmatic theology did seek to correlate (deduce) all of the dogmatic areas from the idea of the kingdom of God. He argued that dogmatics was divided

Schleiermacher is content to arrange the specific doctrines in as coherent a manner as possible. The distinctions Schleiermacher develops between ecclesiastical and scientific dimensions of dogmatics and Drey employs between symbolic and scholastic sides of dogmatics provide a framework for understanding the creative and constructive tasks, but also the dangers, of dogmatic theology. For both, trouble arises in dogmatic theology when either one side or the other takes exclusive control.

Schleiermacher's insistence that dogmatic propositions must retain their ecclesial worth by remaining bound by and faithful to the limits of ecclesial piety, rather than transgressing those limits into philosophical speculation seems to stand at odds with Drey's discussion of the task of *Scholastik* as one of speculation.[117] It may be only an apparent difference, however, because Drey uses "speculation" to mean a theological opinion that has not been formally accepted by the Church. This usage is consistent with Schleiermacher's recognition that individuals have a creative purpose in the development of doctrines.[118] Drey accepts to some extent the model of speculative rationality and the metaphysics of identity developed by the early Schelling, and as we have seen, there are indications that this influences his dogmatic method, if not its

---

into *Theologia*--claims about God, and *Oeconomia*--claims about the drama of the kingdom of God as it reveals God's plan for history. Under the latter he distinguishes creation, sin, redemption, eschatological fulfillment.

[117]*Christian Faith*, § 16, pp. 81-82., also § 27, p. 117. He recognizes that speculations about God within philosophy might have some import for reflection about the Supreme Being, but they must not make any inroads into the system of doctrines. Gnosticism fostered speculation in theology, but "in the dogmatic developments of the earliest centuries . . . the influence of speculation upon the content of dogmatic propositions must be placed at zero" (82). It is during the Medieval period that the speculative interest begins to influence dogmatic language and there arises "a confusion of the speculative with the dogmatic, and consequently a mingling of the two, was almost inevitable" (82).

[118]*Brief Outline*, § 199.

content. Schleiermacher explicitly rejects speculative metaphysical claims within dogmatic theology, but acknowledges that current philosophies will leave their mark on dogmatic propositions.

Dogmatic theology for both Schleiermacher and Drey further promotes the development of doctrine by way of the thorough treatment of the individual Christian doctrines in relation to one another as they form a whole system of doctrines. In Drey's work, the individual doctrines are shown to be necessary insofar as they are deduced from the idea of the kingdom of God as a part of the historical plan of salvation. Accordingly, doctrines correlate with the mystical and historical experience of the Church, i.e., these ideas must become real within the Church. For Schleiermacher, the individual doctrines are dialectical presentations of the consciousness of the Church. These doctrines must correlate with the religious affections of the Church and they must cohere with confessional statements, the New Testament witness and, in numerous instances, the original presentations of the kingdom of God.

Schleiermacher's and Drey's understandings of "science" are divergent and their understandings of the method of dogmatic theology are in some ways distinct. Yet, the question can be asked: do their kindred attempts to mediate between Christian faith and modern thought and their efforts at correlating religious doctrinal propositions with the experience of the Church offset these differences? Even though Schleiermacher rejects Schelling's distinction between the ideal and the real, could one not argue that Drey begins with the ideal (linguistic) presentation of the kingdom of God and correlates it with the real, whereas Schleiermacher begins by describing the Church (the real manifestation of the kingdom of God) and then correlates this description with the ideal (linguistic) formulation of the kingdom of God as found within the Scriptures?

Is it possible that one of these dogmatic methods fosters more doctrinal change than the other? Will one method permit the theologian to say more about God, the Trinity, the person and work of Christ, and the nature of the Church and the sacraments? Both theologians promote doctrine development, but without a doubt Schleiermacher's written legacy is more reform-minded. Drey's dogmatic method is more definite about the inner nature of God and the Trinity, about the importance of Christ's death and resurrection in the plan of salvation, and about the infallibility of the historical Church. By way of contrast, Schleiermacher's dogmatic theology remains a theology of limits. His claims about God, the Trinity, the person and work of Christ, and the Church are not devoid of content, but they are bound by the Church's piety, both by what that piety requires and by the limits of the knowledge which that piety yields.

The Theologian As Organic Leader

Schleiermacher and Drey agree that theologians need to acquire certain proficiencies in language, history, philosophy, and the sciences and that they should cultivate specific talents or skills in order to interpret, criticize, and creatively systematize Christian doctrines. These abilities are required for the scientific nature of the theology to be maintained and advanced. But besides these scientific qualifications and interests, the theologian needs to be in a life-sustaining relationship with the Christian community. This organic bond with a community of faith is considered a prerequisite for the theologian in order to discern and articulate the essence of Christianity within apologetics and dogmatics. Whether the theologian is interpreting, criticizing, or scientifically organizing, Schleiermacher and Drey suggest that the theologian's highest calling is to be an organic leader within this community."[119] It is

---

[119]My use of the phrase "organic leader" to designate Schleiermacher's and Drey's understanding of the role of theologian is inspired by the Italian social theorist, Antonio Gramsci, who contrasted "traditional intellectuals" with "organic intellectuals." This is by no means to suggest that Schleiermacher's and Drey's understanding of the theologian as a Church leader is precisely equivalent to Gramsci's "organic intellectual."

by fulfilling this mission of organic leadership that the theologian fosters the development of doctrine and the vitality of Christian life.

Organic leadership can be contrasted with a traditional model of leadership. In the traditional model the theologian is accountable to authorities: the Bible, creeds and other official Church pronouncements, the Fathers, and respected theologians. This model of theology always assumes and sometimes expresses the communal context and commitments incumbent upon the theologian, but the emphasis is placed on the powerful and binding character of the biblical and ecclesial traditions. With Schleiermacher and Drey a subtle and important transition occurs that alters, deepens, and reformulates the older use of theological criteria and authorities, and the nature of theological discernment. The theologian and these authorities are now situated explicitly in relation to the community of faith. Or to state it differently, the theologian is placed within a mutually life-sustaining web of relationships in a historical community of faith. In the classical model of theology, theologians are traditional leaders, whose primary responsibility is to articulate the past authoritative witnesses to the present community. For an organic leader, however, these traditional authorities must be examined and evaluated historically and socially, that is, in relation to the past and present experience of the community. Such an organic model of leadership is often contrasted with a strictly hierarchical model of organization or social structure. In fact, one finds Schleiermacher and Drey promoting fuller participation of all community members in the life of the Church. But these impulses for ever greater

---

Schleiermacher, Drey, and Gramsci (1) share the use of organic metaphors to understand communal relationships and leadership; (2) recognize the need for elites of one type or another within a community; and (3) employ an ascending model as well as a descending model of power. Schleiermacher and Drey do not speak of economic or class interests in their analysis of ecclesial leadership. See Gramsci, *Selections from the Prison Notebooks*, ed. and trans. by Q. Hoare and G. N. Smith (New York: Inter- national Publishers, 1971), 3-23, 26-43, 323.

ecclesial participation do not in the case of Schleiermacher and Drey mean rejecting structured relationships of a hierarchical nature with specific roles and functions. For both Schleiermacher and Drey the theologian has a vocation to be an organic leader, and this responsibility is as important for doctrinal development, if not more so, than interpreting, criticizing, and systematically creating doctrines.[120]

Schleiermacher and Drey portrayed the theologian as one with a wide range of knowledge and skills. Both thinkers firmly grasp the fact that religion and theology is field-encompassing--it touches every aspect of life and every area of learning. This places educational demands on the would-be theologian. It is important for the theologian to have a broad background in history so that one can understand the history of religions, the historical context of the Scriptures, and the history of Christianity. A background in philosophy and science is required in order to develop the abilities to reason, to communicate clearly and forcefully, and to clarify the relation of theology to the other disciplines in the university. It is likewise essential to know biblical and non-biblical languages and to have a firm grasp of the skills and talents required for critically reconciling data, analyzing and evaluating texts and traditions within and beyond the canon of Scriptures. The theologian must have dis-

---

[120]As previously noted, John Thiel argues that Schleiermacher and Drey present the theologian as a "romantic genius" or a "romantic hero" with technical skill, even virtuosity, who strives to reenter the mind of the original geniuses who have inspired the Christian witness and who become the new creative geniuses who redirect the course of history; e.g., "Theological Responsibility: Beyond the Classical Paradigm," *Theological Studies* 47 (1986): 573-598. The technical and creative dimensions of this portrayal of the theologian cannot be denied. But these dimensions can only be seen in their proper perspective when the relationship between the theologian and the community is more clearly drawn.

cipline, a mastery of historical materials, as well as critical, interpretative, and administrative talents and skills.[121]

But well-educated individuals are not theologians until they have properly comprehended and cultivated their relationship to the ecclesial community. Hence, whether the theologian is interpreting, discerning, or creatively exploring and systematically presenting the Christian faith, or challenging deviations, specific skills and methods of theology are always guided by the mission of the organic leader: to serve the common spirit of the community by discerning the essential character of the faith of this community.

The contention that Schleiermacher and Drey have a comparable understanding of the theologian as organic leader is based on their theology of the Spirit and their organic understanding of the Church.[122] Both Drey and Schleiermacher make important statements about the role of the Holy Spirit as a "common spirit" (*Gemeingeist*) that animates the Church. Surprisingly, Drey's writings on this subject suggest no engagement with Schleiermacher's provocative statements about the "common spirit" in the

---

[121]For pertinent texts, see *Brief Outline*, on general background in human sciences (ethics), history, and languages, §§ 4-6, 29, 35; on criticism, philology, and on interpretative and administrative skills, §§ 89, 102, 125-131, 132, 138-140, 155, 218, 265-266; *Kurze Einleitung*, on general preparatory knowledge and scientific background (*Bildungsmittel*) and specific scientific expertise (*Hülfsmittel*) in history, science, philosophy, languages, §§ 89-106, 147-151; on criticism, philology, interpretative and historical skills, §§ 141-142, 146, 152-161, 45-47, 56; on administrative prudence, skill, and virtuosity, §§ 379, 386-387.

[122]For Schleiermacher on Spirit see *Brief Outline*, § 180, also n. 129, §§ 234, 313; *Christian Faith*, §§ 116, 121-123, 148; for his early treatment of the *Gemeingeist* theme, see the first edition of *Der christliche Glaube*, §§ 134-135, 140-145. I have only located one text, and an early one at that (1819)--before the first edition of Schleiermacher's *Glaubenslehre*--where Drey uses the term "common spirit" and this is identified with the Spirit of Christ in "Vom Geist und Wesen," 229; also see from 1812-1813, "Ideen zur Geschichte," 246, 276-279, 302-305; *Kurze Einleitung*, §§ 214, 233, 286, 293; *Apologetik*, 3:127-141, 284-290.

Glaubenslehre.[123] Nevertheless, they both treat the Spirit as Holy and common, and they emphasize the role of the theologian in promoting the life and unity of the Church.

Drey and Schleiermacher construct a christocentric model of ecclesial authority based on the foundation of the Church by Christ and the prophetic office of Christ, which is mediated by the ministry of word and sacrament.[124] Clerics have legitimate authority and the Church needs leaders to teach and govern.

However, their christocentric interpretations of the Church and authority are also developed in relation to their pneumatologies. These theologies of the Holy Spirit offer a significant counterweight or complement to a purely christocentric model. This theological contribution authorizes and generates their conceptions of social relations. These views of communal organization are indicated by their model of the theologian's relation to the community. Both reject a purely descending model of organizational power and they develop a model of organic leaders, who derive their power from the ecclesial community--the kingdom of God on earth, the outer expression of an inner unity borne of the Holy Spirit--in an ascending fashion. However, neither theologian promotes a simple democratic structure within the church. Both recognize the role of

---

[123]This is surprising because of J. A. Möhler's use of the term "common spirit" in *Die Einheit in der Kirche oder das Prinzip des Katholizismus, dargestellt im Geiste der Kirchenväter der drei ersten Jahrhunderte* (Tübingen, 1825). On the relationship between Möhler's, Schleiermacher's, and Drey's usage of the term and on ecclesial unity, see Harald Wagner, *Die eine Kirche und die vielen Kirchen. Ekklesiologie und Symbolik beim jungen Möhler*, Beiträge zur ökumenischen Theologie, vol. 16 (Paderborn: Verlag Ferdinand Schöningh, 1977), 92-99, 105-118, 197-199; 262-67.

[124]"Ideen zur Geschichte," 302-5, *Apologetik*, vol. 3. Schleiermacher acknowledged that there have been occasions when the majority opinion has gone against the authentic articulation of the faith. More often it is the case that individuals need to be purified by the work of the whole community working through ecclesial leaders. See *Christian Faith*, § 22, p. 96; *Die christliche Sitte*, 89-90, 122-124.

elites in the ministry of theologians and ecclesiastics. But the authority of these elites flows both from the community and from the essence of Christianity, which warrants the legitimacy of both ascending and descending dimensions of ecclesial power. Although this argument about an organic model of leadership can be more clearly defended in the case of Schleiermacher, there is ample evidence to support it in Drey's writings prior to *Die Apologetik*; if you include his later work, the argument is more tenuous.[125]

The theologian must be motivated, Schleiermacher maintained, by an ecclesial interest that provides direction for the scientific skills and talents the theologian has developed.[126] He coined the phrase "prince of the church" to designate the cleric and theologian in whom there existed a harmonious balance between the practical concern for the church and the utilization of scientific skills, methods, and theories.[127] Schleiermacher insisted that the theologian is best understood as one who balances these dimensions of theology. To say that the theologian as a prince of the church is an organic leader is to underscore Schleiermacher's conviction that in every branch of theology the theologian needs to promote the common spirit of the Church which embodies the essence of Christianity at the present time.

Schleiermacher portrays the theologian as one who strives to see parts in relation to the organic wholes. The theologian should strive to understand the entire history of the Christian community of discourse and action, in its continuous essence, its development, and its deviations.[128] The dogmatic theologian needs to describe how the essence of Christianity is being more fully understood and

---

[125]A more strictly christocentric, confessional, and descending ecclesiology emerges in Drey's later work, *Die Apologetik*, volume 3. Here he defends the hierarchy of the Church. Pneumatology receives little attention, but when it is discussed, the role of the Spirit is restricted to guiding and affirming the teaching authority of the Catholic Church.

[126]*Brief Outline*, §§ 9. 12, 13, 258.

[127]*Brief Outline*, §§ 1, 9-12, 251, 258, 270.

[128]*Brief Outline*, § 100.

developed on all sides.[129] This commitment to the full range of past and present voices in the Church requires that a theologian recognize what has "been most determined by the Church," as well as the role of the individual who "opens the way for a future course."[130] The role of the individual theologian is important for Schleiermacher, but that individual is important only insofar as she or he clearly expresses the faith consciousness of the Church and strives for consensus in the Church.[131] Schleiermacher concludes that "[e]very dogmatic theologian who either innovates or exalts what is old, in a one-sided manner, is only a very imperfect organ of the Church."[132] The implication to be drawn is that for Schleiermacher an organic leader is committed to listening and responding to the whole: the social whole of the contemporary Church, the historical whole of the Christian community extended through time, and the intellectual and practical whole of the essence of Christianity.

Finally, for Schleiermacher, theologians should be like the "great persons" in history because they are above all in touch with the masses--they are in a living relationship with a community and they articulate was it valid and vital about that community.[133] So

---

[129]*Brief Outline*, § 198.

[130]*Brief Outline*, § 199.

[131]*Brief Outline*, § 202. For the consensual character of Christian doctrines also see *The Christian Faith*, §§ 153-155, esp. § 155, p. 691: "error is restrained by two forces prevalent in different degrees at different times: in the individual whose errors are peculiar to himself, it is restrained by the influence of public thought, which makes its pressure felt on him from every side, while in the mass of believers it is restrained by the influence of men of spiritual distinction, spreading clear views ever more widely."

[132]*Brief Outline*, § 208.

[133]"[A]ll genuine Church leadership is founded on a distinct formation of the original contrast between prominent member and the mass" (*Brief Outline*, § 267); this contrast is also discussed in §§ 268-270; 278-279; 303-308, 312, 315; "Über den Begriff des grossen Mannes," in *Schleiermachers Werke, Auswahl* (Leipzig, 1910) 1:520-531; and in *The Life of Jesus* lectures.

the theologian-clergy need to develop the communicative skills to unite and advance the community. This "religious force of prominent members rouses the mass, and the mass in turn summons forth such leaders"; they awaken or quicken religious consciousness in worship or other meetings, or order and direct through governance.[134] This clerical leader "brings forth something in common," and if someone lags behind, she or he is cared for by the leader.[135] In matters of Church governance, "changes in doctrinal statements and formulas may result from the study of individuals only when such changes have been received as part of the conviction of a congregation. . . ."[136]

Within the Evangelical Church Schleiermacher detected two forms of government, the authoritative form and the discretionary form.[137] The former serves as the basis for the distinction between the governing and the governed, or between clergy and laity. The latter refers to "any free influence upon the whole, which any free individual member of the Church may undertake who believes himself called to do so."[138] Both forms of government have the same aim: "to represent ever more authentically the idea of Christianity within the evangelical Church according to that Church's distinctive conception of it, and to gain increasingly greater support for this idea."[139] This conveys Schleiermacher's organic model of leadership as it informs both forms of government.

---

[134]*Brief Outline*, §§ 268, 279 respectively.

[135]*Brief Outline*, § 290.

[136]*Brief Outline*, § 323; while this passage is in the context of a discussion of the evangelical union, it is still an illustration of the model of leadership Schleiermacher presents. In the *Glaubenslehre* we also read: "Legislative action is exerted by each through everything he does that goes to form public opinion; and public opinion must always be the living fount of expressly legislative action, for these acts are simply a definitive way of recognition for public opinion in Church affairs" (*Christian Faith*, § 145, p. 667).

[137]*Brief Outline*, § 312.

[138]*Brief Outline*, § 312.

[139]*Brief Outline*, § 313.

However, it is discretionary influence that exhibits most clearly the organic form of leadership in practice. Schleiermacher finds this form most prevalent in the Reformation and reflects on this in several of his writings.

Schleiermacher presents the Reformers and especially Luther as examples of ecclesial leaders. A reformer is neither the creative reclusive genius nor the individual virtuoso who brings about the epochal shift of the reformation through some talent or skill. The spreading of the Reformation message presupposes the following:

> that we not consider Luther in Saxony and Zwingli in Switzerland as those in whom this movement has had its foundation; in them is concentrated only the universal forces as in prominent points. . . . If we consider these forces [of movement of the Reformation], so we must not remain focussed on the individual persons and attribute to them far too much, so many phenomena are also beneath them. There are however always only individual manifestations, in which is concentrated a common spirit and certain principles, otherwise they would not have arisen in such a way and could not bring about these effects.[140]

Luther clearly presents an example of an organic leader, one who senses the changes going on in the community and speaks on the community's behalf. Luther represents the common consciousness of the Church.[141]

Drey also wrote about the relation of the theologian and the community on numerous occasions in his early writings. In his 1812 programmatic essay "Revision des gegenwärtigen Zustandes der Theologie," he narrated the history of theology from the Medieval period down to his own day. There were several lessons to be learned from this history about the excesses of Scholastic, Reformation, and Enlightenment theologies and about the need for

---

[140]*Geschichte der christlichen Kirche*, 575-576.

[141]*Die christliche Sitte*, 125: The excommunication of Luther was "directed against the communal feeling itself which Luther represented."

a vibrant balance between the mystical and the dialectical sides of theology. In this context he suggested that the theologian's proper role is comparable to the politician and the writer of literature in relation to the history of a people. "For what is the scientific condition of a nation other than the highest ideal expression of that which lies in itself, which moves it, as its spiritual life."[142] "The whole mass in a people never thinks or acts, but rather the functions of the whole of life are distributed among certain organs in an individual human being, so it is also, in a people, the eminent individuals through which its life becomes apparent."[143] Theologians in the Patristic and Medieval periods were those eminent individuals who developed theology by uniting piety and dialectic and thus served the people they represented. But in the period of High Scholasticism the balance of piety and dialectic was lost, a problem the Reformers tried to redress.[144]

More than most of his Catholic contemporaries, Drey recognized and publicly admitted that the Protestant reformers were rightly trying to redress the balance that was lost during High Scholasticism.[145] But he also faults the Reformers for cutting themselves off from the Church.[146] From which Church did they cut themselves off? Is it the hierarchy or the community of the

---

[142]"Revision," 85-86. He continues, "[h]ow it [the nation] proves its power through its warriors, its productive skill through its manufacturers, its justice through its legislators, so its actions proclaim itself their action through the public morality, and its thinking through its learned, through the condition of its sciences."

[143]"Revision," 85.

[144]"Revision," 89.

[145]John Thiel has recently drawn attention to Drey's acknowledgement of "einer katholische Protestanismus" in his 1815 journal and of "der innere Protestantismus" within Catholicism in his 1824 article, "Über das Verhältniss des Mysticismus zum Katholicismus." See "Naming the Heterodox: Interconfessional Polemics as a Context for Drey's Theology," (Unpublished manuscript).

[146]"Revision," 91-92.

faithful? Which Church is the theologian supposed to represent and serve? Drey sets up no relevant contrast or distinction in the Church. Throughout his career he defended the hierarchical structure of the Church and its legitimate authority. But in his earlier writings he also suggested that this authority is rightly understood and practiced in close connection with the entire community of faith, that is, the sense of the faithful.[147] The ecclesial hierarchy leads not through force, but through a moral power which forms the "*Gemeinwille*" on the foundation of the "*Gemeinglaubens*" that strives for the "*Gemeinzweck*" through the "*Gemeinsamen Mittel.*"[148] This is the work of the Spirit in the entire community.

The ways Drey employs the contrast between fixed and mobile elements of doctrine and between closed dogmas and open opinions and schools of thought clearly weighted the scales of authority toward the hierarchy of the Church, even if organically understood.[149] Here he stands at a distance from Schleiermacher.

---

[147]For historical observations on "sensus fidelium" see Yves Congar, *Tradition and Traditions* (London: Burns & Oates, 1966), 204, 208, 211. Congar recognizes that Newman's comments on the sense of the faithful lead back to Möhler, but he does not explore the relationships between Möhler, Schleiermacher, and Drey on the theology of the "*Gemeingeist*" and their implications for the "sense of the faithful."

[148]*Kurze Einleitung*, §§ 286, 293, also 54; "Vom Geist und Wesen," 229; "Ideen zur Geschichte," 246.

[149]In his later years, Drey seeks to demonstrate that the teaching office has divinely ordained responsibility of teaching; "Christ has . . . entrusted the indicated powers solely to the college of apostles and not to the entire community of the faithful" (*Apologetik*, 3:188). Catholics for Drey cannot affirm that believers have the right to interpret the Bible without the aid of the hierarchy, nor can they ratify the Protestant principle of "a priesthood of all believers" in any way other than spiritually (3:192-193). Moreover, "The constitution that Christ has given to his Church is not a democracy . . . ; it is however just as little an aristocracy, because the bishops are subjected to the guardianship and reprimand of a communal leader; this latter is likewise not governing as a monarchy, for the bishops govern their dioceses on their

And yet, Drey carves out a place for the theologian as an eminent individual, an organic leader who represents the community and articulates their faith. History has shown, Drey suggests, that "[e]xplanations and investigations by private scholars and writers always precede the determinations of ecclesial doctrines, and most proposals for reforms in liturgy and church discipline, which were actually inaugurated, came not from church prelates, but rather from eager and wise private men."[150] He draws the following conclusion:

> No church government can and may suppress the activity and the effect of individuals, which through spoken or written discourse is directed to the whole church, because through that, it [the Church] would, so to speak, deprive itself of the piety and insight spreading among the masses of its members. . . . It must be the general maxim of Church government to give freedom of expression of religious fervor and insight [and] to prevent the harm which may possibly arise from the Church through suitable means.[151]

Theological opinions, moreover, though voiced by individuals, are addressed to the whole church and can articulate the faith of the Church, even though they have yet to be closed or brought to completion through the process of magisterial pronouncement. The

---

own as the immediate successors of the apostles, and both--bishops and pope are bound to the universal laws" (3:275).

[150]*Kurze Einleitung*, § 342. Drey's recognition of the theologian's organic and critical functions in the Church are evident in his active role in establishing and defining the purpose of the theological journal, *Theologische Quartalschrift*, which fostered free and reform-minded theological discussion on disputed doctrinal and disciplinary issues. Drey also specifically defended the theologian's right and duty to be critical of certain Church practices for the good of the Church. See the discussion of Drey's letter to a local Church authority in *Tübinger Theologen und ihre Theologie: Quellen and Forschungen zur Geschichte der Katholisch-Theologischen Fakultät Tübingen*, ed. Rudolf Reinhardt (Tübingen: J.C.B. Mohr [Paul Siebeck], 1977), 23, 129-140.

[151]*Kurze Einleitung*, § 343.

ultimate criterion in the case of theologian and magisterium is the faith of the Church universal. Thus Drey asserts that "if we speak of the development of certain dogmas in the Church, we can not call it developed until we know it as reflectively recognized by the Church, pronounced as the universal belief of the Church."[152]

In summary, Drey believed, like Schleiermacher, that theology was not merely a matter of scientific methods and skills, but also a calling of the heart to provide a pious rendering of the faith of the community for the community. Drey agreed that the theologian is in an organic and pious union with the community.[153] Finally, Drey concurred with Schleiermacher that the theologian was an eminent individual with an important duty to articulate the community's faith.

---

[152]"Ideen zur Geschichte," 253.

[153]*Kurze Einleitung*, §§ 101-103.

CHAPTER IV

BETWEEN RELATIVISM AND FOUNDATIONALISM: CRITERIA FOR GENUINE DEVELOPMENT

We have examined how Schleiermacher and Drey configure the origins and development of Christianity and how they understand the role of theology in this history. As we have seen, their narrative schemas were intended as an alternative to three interpretations of the nature of revelation and the criteria for judging it. First is the deist and rationalist approach, which sought to discredit the authority of the Bible and Christian beliefs in the interests of rational and moral emancipation. Second is the hyperorthodox position that adhered to a static understanding of the biblical and creedal traditions and promoted an insular mind-set toward the scientific and philosophical changes in culture. The third approach is represented by opposing Christian traditions (primarily cast as Catholic versus Protestant) that use biblical and creedal traditions as polemical weapons.

The plots Schleiermacher and Drey constructed provide the context and the content for their doctrines of revelation and their treatments of criteria for evaluating authentic doctrines. Both figures recontextualize and reinterpret the classic criteria of their respective traditions: Schleiermacher reformulates the *sola Scriptura* principle and Drey the nature of tradition. While Scripture and tradition are retained respectively as legitimate norms, the criteria for judging authentic doctrinal development are broadened on the basis of this contextualization and reformulation. Although neither theologian offers a list of "notes" for determining authentic developments as are offered by John Henry Newman a generation later in *An Essay on the Development of Christian Doctrine* (1845), Schleiermacher and Drey do detect a set of criteria at work in the web of relationships which constitutes the organic community of faith. Their theologies set forth these criteria with some specificity.

Drey and Schleiermacher sought to avoid various extreme positions in their narratives, their doctrines of revelation, and their criteriology for evaluating doctrines. But their own positions have also been judged extreme. Their understandings of revelation and doctrinal development have been accused of relativism on the one hand and foundationalism on the other. Let us briefly consider these lines of criticism.

Schleiermacher and Drey have been charged, on the one hand, with promoting theological relativism or historicism. Some have argued that their positions jeopardize the cognitive and moral norms of the Scriptures and Church teaching. Bretschneider and Alexander Schweizer feared that Schleiermacher's method might justify Roman papalism and other Catholic dogmas and thus sacrifice the normative character of the Bible as embodied in the *sola Scriptura* principle.[1] Owen Chadwick and Jan Walgrave expressed the suspicion that Schleiermacher's approach to doctrines was relativistic and too evolutionary. However, they disagreed on whether Drey and the Catholic Tübingen tradition were guilty of the charge; Chadwick implies that Drey (at least in his early writings) was as inadequate and vague as Schleiermacher when compared with Newman, whereas Walgrave finds in Drey the precursor of

---

[1]See Karl Gottlieb Bretschneider, "Nebst einer Abhandlung über die Grundansichten der Herren Prof. Dr. Schleiermacher and Marheinecke, sowie über die des Herrn Dr. Hase," in *Handbuch der Dogmatik* (3rd edition, 1828); excerpts in translation, "Bretschneider's View of Theology of Schleiermacher," *Biblioteca Sacra* 10 (1853): 598-616; discussed in *On the Glaubenslehre*, p. 97, n. 9. Alexander Schweizer, student of Schleiermacher, also wrestled with this question. See Gerrish, *Tradition and the Modern World*, (Chicago: University of Chicago Press, 1978), 99-150, 224, n. 152.

Newman's position.[2] Barth was the most vociferous critic of Schleiermacher, accusing him of promoting "*Kulturprotestantismus*," accommodating the normative claims of faith to the prevailing cultural currents.[3] Edmund Vermeil judged that the early Catholic Tübingen school paved the way for the Catholic Modernism of George Tyrrell and Alfred Loisy, with the attendant problems of immanentism, subjectivism, and the criticism of doctrines.[4] More recently, Hans Georg Gadamer offered an in depth and influential criticism of Schleiermacher's hermeneutics for its relativism. Gadamer argues that Schleiermacher failed to recognize in language the objective vehicle for tradition, authority, and cultural truth.[5] The theological corollary would, of course, be dogmatic relativism.

On the other hand, Schleiermacher and Drey have been accused of promoting an anthropocentric and rationalist approach to theology and doctrines. With dogmatic norms rejected or relativized in the surrounding culture, according to this line of

---

[2]Owen Chadwick, *From Bossuet to Newman: The Idea of Doctrinal Development*, 104-111, 116,; Jan Walgrave, *Unfolding Revelation: The Nature of Doctrinal Development*, 179-277, 282-289, 331, 401. Yves M.-J. Congar does not treat in detail Drey's understanding of development, but he does state that post-Kantian and post-Schleiermacher liberal Protestant theology was responsible for the modern problems of historicism. "This religious philosophy in one way or another always boiled down to the same thing: the driving in of a wedge between a religious adherence based on faith and the properly intellectual aspect or the forms of expression of religion." *Tradition and Traditions*, 214-215.

[3]See Karl Barth, *Protestant Theology in the Nineteenth Century* (Valley Forge: Judson Press, 1973), 425-473, Barth suspects that with Schleiermacher "theology forgot its own theme over against all world-views" (460).

[4]See Edmund Vermeil, *Jean-Adam Moehler et l'École catholique de Tubingue* (Paris: A. Colin, 1913), 27-30; and Léonce de Grandmaison, "Jean Adam Moehler, l'École catholique de Tubingen et les origines du modernisme," *Recherches de science religieuse* 4(1919): 387-409.

[5]"What is to be understood is not a shared thought about some subject matter, but individual thought that by its very nature is a free construct and the free expression of an individual being"(Gadamer, *Truth and Method*, 188).

argument, Schleiermacher and Drey seek to provide a rational anchor for the Christian faith. They seek to ground the claims of faith in human subjectivity or in an indubitable epistemology in order to adduce rational certainty about matters of faith.

Schleiermacher's *Glaubenslehre* has perennially been hounded by criticisms that the introductory analysis of the nature of religion in human consciousness preestablished the answers for the rest of dogmatics.[6] It is said that his philosophy determines the content of his theology and his transcendental anthropology undercuts the importance of historical revelation. F. C. Baur offered sophisticated version of this criticism in Schleiermacher's own day,[7] as Karl Barth did for another generation.[8] In a similar vein, Vermeil suggests that Drey's brand of theology provides a rationalistic critique of Christianity and even the revered interpreter of the early Catholic Tübingen school, Josef Geiselmann, judged that Drey's theology was semi-rationalist in character.[9]

The accusation of rationalism has been reformulated and refined recently by Ronald Thiemann and Francis Schüssler Fiorenza. They have examined the theological receptions of the

---

[6]See Hans-Joachim Birkner, *Theologie und Philosophie. Einführung in Probleme der Schleiermacher-Interpretation* (Munich, 1974).

[7]F.C. Baur reviews parts I and II of his dissertation in "Primae Rationalismi et Supranaturalismi historiae capita potiora. Pars I. De Gnosticorum Christianismo Ideali. Pars II. Comparatur Gnosticismus cum Schleiermacherianae theologiae indole. Tübingen, 1827," 242, 247. For Schleiermacher's response, see *On the Glaubenslehre*, 76-77.

[8]Karl Barth, *The Theology of Schleiermacher*, 153, 163-164.

[9]Geiselmann, "Die Glaubenswissenschaft der Katholischen Tübinger Schule in ihrer Grundlegung durch Johann Sebastian v. Drey," *Theologische Quartalschrift* 111 (1930): 110. Also see Hermann Joseph Brosch, *Das Übernatürliche in der katholischen Tübinger Schule* (Essen: Ludgerus-Verlag, 1962).

modern philosophical quest for foundations in epistemology.[10] Their work deserves closer scrutiny for the light it sheds on Schleiermacher's and Drey's positions, and for the questions it raises.

Thiemann and Fiorenza adapt the current philosophical claim that foundationalism is an attempt to ground human knowledge in some Archimedean first principle, which is either proven through argument, or immediately certain and self-evident.[11] On this view, foundationalism in theology would be a new brand of rationalism, one seeking to secure the claims of faith and theology in an indisputable epistemology and anthropology.

For Thiemann, a theological foundationalist seeks to justify and criticize Christian beliefs on the basis of a certain self-justified or irrefutable epistemology and anthropology. By so doing, the foundationalist fails to recognize the axiomatic status of theological background beliefs within theology--beliefs known through the primary language of faith as found in the Bible, creeds, and liturgy.[12] Thiemann specifically argues that Schleiermacher has adopted a foundationalist epistemology in order to justify the possibility of revelation, "while denying that revelation grants knowledge of God."[13] Accordingly, religious beliefs are grounded

---

[10]Thiemann, *Revelation and Theology* (Notre Dame: University of Notre Dame Press, 1985); Fiorenza, *Foundational Theology* (New York: Crossroad Publishing Co., 1984).

[11]For the philosophical discussion see Richard Rorty, *Philosophy and the Mirror of Nature* (Princeton: Princeton University Press, 1979), 131-164 and Richard Bernstein *Beyond Objectivism and Relativism* (Philadelphia: University of Pennsylvania Press, 1983).

[12]Thiemann, *Revelation*, 15, 165, n. 40; for his discussion of correlation methods, see p. 186, n. 9.; and for his counter-proposal, see 72-75.

[13]Thiemann, *Revelation*, 24. Thiemann does acknowledge that "Schleiermacher's position is ambiguous on the question of whether that essence [of Christianity] is located *within* those diverse first-order utterances or in a deeper universal and pre-linguistic substratum. Insofar as Schleiermacher asserts the former, his method is supportive of [Thiemann's preferred]

in a set of non-inferential, self-evident beliefs which in turn are "justified immediately by a form of direct experience," that is, a religious intuition. "Though he begins with the particulars of Christian belief and of Christian self-consciousness, Schleiermacher claims to have discerned the formal, universal, precognitive shape of piety-as-such, prior to its combination with particular historical or cultural elements."[14]

Fiorenza examines the history of apologetic theologies and analyzes their assumptions utilizing current philosophical distinctions between soft and hard foundationalism, and empiricist and rationalist forms.[15] The historical approach to fundamental theology tends to presuppose a correspondence theory of truth," which "seeks through historical argumentation to demonstrate a correspondence between belief statements and historical facts that support them either directly or indirectly."[16] The transcendental approach to fundamental theology, which Fiorenza detects in Schleiermacher and Drey, operates with a coherence and disclosure theory of truth, and attempts to correlate present human experience and belief statements. The former historical approach tends toward empirical foundationalism, while the latter transcendental approach tends toward rational foundationalism.

---

descriptive [model of] theology. Insofar as he supports the latter, he gives aid and comfort to foundational theology" (p. 172, n. 5).

[14]Thiemann, *Revelation*, 28, see also 29.

[15]"A soft foundationalism maintains that all noetic structures have a foundation, that is, a set of propositions according to which all others are believed. A hard foundationalism adds to soft foundationalism a set of criteria that defines the allowable basic propositions that can be ascertained as foundational. These criteria are self-evidence, incorrigibility, and evidence to the senses." An empiricist foundationalism grounds basic-beliefs in empirical statements, whereas the rationalist foundationalist justifies these basic-concepts "by a transcendental deduction or through a concept analysis that shows their clarity or intelligibility" (*Foundational*, 283).

[16]Fiorenza, *Foundational*, 270.

Both Thiemann and Fiorenza believe that a non-foundationalist theologian should seek justification for theological arguments in background beliefs, that is, within the first order language of Church faith and practice. Retrogressive warrants may be offered for these positions by employing concepts from experience and non-theological fields, but there are no extra-textual or extra-linguistic referents.[17] Thiemann suggests that any use of a transcendental method in fundamental or dogmatic theology would be foundationalist, while Fiorenza believes that there are foundationalist tendencies with such a transcendental method which can be, and need to be, avoided.[18]

This recent work on foundationalism in philosophy and theology indicates that a shift has occurred. What was most appealing about the world views of Schleiermacher and Drey to those who, earlier in this century, were drawn to Existentialist currents--their anthropological frame of reference, their historical approach, and the subtle relationship they envisioned between inner and outer, transcendental and categorical dimensions of history--has become the target of criticism by those influenced by hermeneutic and neo-pragmatic currents in philosophy and theology for being anthropocentric, relativistic, and foundationalist. Modern appreciation has turned into postmodern suspicion.

---

[17]Thiemann speaks of his position in terms of holism. Fiorenza says his is a reconstructive hermeneutic. Both employ holist forms of justification and retrogressive warrants.

[18]Fiorenza specifies the following weaknesses in the use of a transcendental method in theology: (1) a transcendental argument fails to recognize that "experience and its interpretation have been predetermined by Christian beliefs," (2) the foundations of faith and the foundations of theology become conflated, (3) it "tends to view the Christian tradition primarily as a specification of what is universally experienced as religious," thus minimizing "the historical particularity of the tradition as well as the force of its conflict with experience," and (4) it tends to give too much weight to nontheological disciplines in deciding and adjudicating theological claims" (*Foundational*, 283, 273, 281, 289).

Schleiermacher's and Drey's understanding of revelation and the criteria for genuine development are defensible against the charges of relativism and foundationalism, even if further questions remain and deficiencies or problematic tendencies are discerned. To defend Schleiermacher and Drey on these points is the first line of defense against those who claim a postmodern theology must be radically discontinuous with the mediating and correlating methods of Schleiermacher and Drey and their theological descendants.

Revelation and Doctrine

Schleiermacher and Drey both acknowledge that creation was the original revelation, for God is the cause of all that is.[19] They also recognize diverse revealed historical religions founded on distinctive origins. Their primary attention, however, is given to the positivity of Christian revelation, that is, its historical basis and character.

Schleiermacher and Drey agree that Christian revelation is identified with the historical fact of Christ which stands as the point of origin for what distinguishes the Christian community in relation to all other communities, religious or secular. Revelation is a historical fact which brings about a determinate consciousness within the Christianity community. Thus the religious consciousness of the community--religious affections and religious experience--has its source in the divine (both use the word "supernatural") causality of Christ.[20] This constitutes the positivity or revealed basis of the Christian Church.

---

[19]Schleiermacher refers to Paul's statement in Romans 1:20 that the world is the original revelation of God in *Christian Faith*, § 10, p. 51. In his second letter to Lücke he speaks of "creation" as the original revelation of God (*On the Glaubenslehre*, 79). He also states that the feeling of absolute dependence can be used to designate the original revelation. See, *Christian Faith*, § 4. sec. 4. For Drey, see *Apologetik*, 1:199-202.

[20]*Christian Faith*, § 10; *Apologetik*, 1:226-227, 260-262.

Schleiermacher concludes that the point of origin for Christianity, the fact of Christ, was divinely caused. "[T]he idea of revelation signifies the *originality* of the fact which lies at the foundation of a religious communion. . . ."[21] Divine revelation did not impart inspired thoughts or propositions. Thoughts and propositions are human constructs not divine. "It is obvious," he nevertheless admits, that the influence of the original fact upon the consciousness of the community "does not exclude doctrine, but implies it."[22]

Although Drey gives Schleiermacher credit for defending the supernatural fact as revelatory against deist and rationalist critics, he contests Schleiermacher's claim that the cognitive reception of revelation is merely human.[23] Drey maintains that there is a reception of revelation in immediate consciousness (as a *Gottesgefühl*) and at a level of reflective or mediated consciousness.[24] Religious affections have their source in the supernatural fact of Christ. On the reflective level, however, it is the idea of the kingdom of God which is the central revelation.[25]

This idea of the kingdom of God is subjectively received by the Christian community and becomes objective, real, and concrete within the living tradition of the Church through speech, word, and symbol.[26] The revealed fact and idea of Christianity are

---

[21]*Christian Faith*, § 10, p. 50.

[22]*Christian Faith*, § 10, p. 50.

[23]*Apologetik*, 1:226-227.

[24]*Apologetik*, 1:248, 309-317.

[25]*Kurze Einleitung*, §§ 57-61; also see *Apologetik*, 2:212. In addition to arguing that revelation has its source in a supernatural fact, both Schleiermacher and Drey maintain that the correlation between the doctrines and human experience is a useful apologetic argument. Contrary to Schleiermacher's position, Drey would further claim that there can be (secondary) external proofs from miracles, prophecies, and inspiration.

[26]Drey refers to the traditioning process in terms of *Paradosis* in "Vom Geist und Wesen," 200. The oral, written, and symbolic character of this traditioning process is discussed in *Apologetik*, 1:386-389. For an analysis of Drey's treatment of tradition, see Josef Geiselmann, *Lebendiger Glaube aus*

transmitted through the oral preaching of the apostles, the written form of the gospels and the epistles, and the symbolic tradition, that is, the official teachings of the Church. All genuine revelations are mediated through tradition.[27] Written tradition "binds the original material of tradition, binding the moving speech to the fixed unchanging letter of writing. . . ."[28] The normative authority of the Bible and Church teachings rests ultimately on the revelation of the idea of the kingdom of God in Christ as given to the Church.

For Drey the continuing revelatory activity of God in the Church mediates God's revelation in creation, in the supreme revelation of the fact of Christ, and in the idea of the kingdom of God as enunciated by the life and teachings of Christ. The kingdom is inaugurated by Jesus but it is "a kingdom without limits, its determination is infinite extension, constant expansion, and thus constant extensive and intensive progression."[29] Insofar as original Christianity is grounded in the fact of Christ and the idea of the kingdom of God, it serves as the object of oral, written, and symbolic traditions.[30] The written witnesses of the gospels and epistles provide a historical form to this object, while the judgments of the Church in dogmas provide the criterion of tradition.[31]

Viewed from one perspective, the Bible and Tradition flow from the revealed fact of Christ and the revealed idea of the kingdom of God. Christ and the kingdom are the revealed source. But this fact and idea are always mediated through traditions. Consequently, the Scriptures cannot stand above the transmission or traditioning of the Church. Scripture has "its foundation and presupposition" in this tradition;[32] it receives its "outward attestation only through

---

geheiligter Überlieferung (Freiburg: Herder, 1966), 120-298.

[27]*Apologetik*, 1:381.

[28]*Apologetik*, 1:387.

[29]*Apologetik*, 1:403.

[30]*Apologetik*, 1:386-389.

[31]This constitutes the true "Paradosis" or tradition of Catholicism, "Vom Geist und Wesen," 200.

[32]*Apologetik*, 3:61.

tradition;"[33] and tradition provides "its necessary and only competent interpreter."[34] "[W]ithout tradition there is no Scripture, that is, no authentic, unadulterated, credible Scripture" and "without the Church there is no tradition, that is, no constant, unchanging, and credible tradition."[35]

The Church's hierarchy has a divinely ordained mission in this process of traditioning. The closing of the canon of the Scriptures is one important work of the hierarchy. Beyond that the teaching office of the Church is guaranteed infallibility in fulfilling its charge by articulating explicit dogmas, developing and clarifying implicit dogmas, and pronouncing the Symbols as the objective faith of the Church.[36] The closed canon of the Scriptures and the defined doctrines of the Church are the real objective embodiment of this revelation as it has been passed on by the *lebendige Überlieferung* of the Church. The Scriptures present the revealed fact and idea. Individual doctrines for Drey are deduced from the revealed idea of the kingdom of God, and authentic dogmas are those that have been officially articulated and thereby fixed and closed by the teaching office of the Church. The Scriptures are merely dead letters, unless they are brought to life within the living tradition of the Church.[37] Drey stands with Schleiermacher in affirming the divine fact as the source of revelation and the living community as the historical vehicle for revelation; but Drey's position implies a strong criticism of Schleiermacher's theology for rejecting the fixed, unchanging character of authoritative confessional statements.

Schleiermacher's rejection of a cognitive or linguistic deposit of revelation in favor of the divinely revealed fact does not mean that the Bible and Church teachings leave one agnostic about God, or

---

[33]*Apologetik*, 3:62.

[34]*Apologetik*, 3:64.

[35]*Apologetik*, 3:65.

[36]*Apologetik*, 3:276-312.

[37]Drey states in his journal that "the living tradition gives to the dead letter a lasting meaning," (*Geist des Christentum*, 161); also see "Revision," 92, 96.

that these documents are not normative for the Christian community. The divinely revealed origin of creation, Christ, and the Church does not yield knowledge of God's inner nature in itself. However, "any proclamation of God which is to be operative upon and within us can only express God in relation to us; and this is not an infra-human ignorance concerning God, but the essence of human limitedness in relation to Him."[38] Schleiermacher judged that doctrines cannot express the being of God in itself or the attributes of God except insofar as they are derived from the ecclesial consciousness of faith as it is formed by the divine causality and not on the basis of human speculation.[39] Schleiermacher does claim that a triune God--Creator, Redeemer, and Spirit--is disclosed through a combination of statements derived from the positivity of ecclesial faith. He doubts, however, that the Church is warranted in speaking about the immanent Trinity in terms of eternal distinctions. Any access to the Trinity is through the economy of salvation.[40]

The authority of the Bible and Church teachings rests on the positivity of Christian ecclesial faith, just as the knowledge of God is mediated through this ecclesial faith. The authority of the Bible and Church teachings resides in their adequate presentation of the *Glaubensweise* of the Christian Church. Concrete modes of communal faith, the diverse positive religions, draw their distinctiveness from the original fact at their inception: "the individ-

---

[38]*Christian Faith*, § 11, p. 52.

[39]*Christian Faith*, §§ 30, 50, 51. We read about the ideas of omnipotence and eternity that since they "are here related only to the divine causality, it may at once be proved . . . that the individual attributes in their differences correspond to nothing real in God" (§ 51, p. 201).

[40]See *Christian Faith*, §§ 170-172 and his "Über die Gegensatz zwischen der Sabellianischen und der Athanasianischen Vorstellung von Trinität," *Kritische Gesamtausgabe*, vol. 10 *Theologisch-dogmatische Abhandlungen*, ed. Hans-Friedrich Traulsen (Berlin: Walter de Gruyter, 1988); translated by Moses Stuart in *Biblical Repository and Quarterly Observer* 5 (1835): 265-353; and 6 (1835): 1-116.

ual content of all the moments of the religious life within one religious communion, insofar as this content depends on the original fact from which the communion itself, as a coherent phenomenon, originated."[41] Thus the Scriptures and doctrines are authentic insofar as they articulate the consciousness of the Church.

Schleiermacher affirms with Drey that faith in Christ, even for the earliest Christians, must be mediated by written word or by oral tradition.[42] Still Schleiermacher contends that the Reformation *sola scriptura* principle remains valid since the earliest testimony of the Church presents what is decisive about the community's experience of redemption prior to any interaction with foreign influences.[43] While the Scriptures are the purest articulation of the uniqueness of Christian redemption, that articulation is neither the last word, nor does it present a golden age or archetype, but "the first member of the series."[44] Thus the Scriptures are "the norm for succeeding presentations" and can stand in criticism of erroneous doctrinal development.[45] Yet, doctrines move beyond the language of the Scriptures. Although doctrines are not revealed, they are supra-rational insofar as they ultimately "rest upon a *given*."[46] At the same time, every doctrine is rational insofar as it follows "the same laws of conception and synthesis as regulate all speech."[47]

For Schleiermacher there is no infallible teaching office in the Church, nor are there "closed" dogmas. Nevertheless, he does treat as authoritative the ecumenical councils in his lectures on Church history, and in the *Glaubenslehre* he says that they are "common to the whole Church" when he examines the heretical views of Christ

---

[41]*Christian Faith*, § 10, p. 49.

[42]*Christian Faith*, § 128, p. 592.

[43]*Christian Faith*, §§ 27, 128.

[44]*Christian Faith*, § 129, p. 594. See also *Brief Outline*, § 83.

[45]*Christian Faith*, §§ 129-130.

[46]*Christian Faith*, § 13, p. 67.

[47]*Christian Faith*, § 13, p. 67.

and redemption. Within Protestant churches doctrinal development must be guided more directly by the Evangelical confessional documents.[48] The *Glaubenslehre* refers often to the Evangelical statements as the linguistic heritage which articulates the Protestant Church's faith. Schleiermacher does not deny the authority of the cherished Protestant *sola scriptura* principle and the Evangelical confessions, but he does develop a new approach to them.[49]

Even though Schleiermacher, contrary to Drey, did not believe the idea of the kingdom of God was revealed, it had, quite significantly, an important normative status in his dogmatics. The original presentation of the idea of the kingdom of God is normative, Schleiermacher claims, because in the New Testament "the first theoretical interpretation of Christianity was based upon a comparison of the new Kingdom of God with the old."[50] He

---

[48]*Christian Faith*, § 27. Schleiermacher believes official pronouncements are reformable because they are statements made in the context of controversy and are "presentations put forth by a larger or smaller majority, for controversy more than anything else rouses all those impulses that lead to error." He comments: "Hence we must always reflect with satisfaction that as regards the doctrines which had come to be matters of controversy, the incipient Evangelical Church declined to submit to the decisions of a General Council; but we can no longer approve of its having none the less accepted all the ecumenical Creeds; for these Creeds are but the product of similar Councils, which besides were due to divisions within the Church, and hence were not preeminently fitted for the ascertainment of truth. Similarly, it is a matter for satisfaction that the convictions then held were set forth in brief Confessions for the whole of Christendom, which was the first thing to give reforming influences acting on the whole body their place; but it is a matter of regret that by means of these very documents (as if they had been irreformable) an effort was subsequently made to hinder the performance of the very task to which they owed their birth" (§ 154, pp. 690-691).

[49]This point is effectively made by Hans-Joachim Birkner and John Thiel. See Birkner, "Beobachtungen zu Schleiermachers Programm der Dogmatik," *Neue Zeitshrift für systematische Theologie und Religionsphilosophie* 5 (1963): 119-131; and Thiel, *Imagination and Authority*, 33-62, 194-195.

[50]*Christian Faith*, § 102, p. 439.

shows then how many of his doctrinal formulations cohere with this idea.

Criteria for Authentic Development

Schleiermacher and Drey concluded from their reflections on the historical and developmental character of revelation and doctrines that Christianity was left neither with the radical instability of cognitive and moral relativism nor with a pressing need for a firm and unshakable foundation. They assumed an objective tradition--Schleiermacher's *Glaubensweise* and Drey's *lebendige Überlieferung*--that is attested to by the Scriptures and Church pronouncements and embodied by the Church.[51] Moreover, they argue that the objective tradition can only be critically assessed and affirmed by determining the essence of Christianity. They also believed, however, that the objective faith transmitted by the Church must not be understood statically or only in terms of dogmatic propositions. Consequently, both affirmed the importance of doctrinal development.

At the same time, they accused each other's tradition of lacking the ability to develop. Schleiermacher stated on numerous occasions that contrary to Protestants, Catholics do not accept doctrinal development because they do not recognize the changing character of the Church throughout history.[52] For Drey, Protestants reject doctrinal development by maintaining the *sola scriptura* principle and the freedom of the individual interpretation

---

[51]Objective tradition has, following the Church Fathers, been called the rule of faith. See Congar, *Tradition and Traditions*, 192-193, 199-200, 296-307, esp. 304-305, for rule of faith, 23-35; the use of the phrase "deposit of faith" for objective tradition is discussed on 197.

[52]*Brief Outline*, § 304; *Christian Faith*, § 27, p. 177; *Die christliche Sitte*, 72. See B. A. Gerrish, "Schleiermacher and the Reformation: A Question of Doctrinal Development," *Old Protestantism and the New* (Chicago: University of Chicago Press, 1982), 193.

of the Scripture, whereas Catholics affirm doctrinal development since only they recognize the "living tradition" unfolding in the whole Church and safeguarded by the teaching office.[53]

Yet Schleiermacher did not believe the Scriptures provided the absolute rule of faith, and Drey did not believe the rule of faith was statically preserved in the Scriptures and in tradition, nor did he unequivocally equate the Church that transmits the faith with the teaching authority of the Church's hierarchy.[54] Instead both identified the normative character of faith as everything which is founded on the divine fact of Christ, who is the origin of the Christian community. This objective faith finds its earliest and pivotal formulation in the idea of the kingdom of God and is embodied within the living faith of the Christian community. The Church is the subject of this faith, that is, the vehicle or mediator that transmits this objective tradition and in the process develops it. Schleiermacher's and Drey's ways of thinking about the objective tradition and its transmission yield a variety of criteria for evaluating authentic development.

These diverse criteria indicate, on the one hand, that Schleiermacher and Drey are not radical historical relativists. Although they acknowledge that doctrines are historically relative insofar as they are influenced by diverse cultural and historical sources, they do recognize a normative faith, which governs thought and guides action. On the other hand, the diversity of criteria also suggest that since Schleiermacher and Drey do not ground doctrines in one anthropological or experiential criterion or in an empirical

---

[53]"Vom Geist und Wesen," 202, 225-234; *Kurze Einleitung*, §§ 47, 123; *Die Apologetik*, 3:330.

[54]Congar discusses the deposit of faith understood as the objective content of faith in relation to the deposit of faith as closely associated, if not identified with, the Magisterium of the Church. *Tradition and Traditions*, 197-199.

fact, they are not foundationalists or rationalists in any proper sense.[55]

Criterion of Coherence with Church Confessions and the Bible

Contrary to the claim that Schleiermacher and Drey emphasized the inner faith of the Church to the point of excluding or minimizing the outer linguistic expressions of that faith, we have seen that Schleiermacher and Drey believed authentic doctrinal articulations and development must be appropriate to the primary language of faith, that is, the Bible and Church confessions. Schleiermacher stands opposed to the position affirmed by Drey, that the dogmatic claims of official confessions cannot be rejected; he nevertheless maintains that new doctrinal propositions must be homogeneous with Protestant confessional claims.[56] For both Drey and Schleiermacher, the theologian's efforts at reformulating and clarifying the objective tradition for a new age remains an individual theologian's opinion or an opinion shared by some (e.g., theological schools of thought) until it is accepted by the official church as the faith of the Church. By seeking to harmonize personal positions with the confessions of the Church, a theologian situates herself or

---

[55]My contention that Schleiermacher and Drey are not foundationalists in a proper sense, which I will attempt to demonstrate, is intended to counter the argument that they offer unacceptable foundationalist arguments within their theologies. I do not deny that they employ a transcendental or anthropological form of argument in their criteriology, but this is one of many criteria. Perhaps it might be more accurate to argue that Schleiermacher and Drey are not hard foundationalists, but that they utilize some soft forms of foundational argument within their theologies, which they maintain are entirely appropriate, but not sufficient. Cf. Thiel, *Imagination and Authority*, 167-200, Fiorenza, *Foundational*, 285-311.

[56]See *Kurze Einleitung*, §§ 256-257; *Christian Faith*, § 27 and *Brief Outline*, §§ 209, 211, 212.

himself within a community of discourse. The theologian renders service to the Church mindful that, although it is only a personal position that is offered, his or her intention is to express in doctrinal form what has been implicitly affirmed by the Church and to declare the constant faith as forcefully as possible for the present age.

In addition to official Church pronouncements, the New Testament language of the kingdom of God and its relation to the Old Testament usage provides, as we have underscored, a focal point in their interpretation of the Scriptures. The differences in their respective approaches to this idea cannot be minimized. Drey believed authentic doctrines are deduced from this idea, while Schleiermacher argued that new doctrinal formulations describe the faith consciousness of the Church and must adhere to the idea of the kingdom. In comparison, Drey grants relatively more authoritative weight to the official teachings (dogmas) of the Church since they are, properly understood, deduced from the idea of the kingdom, whereas Schleiermacher views doctrinal statements as the description of the consciousness of the Church at the present time which must also be checked for their homogeneity with previous ecclesial confessions and the New Testament witness, especially the idea of the kingdom.[57]

In practice they both found in the idea of the kingdom of God a multi-valent metaphor that disclosed the plot for Christian history. Through this narrative the identity of God as creator, redeemer, and source of communal unity and moral purpose is made known. The process of human transformation from sinner to saved as mediated through Christ and the Church is indicated through this plot. Further, the eschatological tension between the Christian community and the world is disclosed. This narrative, in short, provides a web of beliefs that is often utilized in their work. The kingdom of God motif provides an important narrative framework

---

[57]See *Christian Faith*, §§ 27, 102, esp. p. 439; *Kurze Einleitung*, §§ 59-60.

for their evaluation of doctrines, but not in isolation from other scriptural and confessional claims.

Thus, coherence to the primary language of faith--ecclesial confessions and the biblical testimony, and in particular, the language of the kingdom of God--serves Schleiermacher and Drey as a key criterion for evaluating doctrines. New doctrinal formulae, inspired by new insights into the constant faith of the Church and refined by being responsive to the contemporary state of scientific and philosophical thought and discourse, must cohere with this linguistic heritage of the Church.

The primary language of faith is one, but not the only, criterion for judging authentic development for Drey and Schleiermacher. As we have indicated, their interpretation of Scripture, especially the idea of the kingdom of God, is a crucial feature in this criterion. For us to acknowledge this fundamental point about their use of Scripture, however, in no way disavows alternative approaches to the interpretation of the Scripture in theology, nor does it addresses the many questions raised by these diverse paradigms [58]

Criterion of Ecclesial Piety

Romanticism in Germany, as in other cultural contexts, is Janus-faced. On the one hand, there is an emphasis on individuality; that is, the unique individuality of persons, cultures, and historical epochs. On the other hand, an organic model for integrating parts within a whole is accentuated. Romantic thinkers can lean one way or the other. For some the part is emphasized to

---

[58]For background on this issue, see David Kelsey, *The Use of the Scripture in Recent Theology* (Philadelphia: Fortress Press, 1975). Schleiermacher is discussed in Hans Frei's work, *The Eclipse of Biblical Narrative* (New Haven: Yale University Press, 1974). For a treatment of the interpretation of the Old Testament by Drey and Franz Anton Staudenmaier, see Elmar Klinger, *Offenbarung im Horizont der Heilsgeschichte* (Zürich: Benziger Verlag, 1969).

the detriment of the whole, the individual person to the exclusion of the community. For others, the organic community and the whole are so stressed as to minimize the significance of the individual. The romantic accent on individuality can promote creativity, but also self-indulgence; the stress on organic relations can support moral and religious consensus, but may be illegitimately controlling. Schleiermacher and Drey wish to affirm the positive aspects of both sides of these romantic motifs, while minimizing their threats.[59] By so doing they set up the problematic which has been at the forefront of doctrinal debate in the modern period: how are we to recognize the diversity of historical epochs, cultures, and individual thinkers, while still acknowledging the continuity of the community and promoting communal unity? Our contemporary formulation is clearly indebted to this romantic problematic: how can we acknowledge plurality without pluralism, and strive for consensus and communication without seeking control through force or domination? In doctrinal matters, Schleiermacher and Drey definitely do not wish to collapse the tension between the individual (especially in terms of individual historical epochs and cultures) and the community. Instead they employ a criterion of ecclesial piety for judging authentic doctrines in an effort to foster

---

[59]For a brief and helpful analysis of romanticism and Schleiermacher, see Richard Crouter's introduction to his translation of *On Religion: Speeches to Its Cultured Despisers* (Cambridge: Cambridge University Press, 1988), 1-39, esp. 32-39. Josef Geiselmann portrayed Drey as an anti-Enlightenment romantic. Abraham Kustermann has challenged this interpretation and contends that Drey's concerns and methods are more closely aligned with the Enlightenment (*Die Apologetik*, 56-66, 75-80). The distinction between romantic and Enlightenment concerns and methods can be made, but the two should not be dichotomized. The influence of one cultural movement upon Drey should not be isolated to the exclusion of the other. Drey's treatment of the positivity of Christianity, kingdom of God, organic life, and education show considerable interest in Enlightenment questions and concerns, even as they also show a commitment to certain romantic formulas.

simultaneously ecclesial consensus and to promote individual creativity in service of the community.

As both writers deem human experience an important source for theology, this criterion of ecclesial piety can be viewed as experiential. In every generation the faith that is handed down in the Church is received differently according to differences of experience due to historical, cultural, and individual determinants. But this formulation of the criterion, in terms of experience, has encountered difficulties. There is reason to fear in the modern period that experience is too often understood as secular human experience, which is evaluated in light of the Enlightenment principle of autonomy from traditions and authorities, rather than assessed by the communal concern for unity and in light of the impact of linguistic traditions that shape human experience.

Nevertheless, it remains important to speak of Schleiermacher's and Drey's use of this criterion in terms of experience, since they attempt to develop a mediating theology that is apologetically persuasive. They pursue this goal on the one hand by showing how there is an inner correlation between doctrines and ecclesial experience: ecclesial experience is expressed in and shaped by religious doctrines. On the other hand, ecclesial experience is also expressed in and shaped by outer cultural influences; scientific, philosophical, and socio-political. Consequently, they also employ an outer criterion of adequacy to modern thought and discourse, which we will examine below. In keeping with both of these criteria, Schleiermacher and Drey seek to indicate the plausibility, adequacy, and indeed necessity of religion, and specifically Christianity, for interpreting and living human life.

Schleiermacher and Drey are primarily concerned neither with individual (i.e., autonomous) human experience nor with experience divorced from a religious context (i.e., secular experience). It is pious or mystical and ecclesial experience that constitutes a criterion for authentic doctrines. Their use of ecclesial piety as a criterion for judging genuine doctrinal development can be appropriately understood as a romantic formulation of the traditional criteria of the *lex orandi lex credendi* principle and the *sensus fidelium*.

To appreciate their focus on ecclesial piety fully, we must first relate it to our authors' convictions about the immediate experience of God available to the individual. Schleiermacher and Drey detect an immediate experience or consciousness that has God as its source (as whence) and term (as *summum bonum*), but, as we shall see shortly, this type of experience is not simply equated with ecclesial piety for either figure. Such an immediate experience constitutes a transcendental characteristic of the human person that is abstracted, but not separated, from concrete or categorical acts of thinking and doing. Both identify this immediate experience in human consciousness with the affections.[60] Schleiermacher speaks of this immediate self-consciousness in terms of the feeling of absolute dependence.[61] Drey concurs, calling it the primitive element of religion.[62]

Important differences between Schleiermacher's and Drey's positions emerge at this juncture, which have ramifications for the criterion of ecclesial piety. Schleiermacher argued that admitting the immediate experience of the feeling of absolute dependence does not entail affirming some previous knowledge of God. He does not wish "to dispute the existence of such an original knowledge, but simply to set it aside as something with which, in a system of Christian doctrine, we could never have any concern, because plainly enough it has itself nothing to do directly with piety."[63] The feeling of absolute dependence indicates a

---

[60]Schleiermacher's classic formulations are found in *On Religion*, 41-46, and *Christian Faith*, § 3; for Drey see "Über das Verhältnis des Mysticismus zum Katholicismus, mit Nuzanwendungen für unsere Zeit," *Theologische Quartlalschrift* 6 (1824): 219-248, reprinted in *Revision von Kirche*, ed. Franz Schupp, 25-54, see 28; *Kurze Einleitung* §§ 1, 101-102; "Vom Geist und Wesen," 213; *Die Apologetik*, 1:88.

[61]*Christian Faith*, § 4.

[62]*Apologetik*, 1:116. We will examine this passage below.

[63]*Christian Faith*, § 4, p. 17.

relationship to God, as distinct from world (against pantheism) and as distinct from self (against the divinization of the human subject). However, his formulation of this immediate consciousness is in opposition to the claim that such feeling "is itself conditioned by some previous knowledge of God." The idea of God "is nothing more than the expression of the feeling of absolute dependence..., the most direct reflection upon it and the most original idea with which we are here concerned, and is quite independent of that original knowledge (properly so called), and conditioned only by our feeling of absolute dependence."[64]

In the first edition of *Über die Religion*, Schleiermacher often linked feeling (*Gefühl*) and intuition (*Anschaaung*). Through feeling and intuition, the human grasps the parts in relation to the whole and the finite in relation to the infinite. There is in the universe a unity in plurality and this religious feeling or intuition guards against losing the underlying unity of reality. In later editions of *Über die Religion* and in the *Glaubenslehre*, Schleiermacher rejected any identification of feeling and intuition, because he sought to differentiate his position from Schelling's "intellectual intuition" into the *Urwissen*.[65] While knowing and doing are interrelated with the affections for Schleiermacher, religion itself is not dependent on

---

[64]*Christian Faith*, § 4, p. 17.

[65]Süskind and Brandt point out that Schelling found the first edition of Schleiermacher's *On Religion* to his liking on the subject of intuition. He agreed with Schleiermacher that through intuition the unity of the parts was recognized. For Schleiermacher this unity was mediated through religion, while for Schelling it was through science. It is fair to conclude with Süskind and Brandt that Schleiermacher wished to distance his definition of religion from Schelling's understanding of science in order to maintain the *sui generis* character of religion in relation to science and morality. Süskind, *Der Einfluß Schellings*, 100-109, 226-275, especially 274-275; Brandt, *The Philosophy of Schleiermacher*, 145-200; see Schelling, *System of Transcendental Idealism*, 27-29, 231-233, and *On University Studies*, 46, 49-50, 73-76. Also see the recent study by Maureen Junker, *Das Urbild des Gottesbewußtseins. Zur Entwicklung der Religionstheorie und Christologie Schleiermachers von der ersten zur zweiten Auflage der Glaubenslehre* (Berlin: Walter de Gruyter, 1990).

ideas about God. Schleiermacher did not believe that piety is antithetical to rational inference or dialectical method, but he did wish to avoid the intrusion of speculation into his dogmatic method.[66]

Drey did not follow Schleiermacher at this point. Drey acknowledged the affective character of religion, but, contrary to Schleiermacher's later formulations, he insisted upon the cognitive, reflective dimension of religious consciousness.[67] Religion is a "dark presentiment or a feeling, in which the human grasps for the first time the being of an invisible world, of a higher power in that invisible world, his dependence on it, it is the presentiment and feeling in his breast."[68] But Drey adds that "religion steps out of the sphere of feeling into the sphere of thought and recognizes itself there."[69] It is in this sphere of thought that there is a specific consciousness of God through ideas. According to Drey,

> Schleiermacher puts religion in consciousness or in the pious feeling of absolute dependence on God. Now indeed the consciousness of our dependence is an essential fact of religious consciousness and in relation to the other [facts] I have called it the primitive element, but it is not the only element.[70]

Drey prefers to speak of religion as "the universal determinate essence of humans through the original consciousness of God;" a consciousness which includes feeling and thinking.[71] His insistence on an element of reflective consciousness at the basis of religion places Drey in opposition to Schleiermacher's later position and

---

[66] *Christian Faith*, §§ 15, 31.

[67] *Kurze Einleitung*, § 21, *Apologetik*, 1:309-316.

[68] *Apologetik*, 1:87-88.

[69] *Apologetik*, 1:89.

[70] *Apologetik*, 1:115.

[71] *Apologetik*, 1:118, 115-117. Hegelian theologian Marheineke is accused of the opposite problem: reducing religion to thinking while rejecting the dimension of feeling.

closer to Schelling and the early Schleiermacher. There is an intellectual intuition which unites us with *Wissen* and within Christianity this is further determined by the grasping of the idea of the kingdom of God.[72]

If we recall several key differences between Schleiermacher's and Drey's theologies--on the nature of religion as feeling and knowing, on the status of official ecclesial pronouncements, and on their approaches to dogmatic theology--there may be sufficient warrants for claiming that Schleiermacher lays relatively more weight on the criterion of ecclesial piety than does Drey. Schleiermacher views doctrines as articulations of ecclesial religious affections and theology's primary task is to provide a description of ecclesial consciousness. Drey, on the other hand, views dogmas as deduced from the idea of the kingdom of God and affirmed by the Church, and theology as a construction out of the idea of the kingdom of God. Although we have stressed that Schleiermacher's descriptive approach to dogmatic theology is structurally parallel with Drey's construction, Schleiermacher's descriptive and correlative method remains in tension with Drey's deductive and correlative method.

For Schleiermacher, the feeling of absolute dependence serves as a criterion for the doctrine of creation, but this feeling always presupposes and is further specified by the modification of ecclesial consciousness under the conditions of sin and grace.[73] "The piety which forms the basis of all ecclesiastical communions is, considered in itself, neither a knowing or a doing, but a modification of feeling, or of immediate self-consciousness."[74] To grasp the entire content of ecclesial piety requires that one not separate the feeling of

---

[72]On *Wissen*, see *Kurze Einleitung*, § 45 The idea of the kingdom of God was the original revelation in the world which is historically unfolding up to Christ and it is the highest revelation; see *Kurze Einleitung*, §§ 27, 32-33, 65. On religious consciousness in Drey, see Kustermann, *Die Apologetik*, 262-267; Tiefensee, *Die religiöse Anlage*, 138-155.

[73]*Christian Faith*, §§ 36, 62-64.

[74]*Christian Faith*, § 3, p. 5.

absolute dependence from the consciousness of sin and grace available to the Christian. "There is no general God-consciousness which has not bound up with it a relation to Christ, and no relationship with the Redeemer which has no bearing on the general God-consciousness."[75] Dogmatic theology arranges "the different modifications of this fact [of Christian ecclesial piety] according to its differing relations with the other facts of consciousness."[76]

Drey spoke in numerous contexts of the importance of piety and mysticism for Christian theology and for the life of the Church.[77] Mysticism and dialectic are both required for the work of theology. Mysticism, not science, is the weapon needed to combat the excesses and decay of scholasticism. Drey believed the Reformers understood this, but what they failed to understand was that this mysticial intuition must not be cut off from the objectivity of the living communal tradition.[78] Drey specifies one instance--a significant one at that--when this mystical ecclesial consciousness provided the primary source for dogmatic development: in the ecclesial articulations of the nature of grace and salvation.[79]

One important reason why ecclesial piety is not more of a source for theology in Drey's system, but is rather the framework for reflection, is his idealist formulation of the nature of

---

[75]*Christian Faith*, § 62, p. 261.

[76]*Christian Faith*, § 28, p. 121.

[77]"Revision," 85-97, esp. 88-89, and "Über das Verhältnis des Mysticismus zum Katholicismus," 25-54.

[78]"Revision," 93; also "Vom Geist und Wesen," 203-206, and "Über das Verhältnis des Mysticismus zum Katholicismus," 36-39.

[79]"Ideen zur Geschichte," 252. In this work Drey divided the history of Catholic dogmas into four periods. The first dealt with the relation of Christianity to the ancient world and especially to Judaism, Paganism, and Gnosticism. The second period concerned the essence of Christianity in terms of Christology. The third period treated the nature of grace and salvation. The fourth is constituted by the debates between Protestants and Catholics.

Christianity. Piety is for Drey the concrete realization of the idea, the content, and the object of Christianity.

> The religious ideas, the object, and content of that belief, demand for themselves their own realization in the individual and in the whole of the Church. Religious belief must pass over into religious disposition, religious life--using a German word--into piety (*Frömmigkeit*). Piety, with all that belongs to that, is the purpose of the Church. Everything that furthers piety, and that can be conceived under the general expression devotion, is the means to the end. However, piety as actually existing depends above all on those ideas present within a Church, whose realization it is. Therefore, just as the religious ideas, although referring to the one [Church], can differ in regard to their form into the different Churches, so piety itself (the spirit of piety), too, is different from one Church to the other, just like devotion.[80]

Different ideas of Redemption and the Church yield different forms of piety and devotion. Yet for this very reason, piety and devotion also serve as a way of evaluating the adequacy of a given doctrine. Doctrines are confirmed in the piety of the Church.[81]

Drey is clear that the experience of the Church does not simply reflect dogmatic norms; ecclesial experience changes according to the conditions of time and location.

> The same word of Christ is proclaimed by the Church at different times and among different people in different forms and with different accents. Thus, the Church constitutes itself differently from age to age. However, each time it does this according to the needs of the people, the exigencies of their purposes, and according to the spirit of the times. Each one of these forms is good, as long as it is in accordance with the requirements that have been indicated; they cease to be good when the conditions are otherwise.

---

[80]*Kurze Einleitung*, § 269.

[81]See *Apologetik*, 1:363-380, especially 367-374. This section has been examined in Chapter III.

> Thus, the further development of the essential [nature of the Church], relative to this essence, which always must remain unchanged, is something non-essential. Yet, it is still not accidental, it has a relative necessity. Even though not enduring, it must, nonetheless, be up to date.[82]

Ecclesial piety is influenced not only by the constant proclamation of the Church, but also by the various conditions of time and location. Accordingly, the historically and culturally determined experience of the Church calls forth the reinterpretation of received dogmas and the proclamation of the Church according to the spirit of the times. Ecclesial piety is a source and criterion here, but, as we will discover, it must be augmented by an outer criterion.

Both thinkers contended that ecclesial piety must remain a source and criterion for authentic doctrines within theology. Ecclesial piety guards against scholasticism and curious speculation. However, they recognized that religious piety or mysticism can be fanatical and problematic if it is not governed by dialectical (logical, scientific) analysis and evaluation in terms of what constitutes the identity of authentic Christian piety.[83] It merits repeating that Schleiermacher's and Drey's criterion of piety is ecclesially understood. There can be fanatical individuals and groups, just as there can be a piety that unites and forms a consensus. For Drey the basic intuition of Christianity is not merely the subjective faith of the individual, but rather it is an intuition that unites the individ-

---

[82]"Vom Geist und Wesen," 231; Drey also states that "[a]s the essential [elements of the Catholic Church] have been formed further according to the needs of the times, places, and persons, likewise it may be further formed, which holds for something non-essential, however for that reason is still not accidental" (277).

[83]Schleiermacher spoke of religious emotions at variance with the true essence of Christian piety and of a recession of vitality in the affections. See *Christian Faith*, § 21, p. 96, and *Brief Outline*, § 54. For Drey, see "Über das Verhältnis des Mysticismus zum Katholicismus," 40-42.

ual to the objective faith carried on in the Church.[84] "If we thus speak of the development of a certain dogma in the Church, we could not call it developed until we recognize it as reflectively reflectively known by the Church, as pronounced the universal belief of the Church."[85]

The objective faith for Drey is present in the whole Church, is witnessed to in the Scriptures, and is officially articulated by the teaching office of the Church.[86] He consistently defends the infallibility of the Church and the legitimacy of the hierarchical office of teaching, while discerning the limits within which this authority should be practiced.[87] Whereas the inner constitution of the Church is one of equality, the outer constitution of administration is not. Christ willed the "higher authority" of the teaching office as a necessary external authority which affirms and speaks the inner faith of the Church, which has the Spirit as its source of unity.[88]

Schleiermacher would concur that faith is always corporate and that doctrinal formulations must foster consensus, but he eschews the language of intuition and in this context he does not draw a distinction between subjective and objective. Moreover, although Schleiermacher affirms the importance of ecclesial leaders as representatives of the community and the infallibility of the invisible Church, he rejects the Catholic doctrine of the teaching office of the

---

[84]"Vom Geist und Wesen," pp. 203-206.

[85]"Ideen zur Geschichte," 253.

[86]*Kurze Einleitung*, §§ 255-262, 273 and *Apologetik*, 3:33.

[87]On the apologetic defense of the Catholic Church, see *Kurze Einleitung*, §§ 233-236 and *Apologetik*, vol. 3.

[88]See "Vom Geist und Wesen," 226, *Apologetik*, 3:87, 103. On Drey's ecclesiology, see Chapter V; Raimund Lachner, *Das ekklesiologische Denken Johann Sebastian Dreys* (Frankfurt am Main: Peter Lang, 1986). Lachner situates Drey's ecclesiology in relation to the tensions between the Enlightenment, romanticism, and German idealism; between Conciliarism and Ultramontanism, and between the Napoléon disturbances and secularization as they bear on the relationship of Church and State.

Church as instituted by Christ.[89] For Schleiermacher, the Church's doctrine must be based on "a clear and enlivening description of a *common* inner experience," because "what is possessed is shared in common."[90] Theology presents ecclesial piety, because it is valid or prevalent for the church at the time and "can be put forward as a presentation of its common piety without provoking dissension and schism."[91]

Criterion of Historical Positivity

Doctrines are judged as authentic for both thinkers insofar as they are based on the positivity of Christianity. This criterion for doctrines, understood at its most basic level, is the determinate content of the Christian religion founded on the historical fact of Christ, which stands at the origin of the Christian community.[92] Every legitimate doctrine must have its historical origin in Christ. Contrary to deists and rationalists of idealist or empiricist bent, the divine positivity of Christianity establishes that the historically rooted and determined character of this faith cannot be dissolved into religious or philosophical ideas, nor can it be rejected in favor of natural religion. On this much, Schleiermacher and Drey agreed.

However, Drey extended or, more accurately, maintained the scope of this criterion beyond what Schleiermacher would have allowed. While affirming Schleiermacher's claim that apologetics needs to situate the place of religion in human experience before discussing the essence of Christianity, contrary to Schleiermacher, he retains the traditional external proofs from miracles and

---

[89]See *Brief Outline*, §§ 267, 278-279, 304-308; *Christian Faith*, §§ 133, 144-145, 153-155; and *Die christliche Sitte*, 124-125.

[90]*On the Glaubenslehre*, 41.

[91]*Christian Faith*, § 19, p. 90.

[92]For Schleiermacher, *On Religion*, 213, 233-234; *Christian Faith*, § 10, p. 49; For Drey, *Kurze Einleitung*, §§ 34, 231, 232; *Apologetik*, 1:1-3.

prophecy for the divine character of revelation.[93] These external facts are included to further demonstrate the divine positivity of Christianity. Schleiermacher rejected them because he believed they prove nothing and presuppose, rather than ensure, faith.[94] If this facet of Drey's treatment of the positivity of Christianity were to be viewed in isolation, it would fulfill the requirements of an empirical form of foundationalism by seeking to ground basic beliefs in empirical statements. But that would not be a fair interpretation. Drey minimizes the importance of the external empirical criteria for demonstrating the divine positivity of Christianity, even though they are still affirmed.[95]

Aside from this difference between Schleiermacher and Drey, there is also a different approach employed when addressing the basic issue of the positivity of Christianity. Schleiermacher's and Drey's treatment of the positivity of Christianity is, as we have stated, in opposition to rationalists and deists who argued that the universal religion of the human race is rational and moral, but need not be tied to the cult of arbitrary aspects of Christianity. They agree that the historically concrete character of Christianity has universal import for the redemption of the human race. In other words, the positivity of Christianity implies the affirmation of a concrete universal. The specific character of Christianity remains normative and can never be transmuted into concepts or ideas. It is on this basis that both figures assume and present the absoluteness of Christianity. New doctrinal formulae must be judged on the basis of the concrete universality of Christian faith.

For Schleiermacher what is historically concrete is the fact of Christ as the source of redemption that is mediated through the Church. The religious consciousness and affections of individuals within the Church are also concrete and empirical within his theology. Finally, the ecclesial doctrines and actions of the Church

---

[93]*Apologetik*, 1:204-246, 344-379.

[94]See *Der christliche Glaube* (1st edition), § 21; (2nd edition), § 14; and *On the Glaubenslehre*, 66.

[95]See Fiorenza, *Foundational*, 261, 271-277, 285-291.

are concrete and empirical. Each of the concrete aspects of Christianity have a universal import insofar as they are constitutive of the essence of Christianity. Schleiermacher argued that the positive character of Christianity may appear arbitrary and superfluous, but that "resistance to the positive and arbitrary is resistance to the definite and real."[96] If any religious affection, doctrine, or action is beyond the periphery of this essence, however, it is heretical or schismatic and therefore to be criticized as such.

Drey concurs that the fact of Jesus, ecclesial consciousness, and the doctrines and actions of the Church are concrete aspects of the positivity of Christianity. Moreover, he agrees that what is beyond the pale of the essence of Christianity is not included within the positively determined faith. However, Drey deploys another kind of argument in apologetics and dogmatic theology: what appears as contingent or accidental within empirical Christianity is rationally necessary for salvation.[97] This form of argumentation requires close scrutiny and comparison with Schleiermacher's approach. Drey's mode of argument is similar to Schleiermacher's in that the arbitrary is described as concretely determined and required for salvation. It is dissimilar in that Drey writes with some regularity of the accidental or contingent character of empirical Christianity and its (empirical Christianity's) rational necessity; Schleiermacher in his theological writings did not speak of a connection between

---

[96]*On Religion*, 234.

[97]*Kurze Einleitung*, § 13 discusses freedom and necessity; more importantly §§ 64-65 treat the relation between the historical and the scientific branches of theology. This lays the framework for his argument that the accidental facts of history are "grounded in reason" and necessary; § 234 employs the distinction between accidental and necessary when treating the apologetics for the Catholic Church; the same distinction is implied in § 231 within apologetics for Christianity; §§ 309, 312, 315 offer the clearest summary statements. See also *Apologetik*, 1:4-7, 98-99, 105-109; 3:117-121, 300.

the accidental or conditional character of empirical history and its rational necessity.[98]

Drey's use of the accidental-necessary argument rests on his deductive method. Schleiermacher's lack of this form of argument is consistent with his rejection of a deductive method in favor of a descriptive method within historical and dogmatic theology, and a critical method in philosophical theology. For Drey, historical theology provides the empirical basis for theology, while the fundamental and dogmatic sciences, by way of philosophical construction, demonstrate that what appears accidental is necessary for reason. In this way we move from faith to knowledge.[99] So we read:

> The individual will find the touchstone for his powers in this, if he succeeds in rationally conceiving of each given doctrine of historical theology as something necessary. This conception accomplished through the whole is properly and in the strictest sense the scientific study of theology.[100]

---

[98]As we have indicated, one exception is Schleiermacher's statement that Christianity has "eine notwendige Existenz" in *Brief Outline*, § 56, n. 25. Drey was seriously engaged with the work of Lessing and Schelling. Lessing discussed the accidental truths of history and the necessary truths of reason in "On the Proof of the Spirit and of Power," *Lessing's Theological Writings*, 53. For Schelling the "supreme problem of transcendental philosophy" is how to understand that "freedom is to be necessity, and necessity freedom. . . . It is thus a presumption which itself is necessary for the sake of freedom, that though man is admittedly free in regard to the action itself, he is nonetheless dependent, in regard to the finite result of his actions, upon a necessity that stands over him, and itself takes a hand in the play of his freedom. To account for it by providence or fate is not to explain it at all, for providence or fate are precisely what need to be explained. . . " (*System of Transcendental Idealism*, 204-205).

[99]*Apologetik*, 1:296-307.

[100]*Kurze Einleitung*, § 309.

> However, more important [than the formal and architectonic conception of the theological science[101]], yet also more difficult, is the inner or the real construction. Here the most important thing first of all is to know how to snatch away given Christianity from the form of contingency, in which it appears in ordinary historical intuition like everything given, and how to raise it as a whole to a standpoint of reflection, on which it is conceived of as a necessary phenomenon.[102]

This deductive logic is a centerpiece in Drey's conception of theology as a systematic or scientific enterprise. Within apologetics and dogmatic theology, through scientific construction, one must determine what from within the concrete, accidental, and contingent history of Christianity is necessary and what is not. Schleiermacher, in contrast, argues that apologetics clarifies what is essential for Christianity within its various historical manifestations, without speaking of necessity, although one could argued that to speak of that which is essential in Christianity implies that it is necessary.

Does Drey's methodological difference--as evidenced by his argument from contingency to necessity--constitute a further extension of the criterion of positivity beyond what Schleiermacher would have permitted? It may be considered an extension insofar as Drey recognizes that ecclesially-defined dogmas are fixed, closed, and necessary. His theology supports an accumulation of dogmatic claims, but never their reversibility. His recognition of the problem of hyperorthodox tendencies, while admitting the fixed and closed character of dogmas, suggests that dogmas for Drey must continually be reinterpreted, but never rejected. As we have seen, Schleiermacher does not agree with Drey that dogmas are closed and fixed. He insisted on the fact that we may need to criticize previous

---

[101]See *Kurze Einleitung*, § 310.

[102]*Kurze Einleitung*, § 312.

dogmatic formulae.[103] But while he may be critical of these formulae and reject aspects of them, Schleiermacher always feels obliged to consider and evaluate their import rather than to assume them, deny them, or simply ignore them.[104]

Although Drey would not reject previously affirmed dogmas, he did believe that some accidental or contingent matters of Christian history were not a necessary part of the essence of Christianity, or necessary for salvation. Drey does believe that some things which have been held as normative in the past (e.g., celibate clergy) are not necessary, but have only a relative necessity, and therefore are open to criticism.[105] This kind of judgment could be supported by the use of the other criteria.

Criterion of Adequacy to Modern Thought and Discourse

Schleiermacher and Drey agreed that doctrinal formulations are able to be changed: as they put it, doctrines include mobile elements. Theologians must reformulate the doctrines for their own age, because the church is a historical reality that affects and is influenced by external cultural factors. Accordingly, doctrines are judged not only on the basis of inner-ecclesial criteria. Schleier-

---

[103]"The ecclesiastical formulae concerning the Person of Christ need to be subjected to continual criticism" (*Christian Faith*, § 95); also see § 172 on the Trinitarian doctrine.

[104]*Christian Faith*, § 27.

[105]Drey believed in fact that matters of ecclesiastical discipline and order were in need of and capable of being reformed. For example, Drey defended Johann Baptist Hirscher's criticism of mandatory priestly celibacy. Thus not everything that has taken place can be defended as necessary. See *Kurze Einleitung*, §§ 342-343; *Tübinger Theologen und ihre Theologie: Quellen und Forschungen zur Geschichte der Katholisch-Theologischen Fakultät Tübingen*, 23, 129; M. Seckler, "Johann Sebastian Drey und die Theologie," *Theologische Quartalschrift* 158 (1977):92-109, especially 96-98.

macher and Drey, consistent with what has been called their mediating methods in theology, insist that doctrines must also be evaluated on the basis of an outer criterion. Here outer indicates contemporary modes of thought and discourse associated with science and philosophy. This outer thought and discourse is placed in a tensive relationship with inner ecclesial thought and discourse.[106]

Whether, and if so how, an outer criterion is appropriate for evaluating Christian doctrines has been contested throughout the modern period. Is the truth of Christian discourse susceptible to criticism on the basis of the empirical descriptions or the explanations offered by the natural and the social sciences? Can theology rightfully question the presuppositions of these same sciences? Or, does theology work within a storm-free zone protected from the findings of the various sciences?

The theological justification for permitting an outer criterion is found ultimately, for Schleiermacher and Drey, in their sacramental and organic theologies of history. The relative and not absolute antithesis between the Church and the world in human history and the organic dynamic of inner and outer influences on development warrant for them the contention that the Church needs to be responsive to the changes in scientific and philosophical discourse. This means neither that alien disciplines control the subject matter of Christian doctrines, nor that science or philosophy has a final say in what is valid in the contemporary formulation of faith.

Positively it means for Schleiermacher that the doctrines must be adequate to contemporary philosophical thought and discourse. Generally this means that "the development of doctrine is determined by the whole state of science and especially by prevailing

---

[106]John Cardinal Newman had similarly recognized the "assimilative power" of Christian ideas: "In the physical world, whatever has life is characterized by growth. . . . It grows by taking into its own substance external materials; and this absorption or assimilation is completed when the materials appropriated come to belong to it or enter into its unity." *An Essay on the Development of Christian Doctrine*, 185-186.

philosophical views."[107] This entails that current scientific and philosophical discourse helps in "the continual effort to fasten down [doctrine's] expression more precisely. . . ."[108] In other words, the dialectical or logical discourse of doctrines must be responsive to contemporary parlance within scientific and philosophical communities. Revolutions in dogmatic language often are accompanied by and precipitated by changes in philosophical systems.[109] On this level, scientific and philosophical discourse does not and should not affect the substance of faith that is expressed by dogmatic propositions, rather it influences the precision of the form of this proposition.

Dogmatic theology must be responsive to scientific and philosophical modes of discourse by rejecting past or present doctrinal propositions that indicate the intrusion of scientific or philosophical claims about God, the self, and the world. Schleiermacher's descriptive method for dogmatics was intended as a way of eliminating previous speculative claims that have accumulated within dogmatics and as a limit to and protection against alien content being smuggled into dogmatics. The threat of speculative claims encroaching the limits established by this descriptive dogmatic method is minimized.

Scientific and philosophical modes of discourse are a proper foreign influence on doctrinal propositions. But, the subject matters of philosophy and the sciences are not the subject matter of theology. Hence, "completely external circumstances cannot constitute the true basis for important decisions in the area of doctrine."[110] If "extraneous factors have entered in and have become organized within for their own sake," we find the problem of disease in the church.[111]

---

[107] *Brief Outline*, § 167, also see § 160.

[108] *Brief Outline*, § 177.

[109] *Christian Faith*, § 28.

[110] *Brief Outline*, § 179, n. 17. from the 1st edition.

[111] *Brief Outline*, § 54.

Schleiermacher's responsiveness to an outer criterion for genuine doctrine is also indicated by his often quoted contention that the churches of the Reformation need "to establish an eternal covenant between the living Christian faith and completely free, independent scientific inquiry, so that faith does not hinder science and science does not exclude faith. . . ."[112] Modern science and philosophy does influence the didactic form of doctrinal propositions, but not its content. Dogmatic theologians do not tell scientists or philosophers what to believe, nor vice versa. However, this does not imply that there is a non-aggression pact between theology and these modern disciplines. Philosophical and presumably scientific disciplines that are materialistic and amoral in their assumptions are unfit for use within dogmatics and wrongly "exclude faith."[113]

Drey believed that Christian theology must take shape "according to the spirit of our time and [the spirit] of the present situation."[114] Since doctrines have a mobile character in addition to a fixed one, there exists a constructive influence of science and philosophy upon Christian doctrine and the Church. "Science always provides new inspirations for the development of Christian doctrine, and leads the moving element of this [doctrine] to its closure."[115] Science and philosophy influence the further development and refinement of concepts that aid the formation of Church doctrines.

It is clear from Drey's treatment of the inner history of the Christianity that science and philosophy in general have been "an outer stimulus influencing Christian doctrine," but "external ideas

---

[112]*On the Glaubenslehre*, 64.

[113]*Christian Faith*, § 28, p. 118: Certain philosophical views are unfit for dogmatic use because they "make no separation between the conceptions of God and the world, admit no contrast between good and evil, and thus make no definite distinction in man between the spiritual and the sensible."

[114]*Kurze Einleitung*, § 56, see also §§ 92-96 on the relationship between philosophy and theology.

[115]*Kurze Einleitung*, § 259.

cannot have any genuine influence on the ideas [of Christianity]."[116] External ideas are an outer stimulus, yet not a genuine influence: can it be both ways? External philosophical systems have strongly influenced doctrines in the past. Sometimes these philosophies have aided in clarifying Christian faith for official public discourse; philosophical ideas that are "in the spirit of Christianity and harmonize with it [this spirit]" positively influence doctrinal development."[117] Sometimes philosophies have promoted disadvantageous changes and certain doctrinal developments have been called into question and turned around by the study of the Bible. "Only if they [philosophies] are not [in this spirit and harmonizing with it] can corruption arise; in general the formation of Christian doctrine by ideas is not corruption, but rather the task of science."[118] Thus, heresies arise if "heterogeneous" developments occur, that is, when foreign or extraneous factors exert an influence opposed to the spirit of the Church and its unfolding self-consciousness."[119] Problems arise "partly in the confusion of the form with the essence, and of the subjective temporal forms with the one objective basic form . . . , [and] partly . . . in the false presentation of what philosophy and theology should accomplish."[120]

Drey early in his career expressed his conviction that philosophical influences have proved decisive in many instances in the history of Christian doctrines. They have provided the theologian with the dialectical and speculative acumen needed to clarify mystical knowledge. This is needed in the Church. Dialectic should remain in the service of mysticism, but it has not.[121]

---

[116]*Kurze Einleitung*, § 192.

[117]*Kurze Einleitung*, § 192.

[118]*Kurze Einleitung*, § 192.

[119]*Kurze Einleitung*, § 193.

[120]*Kurze Einleitung*, § 92.

[121]High scholastic theology and Reformation theology drove a wedge between dialectic and mysticism. The former led to a subjective speculation; the latter to a subjective mysticism. See "Revision," 89-92.

There are subtle differences between Schleiermacher and Drey on the nature of the outer criterion. Drey agreed with Schleiermacher that scientific discourse generally speaking (i.e., including philosophy) does provide a source for doctrinal development in that it helps in the dialectical, that is, the logical clarification of the Christian doctrines. Unlike Schleiermacher, however, Drey does not employ a descriptive method within dogmatics as a means of excluding the foreign influences of scientific and philosophical claims. Drey clearly does not intend to permit the foreign contents of alien disciplines to enter into dogmatics. Nevertheless, philosophy and science not only work at the logical level, but they influence how we think about God, world, and self. Still, is this not also the result of Schleiermacher's rejection of foreign speculative claims entering into dogmatics? We are not tied down to outmoded philosophies or scientific worldviews and are therefore able to think of God, world, and self in a way appropriate to Christian piety and adequate to modern thought. In sum, the same ends are intended by their different methods: doctrinal language should be in harmony with modern thought and discourse and the alien content of new philosophies and sciences cannot replace the subject matter of Christianity which is constant and constantly in need of reformulation.

The Criteria and The Essence of Christianity

Schleiermacher and Drey employed these diverse criteria within philosophical (or fundamental) theology and dogmatic theology. These criteria enabled them to determine the essence of Christianity in its Protestant or Catholic forms respectively and to foster an appropriate articulation of this essence for the present time. The essence of Christianity, conceived as the object or the content of Christian tradition, which is actively transmitted through history by the ecclesial community, functions in their theologies in a variety of ways.[122] On the one hand, this essence is the gratuitous and given character of Christian faith as attested to by the positivity of Christianity; on the other hand, the essence is always something which must be reflectively, critically determined within history. Thus, while it is mediated within history through the ecclesial community, the Scriptures, the church's worship, and confessional documents, the essence of Christianity must continually be interpreted, evaluated, and reformulated so that the articulation of this essence can developed.

We have seen that Schleiermacher judged it to be the specific task of apologetics to determine the essence of Christianity. On the basis of this essence, the theologian can, within polemics, legitimately criticize conservative and liberal, hyperorthodox and heterodox deviations from it. Drey initially agreed with this, but he later (unconvincingly) argued that it was Schleiermacher's position that defining the essence of Christianity was the responsibility of apologetics, while dogmatics treats that which is variable. Drey proposed instead that apologetics should present the basic characteristics of Christianity, and demonstrate its divine positivity, while dogmatics should establish the essence of Christianity in terms of its specific doctrines.[123] Drey's complaint is based on Schleiermacher's proposition that "Dogmatic theology is the science which systematizes the doctrine valid in a Christian Church at a given time."[124] However, as we have argued in Chapter III, the

---

[122]It is customary to distinguish within the concept of "tradition" = *traditio*, the "what" or content of the tradition, i.e., the "tradition being traditioned" = *traditum tradendum*, and the "that" or the "act of traditioning" = *actus tradendi*." See, e.g., Congar, *Tradition and Traditions*, 296-307; and Schubert Ogden, "What is Christian Theology?" (unpublished manuscript); cf. idem., *On Theology* (San Francisco: Harper & Row, 1986), 35-41.

[123]Even in the *Kurze Einleitung*, Drey stated that fundamental theology provides the scientific investigation of the essence, while dogmatics scientifically presents this essence (§ 221). For his revised position see *Apologetik*, 1:iv-v.

[124]*Christian Faith*, § 19.

essence of Christianity is the subject matter of both apologetics and dogmatic theology for Schleiermacher and Drey, even though different types of arguments are employed in the two disciplines.

There is a difference between Schleiermacher and Drey on the status accorded the essence of Christianity, aside from Drey's description of their differences, which I have not found entirely convincing. Both thinkers suggest that the essence of Christianity is the same over history and that the articulation or formulation of this essence develops over time. There is something fixed and something mobile about the nature of Christianity. Neither scholar strictly identified the essence of Christianity with the official dogmatic expression of it. Yet Drey argues that officially-pronounced dogmas are not only the most authoritative articulation of Christianity's essence, but closed and fixed, and therefore unable to be rejected. They can be reformulated and further developed, but they are not reversible. Although Schleiermacher would agree that official confessions are the most authoritative articulation of the essence of Protestant Christianity, they can be erroneous, in need of criticism and therefore in need of reformulation or reversal.

One can conclude that the essence of Christianity works on a number of different levels in Schleiermacher's and Drey's theologies. First, the essence of Christianity is the objective tradition which remains the same through history. Second, the linguistic (doctrinal) formulations of the essence of Christianity develop throughout history: doctrines develop by more clearly articulating the essence of Christianity. Third, the essence of Christianity serves a crucial critical purpose: it provides a basis for criticizing heretical formulations. While Schleiermacher and Drey generally agree on all three aspects, on the final critical dimension there is a difference on whether criticism of dogmas is permissible and on the limits of such criticism.

The critical task served by the essence of Christianity in Schleiermacher's and Drey's theologies takes on considerable importance for modern and postmodern theology because it provides a *theological* basis for criticizing ecclesial traditions.[125] In so doing, the formulation of the essence of Christianity offers an alternative to the Reformation critique of ecclesial doctrines and practices on the basis of the *sola Scriptura* principle, and to the Enlightenment critique of traditions and authorities based on autonomous and secular reason.

Both Schleiermacher and Drey argue that the Scriptures provide an important norm for theology, alongside of ecclesial confessions. But neither believe that the Scriptures are the sole basis for evaluating new doctrinal formulae, even though doctrinal formulations must cohere with the New Testament witness, especially the idea of the kingdom of God. Even though Schleiermacher affirms the sufficiency of the Scriptures as "the norm for all succeeding presentations" of Christian doctrines,[126] he further asserts that it must still be considered only "the first member in the series, ever since continued, of presentations of the Christian faith."[127] Drey recognizes that the Reformers had legitimate reasons for complaining about Scholastic speculation and dangerous Medieval practices and he concurs that the Word of God and mysticism were the correct medicine for the disease, but by leaving the community, he believed, the Reformers had prolonged the problem. Drey's conclusion that the Reformers' *sola Scriptura* principle made the

---

[125]For historical treatments of the essence of Christianity, see Ernst Troeltsch, "What Does 'Essence of Christianity' Mean?" *Troeltsch: Writings on Theology and Religion*, ed. R. Morgan and M. Pye (Atlanta: John Knox Press, 1977), 124-180; Stephen Sykes, *The Identity of Christianity*; Edward Farley, *Theologia*; and Avery Dulles, *The Catholicity of the Church* (Oxford: Oxford University Press, 1985). For constructive statements on the subject, see Edward Farley, *Ecclesial Reflections*; David Tracy, *Analogical Imagination* (New York: Crossroad, 1981), 317-329; and Francis Schüssler Fiorenza, *Foundational*, 304-306.

[126]*Christian Faith*, § 129. He also states that "through our use of Scripture the Holy Spirit can lead us into all truth, as it led the Apostles and others who enjoyed Christ's direct teaching." *Christian Faith*, § 131, p. 606.

[127]*Christian Faith*, § 129.

Word of God a dead letter for Protestants, cut off from the community, does not apply to Schleiermacher nor to many Protestants.[128]

On what basis do Schleiermacher and Drey make their appeal when they evaluate Christian doctrines? On what authority can they criticize doctrines? If not on the authority of autonomous reason or secular experience, then on what? For Schleiermacher and Drey doctrines are criticized on the basis of the essence of Christianity which is mediated by the ecclesial community. The essence of Christianity provides both theologians with a way of criticizing doctrines without succumbing to the strategy of the Enlightenment critique of religion. Neither wishes to base the critical function of the essence on the authority of an autonomous reason. Neither wishes to battle against tradition in itself. Neither denies the legitimate authorities of the past or the present. Rather the essence is defined for them in the service of ecclesial faith in order to fight against inappropriate intrusions from external fields of inquiry and against unwarranted accretions within the doctrinal heritage. Their endeavor to determine, defend, and more clearly articulate the essence of Christianity within philosophical (or fundamental) theology and dogmatic theology cannot be convincingly construed as the attempt to reduce Christianity to its lowest moral, intellectual, or affective denominator. Rather, in dialogue with the entire history of Christianity, the theologian must assess what the ecclesial community in its contemporary form should retain and what no longer adequately serves the faith.

Does the essence of Christianity function as a separate criterion for evaluating doctrines alongside of the four we have considered? Clearly not. Their articulations of the essence of Christianity are

---

[128]Catholic polemics against the *sola Scriptura* principle were fueled in part by some statements by Luther. The later Luther, and Calvin throughout his career, clearly envisioned the word of God as received within a community of faith and recognized the importance of ecclesial leaders in interpreting this word of God. See B. A. Gerrish, *The Old Protestantism and the New*, 51-68.

based on the four criteria we have explored: the three inner criteria--coherence with Church confessions and the Bible, ecclesial piety, and the positivity of Christianity; and the fourth outer criterion, adequacy to modern thought and discourse. The essence of Christianity is not reducible to any one of these four. The essence of Christianity does provide the two theologians with a criterion for criticizing heretical doctrines, but this criterion never functions in isolation from the four criteria.[129]

Do historical-critical and hermeneutical investigations of Christian origins and development serve as a basis for criticism of doctrines in Schleiermacher's and Drey's theologies? These methods raise questions about the factual, situational, and personal ingredients in the formulation of traditions, doctrines, and doctrinal formulations. In this way they could be seen as a constitutive

---

[129]Drey and Schleiermacher contend that Christianity in its essence has practical and social implications, but neither establishes a separate pragmatic criterion for evaluating the adequacy of doctrines. See *Christian Faith*, §§ 3, 9, 11, 26; *Kurze Einleitung*, §§ 117, 189, 195, 254-5, 264; *Apologetik*, 1:332, 337-9. The contrast they draw between the Christian idea of the kingdom of God as a moral and religious idea and the Old Testament understanding of God's reign as political and national has several negative tendencies: (1) it fosters an a-political interpretation of Christianity; (2) it diminishes the living and dynamic reality of Judaism as found in the Old Testament; (3) it renders the Jewish milieu of emergent Christianity virtually invisible; and (4) it fails to give full weight to the social-political quality of Jesus' actions, his teachings, and their implications for his death and the mission of the Church. It would be wrong to argue on this basis that Schleiermacher and Drey promote an other-worldly, individualistic, a-political, or anti-Semitic understanding of Christianity. Evaluating doctrines in relation to practical, political, and Jewish concerns have become acute concerns since the Jewish Holocaust and the emergence of various liberation movements. The operative principle here is familiar to Drey and Schleiermacher: external social and political factors legitimately influence how we interpret the Scriptures and develop doctrines. But as important as that principle is, the process of discerning the most adequate interpretation of the Bible and doctrinal formula does not end with that principle.

dimension of the criterion of the positivity of Christianity. But historical-critical and hermeneutical approaches for Schleiermacher and Drey never serve to criticize the basis and formulation of faith from outside of faith and piety, or from outside of the Church. Certainly they could be utilized in this way, but within these theologians' respective theological encyclopedias, such methods and critical questions are placed at the service of an ecclesial faith. For this reason, the questions and criticisms about doctrines raised by historical methods receive their proper weight when viewed from the vantage point of the criteria we have presented above.

It would distort Schleiermacher's and Drey's contributions to theology if we only focussed on the critical function of the essence of Christianity within their theologies. These writers offer much more than negative judgments on the variety of Christian traditions. However, it is precisely this critical dimension of their so-called mediating paradigm of theology that has been persistently contested from the early modern period to our own day. To place their thought in proper perspective, one must attend to their affirmations of the essence of (Protestant or Catholic) Christianity--as objective tradition--as a necessary and significant dimension of theology. This essence is indeed assumed as the continuous tradition of the Christian community that unites and bestows an identity upon this community. But this affirmation of the objective tradition is not based on, nor does it issue in, blind obedience to the Creeds, the Bible, and the liturgical expressions of faith. This essence is mediated through such vehicles, but theologians must also evaluate the meaningfulness, intelligibility, credibility, and the truth of such mediations in light of critical reflection on the essence of Christianity.

The theme of the essence of Christianity clearly emerges in the modern period as a response to historical investigations into this religious tradition and to critical questions raised by those who attempted to discredit Christian faith altogether. The entire problematic of the essence of Christianity is formulated by Schleiermacher and Drey in the language of German romantic idealism; the essence is determined amidst the various historical manifestations or concretizations of this essence. While many raise legitimate and helpful criticisms about the philosophical underpinnings of their respective statements on the subject, there are many among their critics who acknowledge that addressing this subject is crucial if the theological enterprise is to remain cohesive and not sectarian or antiquarian.

CHAPTER V

AFFIRMING AND REFORMING DOCTRINES

Which specific doctrines did Schleiermacher and Drey believe were in need of criticism, reform, and development? This is, of course, the key question that remains to be addressed. The answer to this question will allow us to judge whether, and if so how, Schleiermacher and Drey were actively striving to change the doctrinal formulations of their respective communities, and will shed light on what kinds of doctrinal transformations their theologies of history may justify and require. Unfortunately, such a question can only be broached here.[1] Many others have probed and pondered Schleiermacher's contributions on specific doctrinal issues and a few have examined the contributions of Drey.[2]

---

[1]A fuller treatment would require analysis of Drey's unpublished lectures on dogmatics, "Prealectiones Dogmaticae" and Schleiermacher's "Über die Lehre von der Erwählung," *Sämmtliche Werke*, division 1, vol. 2 and his study, "Über die Gegensatz zwischen der Sabellianischen und der Athanasianischen Vorstellung von Trinität," reprinted in *Friedrich Schleiermacher und die Trinitätslehre*, ed. Martin Tetz [*Texte zur Kirchen und Theologiegeschichte*, ed. Gerhard Rubach] (Gütersloh: Gütersloher Verlagshaus, Gerd Mohn, 1969).

[2]Fehr provides an indispensable treatment of Drey's unpublished "Praelectiones Dogmaticae," (1812-1834) in relation to his other works, *The Dogmatics of Drey*, 178-244; for works on Schleiermacher's treatment of specific doctrines, see Terrence N. Tice, *Schleiermacher Bibliography*,

Without being exhaustive, we can suggest several areas where Schleiermacher and Drey sought to affirm the Christian faith as passed on, while clearly recognizing the need for doctrinal criticism, reform, and development.

We have, in fact, already addressed two areas in which Schleiermacher and Drey did seek to contribute to theological development: theologies of history and the doctrine of revelation. Theologies of history have not been explicitly treated in official ecclesial pronouncements on doctrines, even though the Augustinian (sacramental) model has been dominant. As we have seen, Schleiermacher's and Drey's theologies of history were a development of this older sacramental understanding of history. By wedding the sacramental view of history with organic and pedagogical motifs, they generated new narrative plots and new insights into history, which extended beyond those offered by the older model. They did not explicitly criticize the earlier formulation of a sacramental model of history, but their criticism of intransigent theologians was an implicit criticism of what they both judged to be a weakness of the sacramental model: the inability to acknowledge that "outer" historical change is dialectically interconnected with the "inner" history of the Church.

On the matter of revelation, as we have indicated, Schleiermacher and Drey did not speak with one voice. While Schleiermacher respected the scriptural canon as affirmed by "many Confessions of our Church," he believed that this does not mean the canon should be closed to further critical inquiry and correction.[3] Although Drey agreed that the canon should be historically analyzed, he denied that it was alterable.[4] They held similar stances on official ecclesial pronouncements. Both revered the ecumenical conciliar statements, and they held as normative the confession of

---

Princeton Pamphlets--No.12 (Princeton: Princeton Theological Seminary, 1966) and *Schleiermacher Bibliography (1784-1984): Updating and Commentary* (Princeton: Princeton Theological Seminary, 1985).

[3]*Christian Faith*, § 129, p. 596; § 130, p. 603.

[4]*Kurze Einleitung*, §§ 134-140, esp. 139-140.

their respective denominations. Yet they believed that these official statements should be historically evaluated and that they could be rearticulated in order to address audiences in new cultural and historical contexts. Schleiermacher took a further step and maintained that "[n]o definition of doctrine . . . even when arrived at with the most perfect community of feeling, can be regarded as irreformable and valid for all time" because "no presentation . . . contains pure and perfect truth;" quite simply put, "error is possible."[5] Drey, on the contrary, believed once dogmas were officially pronounced, they were complete and closed.[6] The major contribution both make to the theology of revelation is their endeavor to reconceive revelation's historical character and its relation to human subjectivity.[7]

What is clear from these two areas and will be reconfirmed as we proceed is that the full range of criteria that were examined in the last chapter serve both theologians in their criticisms and reformulations of specific doctrines. The outer criterion of adequacy to modern thought and discourse has served as an important impetus for criticism and change, although this criterion has not played the role of a final arbiter deciding the nature of the change required.

A Fundamental Issue: The Theory of the Supernatural

A crucial doctrinal issue for Schleiermacher and Drey concerned the relationship between the supernatural and the natural. At the time, debates were taking place between those adhering to what has been called an extrinsicist theory of the supernatural and rationalists who rejected supernatural explanations

---

[5]*Christian Faith*, § 154, p. 690; § 153.

[6]*Kurze Einleitung*, §§ 256-257.

[7]Their contrasting approaches to inspiration will be examined in the next section.

for miracles, prophecies, and the inspiration of the Word of God.[8] Technically speaking, of course, beliefs about the supernatural associated with God's action in nature and history are not included in the dogmatic heritage of the Christian confessions. However, such beliefs stand as dominant assumptions at work in many different doctrinal domains.

God's supernatural intervention in the world of nature and history is presented in the Bible with the use of metaphors and narratives depicting supernatural events, persons, and messages. In earlier Christianity these presentations of supernatural occurrences were understood as an essential indication of the divine plan, and as testimony to the power of God's grace to save those who believe from the power of sin and death. During the medieval period the distinction between nature and grace gained dominance over the model of sin and grace bequeathed by prominent early Church writers.[9] The medieval formulation of nature and grace was constructed on the basis of a metaphysical doctrine of the supernatural in the twelfth and thirteenth centuries and operated as a pivotal assumption for later medieval theology and subsequent

---

[8]The early nineteenth century debate about supernaturalism and rationalism received its impetus from theologians at the University of Tübingen, chiefly G. C. Storr, J. Flatt, F, Süskind, and J. Steudel, who sought to defend the supernatural character of the Bible against the then burgeoning rationalist critique of the Scriptures. The rationalist critique was inspired by Kant's *Religion innerhalb der Grenzen der bloßen Vernunft* (1793), as illustrated by the work of H. Henke, W. Krug, J. Tieftrunk, J. Röhr, J. Wegscheider, and also fostered by the historical-critical study of the Bible initiated by J. Semler and J. Michaelis, as seen most notably in the work of H. Paulus. D. F. Strauss's later work lent further momentum to the rationalist argument. In 1826 F. C. Baur joined the faculty at Tübingen and inaugurated a shift away from the older Tübingen views on supernaturalism associated with Storr and his followers. See Emanuel Hirsch, *Geschichte der neuern evangelischen Theologie*, 5:3-144.

[9]Jaroslav Pelikan, *The Christian Tradition: A History of the Development of Doctrine*, (Chicago: University of Chicago Press, 1971, 1978), 1:132-144; Vol. 3:284-293.

Catholic thought.[10] The Protestant Reformers made selective use of scholastic logical distinctions about nature and grace, preferring a basically Augustinian understanding of sin and grace. Regardless of what scholastic distinctions were questioned, Reformation thinkers continued to assume the influence of the supernatural in the processes of biblical inspiration and of justification by faith. For both Protestant and Catholic theologians in the post-Reformation scholastic period, the supernatural continued to be associated with miracles, the events of Christ's life, death, and resurrection, and with positive verbal revelation. It was the rationalist critique of miracles, prophecies, and inspiration that inspired the modern debate about the natural and the supernatural.

Schleiermacher and Drey endeavored to reconceive the relationship between the natural and the supernatural. Both were critical of an extrinisicist understanding of the supernatural which emphasized God's transcendence to such an extent that any manifestation of God in natural and historical arenas superseded and violated the natural order and human capabilities. They were even more critical of rationalists whose attempts to respect the natural and historical order of things limited the presence of the supernatural to the moment of creation.

Schleiermacher on numerous occasions voiced his dissatisfaction with the polemical opposition between rationalism and supernaturalism and between naturalism and supernaturalism.[11]

---

[10]See Bernard McGinn, "The Shape of Medieval Doctrine," a review of Jaroslav Pelikan, *The Christian Tradition: A History of the Development of Doctrine*, vol. 3, in *The Journal of Religion* 60 (1980): 198-204, esp. 202; Henri de Lubac, *The Mystery of the Supernatural* (Montreal: Palm Publishers, 1967); Karl Rahner, "Some Implications of the Scholastic Concept of Uncreated Grace" in *Theological Investigations* (New York: Seabury Press, 1974), 1:319-346, and "Nature and Grace," *Theological Investigations* (New York: Seabury Press, 1974), 4:165-188.

[11]See *On the Glaubenslehre*, 88-89; *Christian Faith*, §§ 13, 23, pp. 100-101, § 88, esp. p. 365; *Die christliche Sitte*, 313-315; *On Religion*, 256-257, n. 5. In the latter he says that "[t]here is some sense, and more perhaps than is

He judged that "the entire issue is a misunderstanding" and insisted that the "names of the contending parties are most unfortunate." They are unfortunate because "the one refers to the nature of the event and the other to the source of knowledge of doctrine."[12] Schleiermacher asks:

> Why is it impossible for persons to be convinced that certain events are supernatural and yet to maintain that they cannot be asked to accept doctrines that are unintelligible and cannot be rationally reconstructed? And why is it impossible for others to say that they are inclined to accept certain doctrines that are consoling, even though they cannot incorporate these doctrines into the general context of the teachings of reason, as long as these doctrines have a definite meaning? Nonetheless, they are not prepared to form representations about facts that cannot be assimilated into the overall fabric of experience as long as it is possible to form another representation about them.[13]

Schleiermacher's problem with the antithesis between naturalism and supernaturalism is that it fails to articulate adequately the God-world relationship. The supernatural character of creation, christology, and the Church should continue to be affirmed, but it should be conceived in such a way that permits the recognition of their natural determinants. He explains his position, "[w]henever I speak of the supernatural, I do so with reference to whatever comes first, but afterwards it becomes something natural. Thus creation is supernatural, but it afterwards becomes the natural order. Likewise, in his origin Christ is supernatural, but he also becomes natural, as a genuine human being. The Holy Spirit and

---

usually thought, in opposing reason to revelation, but there is no ground for a contrast between nature and revelation. For this antithesis the biblical foundation, to which a Christian will always return, entirely fails, and the more a matter is discussed from such a standpoint the more perplexed it will become."

[12]*On the Glaubenslehre*, 88.

[13]*On the Glaubenslehre*, 88.

the Christian Church can be treated in the same way. Thus I would prefer that one devise for me a position where what is supernatural can at the same time be natural."[14] By arguing that something is supernatural in its cause or origin and natural afterwards, Schleiermacher sought to maintain that something can be natural and supernatural simultaneously. This does not mean that God "intervened" in the course of nature through creation, Christ, and the Church. Indeed, God's activity at these moments cannot be abstracted. Objectively this is so because we cannot have knowledge of God in God's self but only as God determines and orders the whole of history; subjectively we cannot explain God's activity on the basis of the sinful condition of humanity. We are left to describe what has taken place within the course of history. Thus, Schleiermacher's configuration of the relationship between the natural and the supernatural paves the way for utilizing a descriptive method in theology; it also lends credibility to the integrity of theology as a scientific inquiry.[15]

Schleiermacher resolutely rejected the older model of the supernatural as it evidenced itself in the defense of miracles, prophecies, and inspiration as external proofs of the truth of Christianity.[16] Yet he did not wish to do away with the concepts of miracle, prophecy, or inspiration. These concepts could be reinterpreted within the context of faith so that the supernatural

---

[14]*On the Glaubenslehre*, 89. Cf. *Christian Faith*, § 100, p. 430: "The maxim everywhere underlying our presentation [is] that the beginning of the kingdom of God is a supernatural thing, however, [it] becomes natural as soon as it emerges into manifestation; for this . . . view makes every significant moment a supernatural one."

[15]Herein lies a key reason for Schleiermacher's use of general principles of hermeneutics in the interpretation of Scriptures rather than basing biblical hermeneutics on special exegetical principles. This approach to the supernatural also underlies his attempt to articulate an eternal covenant between theology and the sciences.

[16]*Der christliche Glaube* (1st edition), §§ 18-21; (2nd edition), §§ 11-14, 47; *On Religion*, 88-89, 113-114; *On The Glaubenslehre*, 61, 66.

significance of natural events could be clearly affirmed. It is necessary to interpret these concepts "so that faith does not hinder science and science does not exclude faith."[17] To do otherwise would be to barricade oneself off from the advances of science.[18]

Schleiermacher's approach to the supernatural extends to his treatment of the nature of piety. Originally in *Über die Religion* Schleiermacher spoke not of cause and origin, but of the presence of the infinite as manifest in and through the finite--in the world, history, and humanity. The piety which stands at the core of religion finds the unity of these partial manifestations in the whole which lies behind and beyond them. But in the *Glaubenslehre* this uniting of diverse positive determinations of pious consciousness is described as "the feeling of absolute dependence."[19] Schleiermacher's analysis of self-consciousness in terms of a self-caused element and a non-self-caused element, activity and receptivity, set the terms for discussing God as the co-determinant of consciousness, and as the whence of the experience of absolute dependence. Here the supernatural cause or origin is discerned in the natural state of consciousness, not only as a temporal point of origin, but as a sustaining cause.[20]

Drey's treatment of the relationship between the natural and supernatural moved in the same direction as Schleiermacher's: he sought to show the limitations of both rationalist and supernaturalist positions. But while Drey respected Schleiermacher's position

---

[17]*On the Glaubenslehre*, 64.

[18]So we read: "The complete starvation from all science, which will follow when, because you have repudiated it, science will be forced to display the flag of unbelief! Shall the tangle (*der Knoten*) of history so unravel that Christianity becomes identified with barbarism and science with unbelief" (*On the Glaubenslehre*, 61)?

[19]*Christian Faith*, § 4.

[20]These efforts to redefine the relationship between the supernatural and the natural were judged by some to be pantheistic. Schleiermacher's articulation attempts to avoid the pitfalls of pantheism on the one hand and the divinization of the human subject on the other.

on the question of miracles, prophecy, and inspiration, he took great care to show its limitations. In the end, he judged that Schleiermacher's was the most sophisticated, and perhaps a benign, rather than sinister, brand of rationalism.

Drey addressed the problem, on the one hand, in terms of God's activity in revelation as explained by naturalists and supernaturalists, and, on the other hand, by focussing on the human reception of divine revelation as understood by rationalists and suprarationalists.[21] He argues that rationalism and naturalism share a common principle:

> God is only to be thought of in the act of creation in immediate outward activity, in immediate contact with the world. After the act of creation, however, all union and communication between both [creator and the created world] is allowed to be cut off, the world at once runs alone, develops alone, and God is to be only a spectator.[22]

---

[21]See *Apologetik*, 1:178-185, 247-324. On nature and the supernatural, see Fehr, *The Dogmatics of Drey*, 30-44; Geiselmann, "Das Übernatürliche in der Katholischen Tübinger Schule," *Theologische Quartalscrift* 143 (1963): 422-453; idem., *Die Katholische Tübinger Schule*, 426-503; Elmar Klinger, *Offenbarung im Horizont der Heilsgeschichte*, 70-9; Kustermann, *Die Apologetik*, 339-342.

[22]*Apologetik*, 1:262. Drey delineates *three forms of naturalism*: (1) God is pure passivity, while nature actively works, as in the Epicurian school. (2) In the deist form, religion is reduced to the activity of God in nature and the laws of nature, or in reason in the realm of spirit. (3) The finger of God is known in the coincidence and cooperation of special facts of nature and history toward the attestation of a new religion. Schleiermacher is in this last group (1:186-189). *Four forms of rationalism* are also distinguished. The first and purest form of rationalism treats reason itself as self-contained, which parallels naturalists who regard nature as absolutely self-contained. The second form stands with naturalists in disputing the pure reality of revelation in its manifestation. The third seeks a rapprochement with supernaturalism for social and practical purposes, by speaking of revelation and Christ, not as supernatural. but as unusual. In the fourth, the divine

Suprarationalism and supernaturalism likewise share "the application of one principle to two forms of the world, nature and reason. . . ."[23]

> [T]he development of religious knowledge is said to be conditioned through revelation, which consists essentially in an immediate action of God, in an intervention of God both into nature and in the spirit of the human being, the latter and his reason stands receptive to the higher influence, and therefore in the continuing revelation the same relationship is said to take place as in the original one, namely, the dependence of human persons on God, the subordination of reason under revelation; this is said to be what the word "over reason" intends and is supposed to express, which rationalism denies and disputes in totality.[24]

The disputed issue between the rationalists and the suprarationalists, in Drey's estimation, concerns a question of fact: What is the source and origin of all true religion? In other words, from whence come the cognitive, verbal, and historical manifestations which are required for a truly human religious knowledge and life? Suprarationalists derive the universal source of religion and also the specific origin of a historically emerging religion from revelation--the influence of God in the spirit and reason of human persons, whereas rationalists, on the contrary, find or attempt to find both the universal source and the historical origin in reason. Rationalists recognize a dependency of the human person on God in relation to their coming-into-existence, but after this both God and creature are self-contained and independent.

For Drey the suprarationalist position requires that one examine the historical revelation in its external and sensible facts

---

could be none other than the genuinely reasonable and vice versa. This form of rationalism is found in Christianity and Schleiermacher is a representative figure (1:255-258).

[23]*Apologetik*, 1:274.

[24]*Apologetik*, 1:275.

and according to the content of its supersensible ideas.[25] The common conviction that binds various suprarationalists together is that "the source and origin of religion lies above reason in God and his revelation."[26]

Drey agreed with suprarationalism on two counts: God must be recognized as the original source of all truth and of everything good that exists in human reason and in the created spirit, and the immutability of God and God's relationship to the world must be maintained.[27] The problem with suprarationalists is that they do not entirely understand the first claim and they make incorrect use of the second.

> It [historical suprarationslism] believes reason, which was originally open and receptive for the revelation of God, has been able to change its nature and has really changed it; it has become closed and unreceptive to the divine communications; . . . it is unable to understand the communication. . . . Hence, there remains for it nothing further than to believe blindly the mysteries of revelation, and to give in weak-mindedly to the divine influences.[28]

Rationalism, on the other hand, correctly recognizes God as the creator of reason and as the original source of everything in its abiding truth and good aspirations and admits that there is an unchanging character to this. But its error is that "it holds fast to the unchangeability of reason, giving up the unchangeability of the relationship of God to it [i.e., reason] by permitting God as the source of truth for reason only in the act of creation."[29] Thereafter

---

[25]*Apologetik*, 1:276.

[26]*Apologetik*, 1:277.

[27]*Apologetik*, 1:287.

[28]*Apologetik*, 1:288. Drey's description of surprarationalism corresponds to his earlier treatment of hyperorthodox and the problems associated with lagging behind the truth and intransigency; see *Kurze Einleitung* §§ 240, 245-246, 260. Also see the section on fixed and moving elements in Chapter II.

[29]*Apologetik*, 1:288.

God is the source of nothing more; reason becomes the only creator. Rationalism "severs all effective union of human persons with God and only the unliving [union] through thoughts and memory is valid. At the same time it ignores or denies, contrary to history and its own consciousness, each error of reason, in order not to be forced to recognize the necessity of a recurring revelation and the need for the continuing influence of God."[30]

Drey believes that the synthesis of true suprarationalism and true rationalism rests on the proper understanding of the internal and external relationships between God and the world, between revelation and reason.

> Revelation cannot be *against* reason, because it would then have to be against religion as well. In addition, it cannot be *above* reason, that is, be unreachable, unacceptable to it [i.e., to reason], for it could then effect nothing for the best of religion and religious life. It can therefore only be *for* reason. It is *for* reason in such a way that it can be known by this [reason] as such, can be understood in terms of its content, can be conceived in terms of its purposes, [and] can be transformed in terms of its effects in attitudes and life. Revelation is therefore not merely a witness of God externally, it is a power and activity of God internally, and thoroughly *for* reason.[31]

While the internal ground of the synthesis is crucial, the external ground is the most problematic in the modern period. Rationalists deny miracles and special providence, and suprarationalists forget that the revealed teaching has a history and is accompanied by facts which are united with the ideal content of its teaching, and that reason is required to inquire into this subject matter. Hence, revelation is *for* reason insofar as it provides reason with insight into the mysteries of life. Reason requires revelation, for while reason has some natural ability to understand the activity

---

[30]*Apologetik*, 1:288-289.

[31]*Apologetik*, 1:290-291, emphasis mine.

of God in nature and history, it is never able to attain the comprehension which revelation affords.[32]

Drey inscribed his differences with Schleiermacher's method most explicitly in his treatment of the debate between rationalists and supernaturalists. With Schleiermacher, he insists upon the positivity of Christian religion rooted in the fact of Jesus Christ, against the proponents of natural religion. However, Schleiermacher's position must finally be considered, Drey believes, a form of rationalism because it failed to permit external proofs for revelation on the basis of miracles, prophecies, and divine inspiration. Drey contends that by so emphasizing inner criteria in treating Christianity, Schleiermacher undercuts the weight of external criteria, thus minimizing the supernatural and suprarational influence of God.[33] While God might incite revelation in Schleiermacher's schema, in Drey's estimation, the human person is left unchanged in the process, and therefore susceptible to the weaknesses, errors, and sins of humanity.

---

[32]This argument is a direct response to § 4 of Lessing's "Erziehung des Menschengeschlechts," which states: "Education gives man nothing which he could not also get from within himself; it gives him that which he could get from within himself, only quicker and more easily. In the same way too, revelation gives nothing to the human race which human reason could not arrive at on its own; only it has given, and still gives to it, the most important of things sooner." The attempt to show there was no conflict but in fact a harmony between reason and revelation is also framed in terms of the relationship between *Glaube* und *Wissen*; see *Apologetik*, 1:296-308.

[33]Drey examines Schleiermacher's treatment of the supernatural and Christianity from §§ 18-21 of *Der christliche Glaube* (1st edition) in *Apologetik*, vol. 1; on miracles see 214-217; Drey contrasts the old mechanical theory of inspiration with Schleiermacher's position, 227-229, 260-261; Drey calls Schleiermacher's position naturalism, 189-190; and rationalism, 260-261. Although Drey attempts to interpret Schleiermacher's stance fairly, he does not address Schleiermacher's reason for rejecting outer criteria for demonstrating the divine character of revelation: they prove nothing and presuppose faith.

Schleiermacher and Drey highlight the centrality of the problem of conceiving the supernatural for the modern era. This problem was announced by modern philosophy and science. The outer or extrinsic criterion of adequacy to modern thought and discourse provides the impetus for doctrinal questions in this area. Drey agreed with Schleiermacher's strategy against both rationalist and supernaturalist sides of the debate: on the one hand, insistence that the supernatural origin of creation, Christ, and the Church must be clearly affirmed, and on the other hand, the argument that the internal witness within the consciousness of Christians to the supernatural plan of salvation lends credence to the Bible and the doctrines. Drey's disagreement with Schleiermacher about the supernatural did not simply boil down to the issue of external criteria within apologetics: historical proofs from miracles and prophecies. The disagreement went rather to the heart of the matter of dogmatic criticism and development by asking: Are the revealed Word of God and ecclesial confessions the product of human reason or the result of supernatural intervention? Clearly each thinker wishes to claim that revelation is both a supernatural gift and naturally received and conveyed. But Drey believes that the supernatural influence--divine inspiration--guarantees the truth of the Bible and the confessional statements.[34] To deny the ability of the Church to speak infallibly on these matters is to limit the supernatural power of God to guarantee the objectivity of revelation and doctrinal formulations. Schleiermacher resisted this type of formulation, which he found in Catholicism and in some Protestant approaches, averring that, although the Bible and confessions have their source in a supernatural fact and are indispensable for mediating the faith, because individual human thought and communal forms of consensus-formation are involved, they are not immune from error.[35] Drey's position reiterates the traditional Catholic un-

---

[34]*Apologetik*, 1:223-236, 260-261; also see his three part essay "Grundsätze zu einer genauern Bestimmung des Begriffs der Inspiration," *Theologische Quartalschrift* 2 (1820): 387-411; 3 (1821): 230-261; 615-655.

[35]*Christian Faith*, § 154, p. 690; § 155, p. 691.

derstanding of dogmas as eternal, true, and binding because guaranteed by divine inspiration. This stance is justified for Drey by his idealistic deduction of the divine positivity of Christian revelation: the concrete, sensible details of history are deduced from the realm of ideas as necessary and demonstrative for the truth of the ideas. This form of argument is reflected in Drey's position on external criteria (i.e., prophecy and miracles) and in his position on the irreversible character of dogmas. Drey is convinced that it is Schleiermacher's rejection of the supernatural character of inspiration that leaves him with a supernatural source, but only a human imitation of God in revelation, and not, as Drey seeks to affirm, a superhuman meaning.[36] Schleiermacher is willing to concede more than Drey to the outer criterion of adequacy to modern thought and discourse on the questions of miracles, prophecies, inspiration, and on the irreversibility of dogmatic formulae.

---

[36]For Drey's critiques of Schleiermacher's position on inspiration, see *Apologetik*, 1:226-227, 260-1; he refers in both sections to *Der christliche Glaube* (1st edition), §§ 19-20. Drey believes he has solved the "apparent contradiction" that covers the concept of inspiration when "we succeed in the end to the insight that as in miracles the supernatural and the natural are in one another, so too in inspiration the superhuman and the human are in one another." Thus Drey defines inspiration: "it is to be imagined as such an immediate effect of God on the human spirit, which through elevation of the same [human spirit] over itself, and the bestowing of powers on his faculties brings forth effects which may be recognized in relation to the natural faculties as of divine origin" (p. 229). According to Drey, Schleiermacher's attention to the supernatural origin in revealed facts means that the content of revelation is not supernatural or only imperfectly so and that it is a human formation, an imitation which presents this effects of this supernatural origin (cf. *Glaubenslehre*, 1st ed., § 19, sec. 3). This undercuts for Drey key superhuman facts; the incarnational character of God in Christ and the incarnational dimension of creation with the image of God in the first humans. By so doing Schleiermacher fails to recognize that God condescends to humans and that God raises the spiritual powers of human thought, decision, and feeling as a product of this activity. Rationalists deny any immediate influence of God (*Apologetik*, 1:227-230).

There is a real difference between Schleiermacher and Drey on the concept of inspiration which has significant ramifications for their understandings of revelation, but what can be underscored is their common desire to reconceive the relationship between the natural and the supernatural so that one can affirm both working together at the same time. This strategy aims at avoiding an extrinsicist understanding of the supernatural and the rational rejection of the supernatural influence beyond the origin of the world. Their positions on the supernatural and the natural are determinative in their reflections on creation, christology, and the Church.

Creation and Sin

The doctrine of creation is a focal point for addressing the relationship between the supernatural and the natural. Both Schleiermacher and Drey resisted the alternatives posed by supernaturalism and rationalism: to defend the biblical myths of creation as historically accurate and supernaturally safeguarded or to commend a mechanistic view of nature as initiated by a divine source but left to its own devices once begun. Schleiermacher and Drey both conceived of creation as the original revelation, wherein the supernatural and the natural are interrelated and interdependent.

Schleiermacher disallowed within the confines of dogmatic theology any speculation about the origins of the world generated from science or myths. Following his descriptive method, the doctrine of creation begins with "the immediate feeling of absolute dependence [that] is presupposed and actually contained in every religious and Christian self-consciousness."[37] In order to account for this feeling Schleiermacher indicates that one must infer that God is the whence of this feeling because God creates the world

---

[37] *Christian Faith*, § 32.

and sustains it, even though we are at the same time co-determined by "a universal nature-system." The causality of God and the causality of the natural order are equally comprehensive in their effect upon self-consciousness, and yet they must be distinguished in order to resist the charge of pantheism. His efforts to speak of the co-extensiveness of the divine causality and natural causality have been viewed as promoting doctrinal development by reconceiving the immanence and transcendence of God in relation to the world, but his success in distinguishing God and world in their effectiveness upon the human subject has remained in doubt for many since the time of the original publication of *Über die Religion*.[38] Also his emphasis on the divine causality coupled with his conviction that Christian theology must treat the Trinity not as a separate and primary subject, but as a composite idea of God derived from various dimensions of ecclesial consciousness led some to raise this question: Is Schleiermacher's theology a radical monotheism that leads necessarily to an untenable modalist trinitarianism?[39] Schleiermacher persistently argued that he neither rejected the freedom of God in creation, nor the appropriateness of trinitarian distinctions; rather he rejected the legitimacy of speculation on the inner life of God within the confines of dogmatic theology.[40]

Drey's treatment of the doctrine of creation affirms that God's free creative activity is a "transcendent fact" which is cloaked in

---

[38]See *On the Glaubenslehre*, 47-51; *On Religion*, 24, 97, 115-116.

[39]*Christian Faith*, §§ 10, 170-172; See Robert Williams, *Schleiermacher the Theologian* (Philadelphia: Fortress Press, 1978), 139-159; Claude Welch, *The Trinity in Contemporary Theology* (London: SCM Press LTD, 1953), 4-9; William Hill, *The Three-Personed God* (Washington, D.C.: Catholic University of America Press, 1982), 84-91.

[40]*Christian Faith*, §§ 31, 50-51. See Claude Welch, *Protestant Thought in the Nineteenth Century* (New Haven: Yale University Press, 1972), 1:76-81.

mystery.[41] He resists three alternatives: the idealist tendency to conceive of creation as the necessary objectification of the absolute; the naturalist reduction of creation to the point of origin; and the supernaturalist defense of the violability of the natural realm. Drey contends that an absolute opposition between the supernatural and the natural prevents one from correctly conceiving of creation and the God-world relation. "Since in the end no one will want to deny that the supernatural and the natural were in one another in the original creation, the one as that which revealed itself, the other as that through which it revealed itself, so will both [the supernatural and the natural] also be in one another in the continuing creation, in the gradual historical revelation, and one will with full authority be able to say of it that it is at the same time supernatural and natural, that in its principle, this in its product."[42] Drey is never suspected of pantheism because although he emphasizes the close abiding connection between God and world initiated in creation as the first phase of development of the kingdom of God, he insists that creation is the free and inscrutable action of the personal and Trinitarian God.[43] Creation is the point of origin and dependency of creation upon God; creation provides the unity of world history which is ultimately brought to completion in Christ.[44]

---

[41]*Apologetik*, 1:284; on creation and nature, see 1:109-113, 178-207. Fehr provides a helpful analysis of Drey's doctrine of creation, see *The Dogmatics of Drey*, 30-44, 168-172.

[42]*Apologetik*, 1:181.

[43]*Apologetik*, 1:182, 284. Drey divides his lectures on dogmatics into *theologia*, which treats God in God's self, and *oeconomia*, which concerns the world in relationship to God. See the selection from Drey's lectures in Geiselmann, *Die Katholische Tübinger Schule*, 110-123, also see Fehr's analysis, *The Dogmatics of Drey*, 168-172, 182-198, 207-215.

[44]On the unity of history in creation, see Franz Schupp, "Die Geschichtsauffasung am Beginn der Tübinger Schule und in der Gegewärtigen Theologie," *Zeitschrift für katholische Theologie* 91 (1969): 150-171, esp. 162-163.

What stands as innovative and troubling for many in Schleiermacher's and Drey's treatment of sin is the apparent necessity of sin in the divine plan of salvation. It is not simply that these two theologians claim that the Incarnation was required because of sinful humanity, as is emphasized among Western, Latin, and Thomist approaches to the Incarnation, and not emphasized by Eastern, Greek, and Scotist approaches. Rather it is the conviction expressed by Schleiermacher and implied in Drey's work that God wills sin and evil in order to fulfill the created order. Schleiermacher resisted the traditional (Augustinian) efforts to define the fall in relation to a prior temporal state of original righteousness as an event of an evil human will motivated by pride and resulting in personal, natural, and social evil as the consequences for sin.[45] In its place Schleiermacher developed a doctrine of original and personal sin inspired by his analysis of the Christian community's conscious coeval experience of self in relation to God and world.[46] The human consciousness of the world indicates the original perfection of the created world insofar as it manifests the predisposition of human consciousness to God-consciousness. But this potentiality is not immediately actualized because we are born into the corporate consciousness of sin, wherein sensuous world-consciousness is more dominant than God-consciousness. Schleiermacher speaks of this dynamic in terms of the Pauline motif of the struggle of flesh against spirit.[47] Sin and evil are relational terms which can only be understood in terms of grace and human development. Thus sin and evil are inevitable and logically necessary in the developmental process of redemption and the consummation of the world, even though we remain personally

---

[45]On original perfection as a temporal category, see *Christian Faith*, § 57, pp. 234-5, on original sin, against monogenetism, §§ 70-72; God as the author of sin, § 81.

[46]See John Hick's interpretation of Schleiermacher's position on sin and evil in *Evil and the God of Love* (San Francisco: Harper and Row, 2nd revised edition, 1978), 220-235.

[47]*Christian Faith*, § 66.

responsible for sin. God, in Schleiermacher's schema, must be understood as the ultimate author of sin and evil in order to account adequately for the inevitable character of sin and evil in the development of the kingdom of God in relation to the world.[48]

Drey judged that "the Fall is to be regarded as one of the great divine decrees, by which God educates human persons in His kingdom."[49] Sin and error consist in the free human rejection of dependency upon God as creator and sustainer, by contradicting the true nature of reality, through the assertion of self-sufficiency.[50] The biblical testimony of the Fall provides the key to our inner subjectivity, "in which the consciousness of our sinfulness is bound together at the same time with the developed self-consciousness" and it illumines the mysterious character of external history "in which no one appears without sin; [external history is] the interweaving of good and evil . . . [as long as it] is not sublated through the entrance of God into history--through revelation."[51] Thus, even though Drey wishes to affirm the accidental character of sin and the fall,[52] what seems to be accentuated is that the Fall and sin are a necessary part of the redemptive plan of the kingdom, and that evil is required to fulfill the divine purposes.[53] Although God

---

[48]*Christian Faith*, §§ 79-83.

[49]This marginal note from the "Praelectiones Dogmaticae" is quoted in Fehr, *The Dogmatics of Drey*, 221; see Fehr's discussion of sin, 209-228. Also see Drey's treatment of "Die Erbsünde" in "Aus den Tagenbüchern über philosophische, theologische und historische Gegenstände," *Geist des Christentums und des Katholizismus*, 142-145; and "Ideen zur Geschichte," 281-294.

[50]*Kurze Einleitung*, §§ 12-15, 19, 29; *Apologetik*, 2:1-30.

[51]*Apologetik*, 1:170.

[52]See *Apologetik*, 1:139-140.

[53]In Drey's review of Dobmayer's dogmatics we read: "The Fall and its consequence belong thus with the plans of the kingdom of God, representing in its history a special period, to which is connected the period of Christ, not in order to restore the kingdom of God lost in the previously past [period] of the kingdom of God, but rather to begin and to continue that new

is not explicitly called the "author of sin and evil," as in Schleiermacher's *Glaubenslehre*, by speaking of sin and evil as a necessary decree of God, Drey makes the same contention.[54]

Schleiermacher and Drey never framed their positions in terms of breaking with the biblical and ecclesial statements about creation, even though their reformulations did not simply affirm the supernatural and transcendent activity of God in creation and providence as the scriptures and creeds affirmed. They never denied the freedom of God in the act of creation. Also neither believed they were affirming pantheism by stressing the coextension of the divine causality and natural causality. The historical referent of the Genesis account was no longer an issue for Schleiermacher and Drey.[55] More importantly, their attempts to reformulate the doctrine of creation are offered in response to critical philosophical and modern scientific questions about the natural world, i.e., the outer criterion of doctrinal development: adequacy to modern thought and discourse. This is acknowledged by Schleiermacher and Drey.[56] But any judgment about the adequacy of a doctrinal formulation reached on the basis of the outer criterion is not

---

development prepared by that particular turn. . . . That is exactly the triumph of theodicy and the shaming humiliation of human wisdom . . . that the kingdom of God requires evil as manifestation in the world just as it requires good; that however, which is in evil, the essentially evil, the inverted meaning and will of individuals, is eternally outside of the world and the kingdom of God, that is, lacking all truth and true reality" (in *Theologische Quartalschrift* 7 (1825): 129, cited in Fehr, *The Dogmatics of Drey*, 222, nn. 99-100).

[54]Fehr criticizes this aspect of Drey's thought, *The Dogmatics of Drey*, "There seems to be an inconsistency in Drey's view of this problem" (221); "Is sin to be considered as part of the divine essence's self-manifestation in finite reality? (This is clearly unacceptable to Christian theology)" (222). Rief voices a similar concern, *Reich Gottes und Gesellschaft*, 96.

[55]*Christian Faith*, § 72. Drey does not address the subject of the historical veracity of the Genesis account; cf. *Apologetik*, 2:1-30.

[56]See *Christian Faith*, § 49, esp. p. 193 and *On the Glaubenslehre*, 60; and Drey, *Apologetik*, 1:106.

sufficient in itself; it must be corroborated for Schleiermacher and Drey by the inner criterion of ecclesial piety and optimally it should cohere with the primary language of faith of the Bible and Church Confessions.

On the fall, sin, and evil, both thinkers stood in tension with scriptural and confessional traditions. Schleiermacher readily acknowledged this. While adhering to the communal and individual character of original sin, Schleiermacher rejected the necessity of monogenism; in his view, the biblical and creedal statements about original sin entering the world through the first pair need no longer be affirmed. More significantly he believed that the Church's efforts to argue that God is not the author of sin and evil, though understandable, were wrong and needed to be criticized and reformulated.[57] He argues on the logical cogency of his position, not by referring to the outer criterion. Drey on this score remained mute. While his theological position suggests that God is the author of sin and evil, he nowhere states it explicitly, nor does he call the Church's teaching on this matter into question.

The Person and Work of Christ

It is often claimed that Schleiermacher inaugurates the modern approach to christology: proceeding from soteriology to christological claims rather than the opposite, adjudicating the claims of faith with the historical life of Jesus, and working with a critical posture toward the christological dogmatic heritage.[58] Although Drey's christology has received scant attention,[59] it offers

---

[57]*Christian Faith*, §§ 79-82.

[58]Walter Lowe, "Christ and Salvation," *Christian Theology: An Introduction to Its Tasks and Traditions*, ed. P. C. Hodgson and R. H. King (Philadelphia: Fortress Press, 2nd edition, 1985), 238.

[59]See Fehr, *The Dogmatics of Drey*, 225-236; Franz-Josef Niemann, *Jesus als Glaubensgrund in der Fundamentaltheologie der Neuzeit. Zur Genealogie eines Traktats*, Innsbrucker theologische Studien (Innsbruck-Wien: Tyrolia-

an impressive Catholic analogue to Schleiermacher's approach. For both theologians, the idea of the kingdom of God provides the linchpin for soteriology and christology, supplying a web of beliefs which serve as a bridge from the historical life and teachings of Jesus to the dogmatic claims about the person of Christ. While Drey criticizes and rejects nothing in his treatment of the christological dogmas, his constructive interpretations of the dignity of Christ and the nature of salvation bear a marked resemblance to Schleiermacher's.

Schleiermacher's christology was innovative in its procedure and formulation. Beginning with a description of the ecclesial consciousness of grace, he inferred the "whence," the nature of the cause of this transformation in terms of Christ and the Spirit-formed Church.[60] This transformation--the nature of salvation--is understood primarily in terms of overcoming sin and ignorance by means of a transition from a life dominated by world-consciousness to one dominated by God-consciousness, from the dominance of the flesh or sensible consciousness to the dominance of spirit. Christ is the second Adam who restores and brings to completion the created human nature which, as the first Adam signifies, has its origins in God and its demise in sin.[61] The movement from sin to grace is determined and made possible by the historical figure of Jesus Christ who effects this transition through his fulfillment of the prophetic, priestly, and kingly offices.[62]

Schleiermacher argued in the *Glaubenslehre* that in order to account for the distinctive identity of Christianity one must trace the external difference of the Christian community back to the founder of this positive religion and then examine the internal difference associated with the concrete, determinate nature of the

---

Verlag, 1983), 301-348.

[60]*Christian Faith*, §§ 86-89.

[61]*Christian Faith*, § 89.

[62]On the transition from the consciousness of sin to the consciousness of grace, see *Christian Faith*, § 86, p. 356; on the three offices, see §§ 102-105.

redemption effected through this historical figure.[63] Schleiermacher contended that the effects evident in the community necessarily lead back to Christ. Christ's mission can only be understood in terms of the historical context in which he emerged, but the distinctiveness of his effect requires that we affirm his perfect God-consciousness, his sinlessness, and the creative divine principle at work in him. Christ is not merely exemplary, he presents the ideality, the archetype (*Urbildlichkeit*). He is influenced by his surroundings but transcends them because of the divine causality at work in him. Thus, "the supernatural becomes natural" in him and this can be spoken of as the one "miraculous fact" of Christianity.[64] Christ can rightly be called divine, because in him the ideal has become historical.[65]

Schleiermacher did not wish to deny the humanity and divinity of Christ, which stand at the center of the ancient christological dogmas, but he did wish to challenge all speculative and mythical assumptions operative in the dogma of the Incarnation.

> The task of the critical process is to hold the ecclesiastical formulae to strict agreement with the foregoing analysis of our Christian self-consciousness, in order, partly, to judge how far they agree with it at least in essentials, partly (with regard to individual points), to inquire how much of the current form of expression is to be retained, and how much, on the other hand, had better be given up, either because it is an imperfect solution of the problem or because it is an addition not in itself essential, and harmful because the occasion of persistent misunderstandings.[66]

This merely reiterates what was stated in his introduction: "Dogmatic propositions have a twofold value--an ecclesiastical and a scientific; and their degree of perfection is determined by both of

---

[63]*Christian Faith*, §§ 10-11.

[64]*Christian Faith*, § 89, p. 365, § 93, p. 381.

[65]*Christian Faith*, § 93.

[66]*Christian Faith*, § 95, p. 390.

these and their relation to each other."[67] As has often been pointed out, Schleiermacher did not wish to criticize dogmas on the basis of historical criticism, for, in fact, he "made only a half-turn to the new nineteenth-century attempt to construct Christology "from below" (*von unten nach oben*) rather than "from above" (*von oben nach unten*)."[68] He was, however, critical of the apologetic use of external proofs from prophecies and miracles; he was persuaded by the arguments of the historical and natural sciences that this mode of argument was not valid.[69] Nevertheless, his positive central christological assertion of the ideality of Christ, which is explicated in terms of the perfection of God-consciousness as a veritable existence of God in Christ, was initially challenged by F.C. Baur and David Friedrich Strauss for not being able to account for the historical character of Christianity.[70] Schleiermacher defended the importance of the historical facticity of Christ in order to account for the origin of the consciousness of grace in ecclesial consciousness,[71] but any description of the consciousness of grace must also be evaluated according to the criterion of the primary

---

[67]*Christian Faith*, § 17.

[68]Claude Welch, *Protestant Thought in the Nineteenth Century*, 1:83. See also Ernst Troeltsch, "The Significance of the Historical Existence of Jesus for Faith," *Ernst Troeltsch: Writings on Theology and Religion*, 182-207; and B. A. Gerrish, "Jesus, Myth, and History: Troeltsch's Stand in the "Christ-Myth" Debate," *The Old Protestantism and the New*, 230-247.

[69]*On the Glaubenslehre*, 61-68.

[70]*Christian Faith*, §§ 93-94. F. C. Baur, "Comparatur Gnosticismus cum Schleiermacherianae theologiae indole," 242, 247 and D. F. Strauss, *The Christ of Faith and the Jesus of History*, trans. L. E. Keck (Philadelphia: Fortress Press, 1977). For Schleiermacher's response to Baur, see *On the Glaubenslehre*, esp. 45-47, 71.

[71]One can acknowledge the legitimacy of Schleiermacher's use of a anthropological and transcendental modes of analysis and argumentation and still have reservations about his interpretation of christology and soteriology. See Thomas Pröpper, "Schleiermachers Bestimmung des Christentums und der Erlösung," *Theologische Quartalschrift* 168 (1988): 193-214, and Maureen Junker, *Das Urbild des Gottesbewußtseins*, 207-215.

language of faith, especially the New Testament presentation of Jesus's teaching on the kingdom. This determines whether the reformulated doctrine coheres with the christological affirmation of the ideality and sinlessness of Jesus as it was affirmed in the early Church.

Schleiermacher's critical assessment of the dogmatic christological confessions was not aimed at their rejection in favor of a minimalistic human and exemplary Jesusology. His christology attempted to respond to the problems raised by modern science and philosophy. Again, the outer criterion of modern thought and discourse provides Schleiermacher with the impetus for his critical evaluation of the dogmatic heritage, but not the sole norm. He was critical of the two-natures formulation, the hypostatic union, and the Trinitarian formula because he found them no longer adequate or intelligible in the modern period. He did not want to deny their historical and dogmatic significance but rather to provide a more adequate formulation.[72] Schleiermacher not only criticized, but also rejected, the dogmatic claims about the pre-existence of Christ and the Virgin Birth, as well as the allegorizing tendency to find some specific causal worth in the death, resurrection, or ascension of Christ as attested to in the Scriptures and affirmed in dogmatic claims.[73]

---

[72]See *Christian Faith*, §§ 94, 96, Schleiermacher hopes his formulation in § 94 lays "the foundation for such a revision, which attempts so to define the mutual relations of the divine and the human in the Redeemer, that both the expressions, divine nature, and the duality of natures in the same person (which to say the least are exceedingly inconvenient) shall be altogether avoided."

[73]On the pre-existence of Christ and eternal distinctions in the Triune Godhead, see *Christian Faith*, §§ 97, 170; on Mary's virginity, see § 97, pp. 403-406; on the resurrection and the ascension see § 99, pp. 419-420: "Belief in these facts (resurrection, ascension, his return for judgement) . . . is no independent element in the original faith in Christ, of such a kind that we could not accept Him as Redeemer or recognize the being of God in Him, if we did not know that He had risen from the dead and ascended to heaven,

Schleiermacher's conception of the work of Christ was based on his interpretation of the salvific revelation of Christ as an educative influence, rather than as specifically effected by the passion and cross of Christ, or by the victory of the resurrection.[74] The death of Christ, in Schleiermacher's view, ought not to be seen in isolation, but in relation to his life and his teaching.[75] People are redeemed when they are incorporated into the power of Christ's God-consciousness: the "advancement" (*Förderung*) of Christ's activity and life takes place within the corporate life of men and women. This community simultaneously provides the medium for communicating the powerful God-consciousness of Jesus Christ to believers. This advancement "is the act of the Redeemer become our own act;" we freely accept the recreative influence of Christ upon us and a person-forming process begins.[76] As people enter into a living relationship with Christ, both the reconciling activity of Christ and his redemptive activity are given immediately. But

---

or if He had not promised that He would return for judgement. . . . Rather they are accepted only because they are found in the Scriptures; and all that can be required of any Protestant Christian is that he shall believe them insofar as they seem to him to be adequately stressed."

[74]On salvation as educative, see *Christian Faith*, § 94, p. 386.

[75]*Christian Faith*, § 101, p. 437: "Now Christ's suffering can be thought of in this connection with his redemptive activity only when regarded as a whole and a unity; to separate out any particular element and ascribe to it a peculiar reconciling value, is not merely trifling allegory if done in teaching, and worthless sentimentality in poetry; probably it is also seldom free from a defiling admixture of superstition. Least of all is it proper to ascribe such a special reconciling value to his physical sufferings" because (1) "these sufferings in themselves have only the loosest connection with his reaction against sin;" and (2) "our own experience teaches us that an ordinary ethical development and robust piety have as their reward the almost complete overcoming of physical sufferings in the presence of glad spiritual self-consciousness, whether personal or corporate." Also see § 104, pp. 457-463.

[76]*Christian Faith*, § 100, p. 425. Also see p. 427 where Schleiermacher discusses the redemptive activity as comparable to the educative intellectual influence and as a person-forming process.

"the reconciling activity can only manifest itself as a consequence of the redemptive activity," for the process of person-formation associated with regeneration and sanctification must be initiated by the gift of redemption: "the old man is put off and a new man is put on."[77] By interpreting the redeeming and reconciling activities of Christ in terms of the communication of the perfect power of Christ's God-consciousness and of his blessedness, Schleiermacher emphasized the soteriological effect flowing from the incarnation (i.e., perfect God-consciousness, the ideal become historical) rather than from the death of Christ. Schleiermacher's soteriology, since it is not based on the death of Christ, became the target of traditional criticisms of the Greek, Incarnation-centered, model of salvation offered by adherents to the Latin model of redemption and to the Lutheran theology of the cross. He did not exclude the redemptive effects usually associated with the cross and resurrection--forgiveness, justification, sanctification, and immortality in a qualified sense--but incorporated them within his incarnational soteriology.

Drey's reflections on christology within his *Apologetik* proceed in a traditional fashion: he defends and interprets the Chalcedonian formulation of Jesus Christ as the Incarnation of God, as the God-man, and from the vantage of Christ's divinity he examines the work of Christ. He questions none of the dogmatic heritage. Unlike Schleiermacher's, Drey's more strictly idealistic assumptions and his specific conception of dogmatic theology enabled him to acknowledge the legitimacy of christological and trinitarian speculation within theology. Thus, Drey affirmed classic christological and trinitarian dogmas and the eternal distinction within the Godhead. However, Drey does not defend Jesus as the God-man by using the traditional Greek categories; rather, like Schleiermacher, he writes of Christ's "divine self-consciousness" as the semantic and theoretical frame of reference for defending and

[77]*Christian Faith*, § 101, pp. 431, 433.

explaining the Incarnation, the union of natures, Christ's sinlessness, and his perfect knowledge of God.

Christology is treated by Drey under the general rubric, "God Incarnate in his manifestation." He first argues for the divine and perfect nature of Christ's revelation as unfolded from the idea of the kingdom of God and mirrored in his life, insofar as it manifests his "personality" and his "divine self-consciousness."[78] The expression of Jesus' consciousness does not merely present a divine envoy or an ambassador of God, but rather he must be recognized as a divine nature, the Son of God, and as God Incarnate.[79] Christ indicates his divine self-consciousness in many ways according to Drey.[80]

Drey contends that Christ's earthly personality, teaching, and life communicates the divine attributes of wisdom, holiness, and omnipotence. His teaching exhibits the nature of God, the ideal embodiment of the spiritual and moral character of the human person, and the universal intent of God's salvific plan.[81] Hence, Christ reveals the ideal of human holiness insofar as he shows his inner relationship to his father "from eternity." "The highest religiosity does not merely manifest itself in Christ; he himself is religion personified."[82] Drey's attention to the teachings and life

---

[78]*Apologetik*, 2:239.

[79]*Apologetik*, 2:240.

[80]Drey speaks of the divinity of Jesus Christ in the following ways: (1) pre-worldly existence and his concern for the world and not for himself (*Apologetik*, 2:240-242, 244, 250); (2) His inner relationship to God (2:242-244); (3) Christ's affirmation that he is the eternal Son of God, the self-revelation of God that transcends the Old Testament idea of the Messiah (2:244-246); (4) as the envoy of God, Christ communicates the divine purposes (a) to announce the kingdom of God, (b) to bring redemption: deliverance from the human annihilation caused by sin and disbelief, (c) to mediate reunion with God, and (d) to return to deliver divine judgement and reward (2:246-249).

[81]*Apologetik*, 2:250-259.

[82]*Apologetik*, 2:266.

of Christ as manifestations of his divine self-consciousness is quite similar to Schleiermacher's approach even though Drey does not follow the same order: first soteriological effects, then christological claims.

However, Drey gives much more attention than Schleiermacher to the death of Christ; it is presented as the supreme action of his life, which discloses God's unlimited love for humans. In the passion Christ is scorned and despised. In the eyes of the world it is a humiliating death. But through it Christ exhibits perseverance, and in it he "died for the honor of God, for the salvation of human persons, and for truth, certainly the most noble way a human being can die."[83] All appeared lost for Christ; his enemies are triumphant. Yet, "he raises his head a last time, unshaken through this all with the same security with which he began and continued and calls out in the sound of victory--it is finished."[84]

Although Drey initially treats this inner nature of Christ as revealed in his life and teachings, he goes on to discuss the external manifestations of Christ's divinity: healings, resuscitations, and nature miracles.[85] These external proofs from miracles indicate without distinction the divine dignity and mission of Christ, but the resurrection and the ascension must be distinguished as external proofs for individual dogmas.[86] As with the death of Christ, Drey affirms the worth of traditional formulas and arguments where Schleiermacher questioned their legitimacy and intelligibility.

---

[83]*Apologetik*, 2:270.

[84]*Apologetik*, 2:270.

[85]Drey ponders various kinds of miracles in the New Testament in light of the modern scientific doubts about their historical veracity, but he claims in the end that these miracles are incontestable; see *Apologetik*, 2:318-328. He also treats miraculous events: the birth of Christ (no mention of Mary's virginity), John's baptism of Jesus, and the transfiguration, but above all the resurrection and the ascension (2:328-337). These miracles provide external proofs of secondary significance--necessary, but subordinate--to the internal proofs of the truth of Christ's person and teaching.

[86]*Apologetik*, 2:340.

The dominant motif in Drey's soteriology is the restoration of human nature through the revelation of the kingdom of God in the person and teachings of Christ. Sin and ignorance of the original dependency of the human on God are overcome through Christ in a "new spiritual creation."[87] Thus, the consciousness of the original union with God--the mark of created human nature, which has become clouded by sin and ignorance--is re-created as the effect of the divine self-consciousness of Jesus Christ and issues forth in a new way of life.[88] The work of Christ serves three purposes: (1) to establish a religious and ethical community founded on his teachings; (2) to bring about a moral re-creation; and (3) to offer forgiveness of and salvation from the destruction caused by sin for eternal happiness.[89] These three purposes are united in the idea of the kingdom of God. Forgiveness of sin is specifically effected through the sacrifice of Jesus' death; it is "the fruit of his death."[90] In Christ's death, he "sacrificed his life for humanity."[91]

Drey's approach to christology and soteriology shares with Schleiermacher's the belief that Christ in his teaching and his actions articulated the kingdom of God and in this manner disclosed the self-identity of Christ and the soteriological nature of his work. Drey speaks of Christ's personality and his self-consciousness, but, even though he does speak of Christ not merely

---

[87]*Apologetik*, 2:237, 279, 284.

[88]Fehr correctly sees the closeness of Drey's formulation to Schleiermacher's position on the nature of redemption in relation to a christology of consciousness and personality. However, Fehr intimates that what distinguishes Drey from his contemporaries (implying Schleiermacher) is that "the alteration or 're-creation' of human nature which Christ brings about is not limited to a new kind of consciousness, but must find its full expression in a new quality of life." *The Dogmatics of Drey*, 225-226, n. 113. It is not clear how or why Drey's position would be distinct from Schleiermacher's at this point. See *Christian Faith*, § 106.

[89]*Apologetik*, 2:278-286, 221-225.

[90]*Apologetik*, 2:224. see also 221-224, 270.

[91]*Apologetik*, 2:242.

as the model but as the ideal of religion and union with God which has become historical, he does not share Schleiermacher's precise formulation of the nature of God-consciousness. Moreover, Drey would never have stated, as Schleiermacher did, that we must continually criticize the doctrinal heritage of christology, even though he affirmed development and sought to reinterpret the traditional dogmas and not merely repeat them. Drey could never be accused of Sabellianism, because he did not share Schleiermacher's critical and apprehensive stance toward the older formulations of the dogmatic tradition, e.g., the pre-worldly and eternal existence of the Son of God, the Incarnate God, the two natures doctrine, the resurrection, and the ascension. While it can be reasonably argued that both Schleiermacher and Drey worked with an incarnational model of christology and that their understandings of salvation rest on this model, when discussing the death of Christ and its influence, Drey stands apart from Schleiermacher. Although Drey, like Schleiermacher, emphasizes the Incarnation and the salvific character of Christ's teaching about the kingdom and his manifestation of this message in his life, he continues to affirm the crucial importance of the cross of Christ and its salvific power. "Where," Drey asks, "is there a death in history which is like the death of Christ?[92]

The Spirit and the Church

Schleiermacher and Drey developed their theologies of the Church mindful of the Enlightenment critique of the Christian Church's use of authority, tradition, and power. They not only gave serious and noteworthy consideration to a theology of the Church as one doctrine among many,[93] but they also insisted that the

---

[92]*Apologetik*, 2:270.

[93]Schleiermacher develops his ecclesiology in the *Glaubenslehre* in the section on "The Constitution of the World in relation to Redemption" (*Christian Faith*, §§ 113-156). Drey touches upon numerous ecclesiological

Church is the fundamental datum of theological reflection.[94] We have already given a great deal of attention to this latter aspect of their thought and will here focus on their contribution to the developing doctrine of the Church.

Neither figure wished to abdicate on any issue that remained under dispute about the nature of the Church from the time of the Reformation. Schleiermacher affirmed the priesthood of all believers and reiterated the Protestant critique of the hierarchical distinction between laity and clergy.[95] Drey defended the hierarchical nature of the Church as instituted by Christ for the salvation of the human race.[96] Yet, their writings on the Church and the Spirit do not merely reiterate past positions. More importantly, each offers important reflections on the foundations, nature, and mission of the Church. The significance of Schleiermacher's ecclesiology lies in his rejection of the doctrine of double predestination and his emphasis on the Holy Spirit as the common spirit of the community. Drey's ecclesiology defends the

---

themes in the third volume of the *Apologetik* (1847), which sought to prove the divine positivity of the Catholic Church. Although Drey acknowledged the aptness of consigning a portion of his dogmatic lectures to the Church and the Sacraments, he never wrote a separate section on this subject. Fehr rightly suggests that this is probably due to Drey's distinction between the "ideal side" of Christianity: doctrines, ideas, and decrees of God which govern world history, and the "real side" of Christianity wherein the realization of the ideas of the kingdom of God take place within the Church. See Fehr, *The Dogmatics of Drey*, 232, 239-244 and *Kurze Einleitung*, § 71.

[94]*On Religion*, 148; *Christian Faith*, § 6; *Brief Outline*, § 33. *Kurze Einleitung*, § 54: "The Church is the true basis of all theological knowledge. From it and through it the theologian receives the empirically given material of it; through the relation to it, all its concepts must extract reality, outside of it they degenerate into vague, detached speculation; his [the theologian's] knowledge has to flow back into it [i.e., the Church] in practical terms otherwise it remains an idle, purposeless drifting around."

[95]*Christian Faith*, §§ 133, 134, 145, esp. p. 666. *Brief Outline*, §§ 267, 307. *Die christliche Sitte*, 175-176, 384-385.

[96]*Apologetik*, vol. 3.

hierarchy of the Church, but not the infallibility of the Pope, and offers a substantive pneumatology that harmonizes with his Christological ecclesiology.

As we have seen, Schleiermacher identifies the Church and the kingdom of God, but this identification is not a complete one supporting a triumphalistic ecclesiology. He discerns three antitheses or polar relationships in his discussion of the origin, the continuation, and the consummation of the Church: the relationship and distinction between Church and world, between the outer and the inner Church, and between the invisible and the visible Church. Each of these distinctions is governed by his doctrine of election.

The distinction between visible and invisible church has its historical basis in Augustine's ecclesiology and theology of election, and is given special attention in Reformation thought.[97] The invisible Church designates the community of believers predestined to be effectively regenerated in Christ. The visible Church is constituted by those elected to be justified and those who are not, even though both groups participate in the external practices of the Church. This distinction arose as a way to combat a rigorist, Donatist understanding of the Church as a morally pure community of true believers, by recognizing that there would be ambiguity and sin in the life of the Church based on the different levels of receptivity and responsiveness of the members. The ambiguity in the life of the Church (and world) was made theologically acceptable or understandable, because it was resolved in the hidden will of God which predestines individuals for glory or misery.

Augustine's late theology of election, forged in his dispute with Pelagianism, can easily draw on the gospel images of heaven and hell, God's judgment, and the division of sheep and goats.

---

[97]See Augustine, *The City of God*, trans. H. Bettenson (New York: Penguin Books, 1972), 1:35. Geoffrey, G. Willis, *Saint Augustine and the Donatist Controversy* (London: S.P.C.K., 1950), 98, 123-125, 174; and on Luther see Herbert Olsson, "The Church's Visibility and Invisibility According to Luther," in *This is the Church*, ed. Anders Nygren, trans. C. C. Rasmussen (Philadelphia: Muhlenberg Press, 1952).

However, it is sometimes suggested that while Augustine brilliantly disputed Gnostic cosmic dualism in his early career, his later fear of Pelagianism often pushed him toward the moral dualism of the once repudiated Manicheanism.[98] Augustine's later doctrine of election held that the evil that exists in the world cannot be attributed to God, but to free will, and yet the hidden will of God predestines all. This later formulation became the dominant theological paradigm on the question throughout the history of Christianity, in opposition to or alongside of the Origenist theology of *apokatastasis*. A few medieval interpreters found in Augustine the basis for a belief in double predestination, a belief which also became an ingredient in John Calvin's theology.[99] Since the Enlightenment, serious questions had emerged about the basis and impact of the Augustinian doctrine of election on the Christian doctrines of God and Church. Schleiermacher did not think that this doctrine of election --usually implied in dogmatic formulas about grace and justification, but never explicitly required for faith--and specifically the Reformed admission of a double predestination was in keeping with the religious consciousness of the Church and with the proper understanding of the kingdom of God in relation to Church and world.

In contrast to the traditional model of election, Schleiermacher argued that "there is only one eternal and universal decree justifying human persons for Christ's sake."[100] By so doing, he sought to

---

[98]See Willis, *Saint Augustine*, 124 and Hans Blumenberg, *The Legitimacy of the Modern Age* (Cambridge: The MIT Press, 1983), 125-136, esp. 133, 135.

[99]Gottschalk (c.804-c.869) developed the work of the anti-Pelagian treatises of Augustine in the direction of a doctrine of double predestination. This position was condemned at the Synod of Quiercy in 849. For Calvin's position see *The Institutes of the Christian Religion* (Philadelphia: The Westminster Press, 1960), 3:21.

[100]*Christian Faith*, § 109, p. 501; also § 119, p. 549, where we read: "If . . . we proceed on the definite assumption that all belonging to the human race are eventually taken up into living fellowship with Christ, there is nothing for it but this single divine fore-ordination."

steer a different course between the "Scylla of Pelagianism, and the Charybdis of Manicheanism" than the one traversed during the later career of Augustine.[101] Schleiermacher proposes the following:

> [I]f the impartation of the spirit to human nature which was made in the first Adam was insufficient, in that the spirit remained sunk in sensuousness and barely glanced forth clearly at moments as a presentiment of something better, and if the work of creation has only been completed through the second and equally original impartation of the Second Adam, yet both events go back to one undivided eternal divine decree and form, even in a higher sense, only one and the same natural system. . . .[102]

Schleiermacher's doctrine of a single divine decree is the key to his treatment of the relationship between the Church and the world, the inner and outer circle of fellowship, and the visible and the invisible Church. Schleiermacher's treatment of the consciousness of sin and grace yields a tension within the individual between God-consciousness and world-consciousness, a tension that also exists within the Church. Thus he states that "faith in the Christian Church as the kingdom of God not only implies that it will ever endure in antithesis to the world, but also . . . contains the hope that the Church will increase and the world opposed to it decrease. . . ."[103] If there is ambiguity in the Church because of the tension between the Church's focus on God-consciousness and the world's adherence to sensuous-consciousness in a struggle for the attention of men and women, there is also a far greater hope that this tension will be overcome thanks to God's work in creation, Christ, and the Church. Although, in the end, the perfection of God-consciousness, the kingdom of God in the Church is to be realized for the whole human race, ecclesiology must deal with the interim period and ac-

---

[101] *Christian Faith*, § 118, p. 544.

[102] *Christian Faith*, § 95, p. 389.

[103] *Christian Faith*, § 113, p. 528.

count for the tensions by speaking of the outer and the inner circle of the Church, and the visible and the invisible Church.

For Schleiermacher "the totality of those who live in the state of sanctification is the inner fellowship; the totality of those on whom preparatory grace is at work in the outer fellowship, from which by regeneration members pass to the inner, and they keep helping to extend the circle wider."[104] This outer circle is constituted by those who are "called," and share a common susceptibility to the influence of the preparatory operations of Christ's grace, while the inner circle of fellowship is constituted by those "elected," who not only share this receptivity to Christ's influence but who also are united in their will for the realization of the kingdom of God. It is this inner circle that constitutes a network of mutual interaction and co-operation, which seeks to bring about the realization of the kingdom of God within the Church and the transformation of the world. There are certainly individuals who do not take part in the activity of the Church, who appear caught in the web of a sinful world, but their antithesis to the kingdom of God is a "vanishing one." "The merely gradual passage of individuals into the full enjoyment of redemption is for our [human] race-consciousness just what the gradual process of sanctification is for our personal self-consciousness, namely, the natural form necessarily taken by the divine activity as it works itself out historically and as we have seen the inevitable condition of all activity in time of the Word made flesh."[105]

The distinction between the visible and invisible Church does not rest according to Schleiermacher on the contrast between the elect and those not elected. The invisible Church is the essential and invariable Church because of "the totality of effects of the Spirit as a connecting whole." It is contrasted with the visible Church, which is mutable and ambiguous because the effects of the Spirit are "connected with those lingering influences of the collective life

---

[104]*Christian Faith*, § 113, p. 525.

[105]*Christian Faith*, § 118, p. 540.

of universal sinfulness, which are never absent from any life that has been taken possession by the divine Spirit."[106] The visible Church remains ambiguous not because it includes those who are not elected, but because the effects of the corporate presence of sin are still present within the community of faith.

The Church has its foundation in Christ and its animating principle in the common spirit, which may rightly be called the Holy Spirit.[107] Every genuine community, be it religious, political, or scientific, exhibits a common spirit--a uniting of individuals into a community of interaction and co-operation--but the Christian community is determined by the positivity of Christianity, that is its external origin in Jesus Christ, and its internal identity is informed by the Christian understanding of redemption. Schleiermacher did not wish to posit a common spirit antithetical to a transcendent Holy Spirit. The supernatural becomes natural through the constant causal activity of God within the community. The common spirit that is universally effective in the Church is also an absolute and particular Spirit which can be called holy. In Schleiermacher's words, the "will for the kingdom of God [within the Christian community] is the vital unity of the whole, and its common spirit in each individual; in virtue of its inwardness, it is in the whole an absolutely powerful God-consciousness, and thus the being of God therein, but conditioned by the being of God in Christ."[108]

Drey likewise constructed his theology of the Church on the basis of the idea of the kingdom of God. His ecclesiology is not determined by the problematic of election as is Schleiermacher's, but was forged in the controversy between conciliarists and

---

[106]*Christian Faith*, § 148, p. 677.

[107]On Christ as the origin of the Church, see *Christian Faith*, §§ 10, 11, 88. Karl Barth expressed doubts about whether the common spirit is the Holy Spirit for Schleiermacher, fearing that here was a further indication of his Sabellianism, see *The Theology of Schleiermacher*, 276.

[108]*Christian Faith*, § 116, p. 536. Schleiermacher's reflections on the Spirit have immense importance for the nature of ecclesial unity and leadership as was discussed in terms of organic leadership in Chapter III.

ultramontanists about the nature of the Church's hierarchy.[109] Understood within this context, Drey's ecclesiology affirms the hierarchical and clerical nature of the Church by basing it in a christological argument about the foundation of the Church, but he complements this christocentric ecclesiology with a theology of the Spirit as holy and common which qualifies and limits the hierarchical nature of the Church. In pursuing this line of reasoning Drey did not wish to repudiate any dogmatic claims, but rather to retrieve and accentuate scriptural and Patristic reflections on the Holy Spirit.

The christocentric character of Drey's theology of the Church is rooted in the kingly, priestly, and prophetic offices of Judaism, which are united in the foundation of the Church by Christ.[110] The organic unity of the Church is however not only based on the institution of the Church by Christ as the head, but also on the continuation of the original form of Christianity throughout history. This continuation is secured internally through the power of the Spirit. "He [Christ] promised and sent to all the Spirit as principle and organ of the inner spiritual unity, . . . who is holy as Christ and one with him, because he [Spirit] is his [Christ's] own; it [the Church] should cohere in mind from within through the holy and Christian common spirit."[111] Externally the unity is found in the organ and middle point of papal primacy.[112] In discussing the

---

[109]Raimund Lachner, *Das ekklesiologische Denken Johann Sebastian Dreys*, Europäische Hochschulschriften (Frankfurt am Main: Peter Lang, 1986), 365-456. Also see Josef Rief's treatment of Drey on Church and State, *Reich Gottes und Gesellschaft nach Johann Sebastian Drey und Johann Baptist Hirscher*, 214-345.

[110]E.g., Vom Geist und Wesen," 226, 228, 229. See also *Apologetik*, 2:278-283.

[111]"Vom Geist und Wesen," 229.

[112]"Vom Geist und Wesen," 230. See *Apologetik*, 3:128-129 where Drey returns to the outer and inner unity of the Church: "Each society and so also each Church is in the first place an outer manifestation, existing in the union of some or many persons for certain purposes by means of a common

holiness of the Catholic Church, Drey admitted that in the Church we find all kinds of sin and misuses from the apostolic times down to today, but held that the power of grace nonetheless extends inwardly in the heart and soul of each member through a spiritual power and externally through word and discipline.[113]

Due to the close relationship he posited between inner and outer aspects of the Church, Drey resisted the distinction between the visible and the invisible Church. Tracing the distinction only back to Luther and the Reformers, rather than back to its Augustinian origins, Drey countered that "this Church is only thought of in the form of a visible society."[114] To oppose the visible with the true and invisible Church yields "the dogmatic development of Protestantism."[115] But for all of their complaints about the visible Church, and Drey agrees with a number of them, Protestants acknowledged the need to construct a visible Church and to regulate its practice as indicated by the Augsburg Confession. This said, however, Drey confesses that "the visible Church also has an invisible side, and has had it since the Ascension of Christ. However, this invisible side does not lie, as Protestants suggest, in

---

working together under common direction. Its unity is therefore in the first place an outer one and must be outwardly perceptible and it will really be given if its members are joined through such social bonds and norms with one another and are held together. . . . This outer unity has however for its foundation still other bonds, which bind the members also inwardly, and these bonds can lie in each society only in the common purposes and interests which all members pursue and on which they accordingly all agree among one another. Thereby the outer unity of the society becomes at the same time an inner unity of individuals, without which the society would be like a mere aggregate of persons. In a Church, as a religious society, the common purposes and interests can lie only in the religious and spiritual goods which it [i.e., the Church] recognizes as the true and the highest." These purposes and interests are identified with the idea of the kingdom of God.

[113] *Apologetik*, 3:146. Drey also acknowledges an inner equality of members in the Church alongside of an outer inequality (3:103-4).

[114] *Apologetik*, 3:160.

[115] *Apologetik*, 3:157.

the invisibly effected faith and the invisibly begotten love, for this faith and this love must make themselves externally visible in accordance with their nature and the demands of the Lord."[116] On the contrary, the invisible dimension lies in the absolutely invisible which resides beyond the here and now. "No one can become a member of any invisible Church, who has not been initiated first into a living community of the visible."[117]

Drey defended the hierarchical nature of the Church and its unchanging form on the basis of Christ's institution and on the soteriological and practical mission of the Church which requires the teaching office, priesthood, and Church government.[118] This is spoken of as the inner organization of the Church. Drey staunchly defended the divinely established character of the authority and powers of the hierarchy. However, he sought to hold the hierarchy responsible for the type of service rendered. In this he promoted an organic understanding of the Church and a theology of the Spirit which supported and legitimated a model of leadership more receptive and responsive to the community of the faithful, rather than authoritarian. The bishops' and pope's authority is not their own, but the power of Christ which comes from God and the Holy Spirit.[119]

---

[116]*Apologetik*, 3:162.

[117]*Apologetik*, 3:162-163. Drey continues, "The invisible Church steps forth into all directions out of the visible, and is properly the emigration of the latter into the world to come." Also see "Der katholische Lehrsatz von der Gemeinschaft der Heiligen," *Theologische Quartalschrift*, 4 (1822): 587-634.

[118]*Apologetik*, 3:163-4. Drey did not believe the unchanging hierarchical structure of the Church precluded the creation of different hierarchical grades to reinforce the unchanging foundation of the ecclesial form of government (3:274).

[119]*Apologetik*, 3:196. Drey also discusses the New Testament references to Spirit as guide, as spirit of Truth (3:287-90). "The effectiveness of the Holy Spirit is thus an inner and subjective one, however it is nonetheless general, because it suffuses all individuals." Drey's immediate point is that

As we have stated previously, Drey thus attempts to hold in tension a descending theology of power based on Christ's institution of the Church and the headship of Christ, which justified the powers vested in the ordained clergy, with an ascending theology of power nourished by a certain organic vision of the Church, and by a theology of the Spirit as the Holy and common Spirit of the community which unites minds and hearts in the common interests and purposes of the kingdom of God.[120] He did not criticize the doctrine of the Church which had developed thus far. But he was fully aware that the doctrine of the Church was a still-germinating doctrine.[121] By holding together a christological and a pneumatological approach to ecclesiology, Drey sought to stake a position between conciliarism and ultramontanism. On the one hand, the Church could not be a democracy.[122] There is not only a need for the leadership of priests and bishops; this is a divinely instituted leadership, as is the primacy of the pope which serves as the symbol and impetus for the unity of the apostolic Church

---

"out of the whole of the biblical presentation arises, however, that the Church was secured in the apostles through the double assistance of Christ and the Holy Spirit against theoretical error and practical aberrations" (3:289-290).

[120]Although I am arguing that Drey holds together in a productive tension descending and ascending models of power, which are authorized respectively by christological and pneumatological arguments, and a hierarchical and communal understanding of the Church, it must also be recognized that in Drey's later writings he stresses a descending model of power and a more christocentric and hierarchical model of the Church. See, for example, his later treatment of power and authority, *Apologetik*, 3:176-192.

[121]"Ideen zur Geschichte," 302-305.

[122]*Apologetik*, 3:274-275. "The constitution which Christ has given to his Church is not a democracy. . . ; it is however just as little an aristocracy, because the bishops are subjected to the guardianship and reprimand of a communal leader; this leader is likewise not governing as a monarchy, because the bishops govern their dioceses on their own as the immediate successors of the apostles, and both, bishops and pope, are bound to universal laws" (275).

spiritually and organizationally. On the other hand, Drey claims that while we cannot simply claim that all are equal in the Church according to function, there is a deeper equality all share. Moreover, although Catholics cannot agree with the assumptions included in Luther's interpretation of the priesthood of all believers, they do affirm a common spiritual priesthood in which all participate.[123] The Church is infallible, but individual bishops and the pope can err in matters of the faith.[124] The original form of the Church as instituted by Christ establishes the college of apostles for carrying out the teaching function of the Church and the primacy of the pope who through his ministry of administration promotes the unity of the Church.[125] However, Drey believed that papal infallibility did not flow necessarily from the salvific purpose bequeathed to the hierarchical authority of the pope.[126]

---

[123]*Apologetik*, 3:192-197; he also speaks of an inner equality of Church members that is inseparable from an outer inequality (3:103-4).

[124]*Apologetik*, 3:308; Drey states "that the promise of infallibility is to be related to the teaching and ruling Church and indeed to the wholeness of its organism, and to this properly" (310).

[125]*Apologetik*, 3:188-191, 210-214; "Primacy must, however necessary, be joined to one person, because only this form expresses the idea of the unity of the Church . . . . The relative (and imperfect) points of unity require always again a central point of unity. So, for example, the unity of the Church presents itself also in the form of a collectivity of the whole hierarchy in a unanimous gathering--a general council, but this itself must have for the purpose of its unanimity, a middle point. Also the hierarchy can represent, as it were, itself through a committee, but this committee requires, even more than the council, an affinity to the central point of the ecclesial unity, if it is meant to represent the whole hierarchy" (3:233).

[126]*Apologetik*, 3:224-227. The Pope is the middle point of unity, and the highest power in the Church has been conferred on him. It is not merely an honorary primacy. "Out of the promises in Matt 16:18-19 and Luke 22:32 may be derived the primacy of the pope, as we have also done, but not his infallibility, for this is not included in the primacy, does not belong to its concept, but rather only the representation of the unity of the Church, the right of surveillance over the bishops, and the right to make general

Both Schleiermacher's and Drey's ecclesiologies proved of decisive importance for the development of this doctrinal area in the modern period.[127] And while we can detect a shared emphasis on the role of the Holy Spirit as the common spirit at work in the Church, and a recognition of the need for leaders in the Church, they clearly differed with respect to the ecclesioligical ramifications of the Reformation agenda.

Schleiermacher's pioneering and constructive ecclesiology emerged from his criticism of the Protestant reception of the Augustinian doctrine of election. This criticism was not explicitly based on the outer criterion of adequacy with modern thought and discourse. Instead Schleiermacher argued that double predestination did not cohere with ecclesial piety nor with the primary language of faith, which spoke of the unfolding of the kingdom of God in terms of the tensive relationship between the Church and the world. Drey constructed his ecclesiology mindful of Reformation, conciliarist, and modern democratic criticisms of the hierarchical nature of the Church. Although he did not find any one of their counterproposals correct, his ecclesiology is responsive to what he believed were their legitimate concerns: it stresses the obligations of the hierarchy to be receptive to the sense of the faithful, the spiritual equality of all believers, and the unity of the Church which is fostered by love and mutual respect and not by force and authoritarianism.

---

ordinances that are necessary for the well-being of the Church" (3:310).

[127]For Protestant thought, see Ernst Troeltsch, "Schleiermacher und die Kirche," in *Schleiermacher der Philosoph des Glaubens*, *Moderne Philosophie*, no. 6 (Berlin-Schöneberg: Buchverlag der "Hilfe," 1910), 9-35; Trutz Rendtorf, *Theology and Church* (Philadelphia: Westminster Press, 1971); and Peter C. Hodgson and Robert C. Williams, "The Church," in *Christian Theology: An Introduction to Its Traditions and Tasks*, 249-273. For Catholic thought one must trace the contributions of Drey and Johann Adam Möhler as they were received and augmented by Josef Geiselmann, Yves-Marie Congar, Henri de Lubac, and Karl Rahner, leading up to the ecclesiology articulated by the Second Vatican Council.

Eschatology

Schleiermacher's and Drey's treatment of the last things--death, judgment, the consummation of the world, and the resurrection of the dead--can be treated as constitutive aspects of their theologies of history. In their grand narratives of sacramental mediation, Christ is the turning point of history and the Church stands at the center of history as the kingdom of God on earth. They both identify the Church and the kingdom, but they also recognize that the kingdom is not fully present in the Church. There is sin, error, and disease in the Church as the body of Christ. This organic community reaches perfection in the fullness of time when all parts are brought into an organic whole. Then this kingdom of God will ultimately come to completion and there will come about a perfect union of all things with God.[128] To this end the Church has the salvific mission to teach all nations and to bring all to faith in Christ.[129] As they constructed this comprehensive plot, both rejected, with little analysis, apocalyptic and chiliastic interpretations of Christ's second coming, thousand year reign, and the end of the world.[130]

---

[128]*The Christian Faith*, §§ 157, 164; *Apologetik*, 2:292-293, 314-215, "Ideen zur Geschichte," 294-295. Drey's "Praelectiones Dogmaticae" states that in "the perfect uniting of all things with God . . . [everything] which is now opposed and hostile to God and the divine decrees will disappear utterly and be removed" (3:68-69, cited in Fehr, *The Dogmatics of Drey*, 237).

[129]*Christian Faith*, § 157: "We therefore cherish the hope that the expansion of Christianity will be accelerated in proportion as the glory of the Redeemer is ever more clearly reflected in the Church itself." *Apologetik*, 2:287: Drey speaks of the work of Christ which dialectically develops as it is communicated to all people on earth at all times. This development through communication proceeds amidst the interruptions and vicissitudes caused by national, cultural, religious, and moral differences.

[130]*Christian Faith*, § 161, p. 708; *Apologetik*, 2:314. Drey indicates that the visible fulfillment of the kingdom of God in the thousand year reign of

Even though their constructions of the history of the world and Christianity are in large measure compatible, when it comes to the nature of the survival of the human personality after death, differences between these two theologians can be discerned. As we have seen, Drey reaffirmed the classic claims about the saving significance of Christ's death and the literal character of the biblical testimony to the miracles of the resurrection and ascension.[131] The key implication of Christ's resurrection for all Christians was agreed upon by the Church Fathers: the body of each individual Christian will be raised.[132] Drey expressed confidence in the accuracy of the biblical testimony about Christ's teachings and prophecies about the future. Christ taught an immortality of the human person, and a judgment of the world that decides the fate of the pious and the godless.[133] Furthermore, Christ clearly foresaw the future and prophesied about the effects of his work, about his imminent death and resurrection, and about the world to come.[134] Certain prophecies by Christ have not yet been fulfilled: the second coming of Christ, the resurrection of the dead, the judgment of all human beings, the end of the present world, and an entirely new condition for all things.[135] God's judgment is not merely an inner-worldly reality, as Drey believes is indicated by Jewish belief. There

---

Christ after the resurrection and before the end of the world "is an interpretation of the fundamental idea of Christianity [i.e., the kingdom of God], which was later rejected." Drey concludes that this chiliastic interpretation was individual opinion held by some, but it was never universally binding in the Catholic Church ("Ideen zur Geschichte," 294-5).

[131]*Apologetik*, 2:331-336.

[132]"Ideen zur Geschichte," 298. Drey acknowledged that the Fathers understood the limits of this individuality differently.

[133]"Ideen zur Geschichte," 296.

[134]*Apologetik*, 2:303-316. Drey also echoes an anti-Semitic theme when he argues that Christ not only foresaw the destruction of Jerusalem and the Temple, but also the "regretful" destruction of the Jews among all peoples, citing Luke 21:24 (306, 311, 313).

[135]*Apologetik*, 2:312.

is also a final judgment of the pious and the godless. Drey finds that in the early history of dogmas the Fathers were in agreement about a judgment at the end of the world, and that the good would be eternally rewarded. Although he does not find total agreement among the Fathers on the duration of the punishment of the godless, Drey does conclude that there is a strong consensus, against Origen, that the punishment of the damned is eternal.[136] While in some passages the universal character of God's salvific plan is suggested, Drey clearly reaffirms not only the possibility, but indeed the reality of temporal punishment for sins and eternal punishment of the damned.[137]

When Schleiermacher turned to eschatology under the aegis of the consummation of the Church, his previous method of procedure no longer sufficed. Eschatological assertions could not be doctrines in his strictest sense--an expression of ecclesial consciousness--because they could not be based on a description of actual consciousness. Statements about the consummation of the Church are "rooted in our Christian consciousness as representing the unbroken fellowship of human nature with Christ, under conditions wholly unknown and only faintly imaginable, but the only fellowship which can be conceived as wholly free from all that springs from the conflict of flesh and spirit."[138] Although Schleiermacher had identified the Church and the kingdom, claiming that the kingdom of God had been inaugurated, thanks to Christ, within the community of believers, this did not imply that the kingdom was fully manifest on earth. The redeeming and reconciling work of Christ would only be fully realized in the end. Like Drey, he described the final consummation of the Church as the kingdom of God in terms of the union of humanity with God. While this

---

[136]"Ideen zur Geschichte," 300-302. Fehr indicates that Drey's treatment of "the last things" in his dogmatic lectures reaffirms the Church's teachings; *The Dogmatics of Drey*, 236-237.

[137]On the universal intention of Christ's work to unite all things, see, for example, *Apologetik*, 2:257-259, 286-290, 315-316.

[138]*Christian Faith*, § 157, pp. 697-698.

consummation of the Church is something we must approximate as an ideal, it is not merely an ideal, but something which lies in the future as a real event.[139]

Schleiermacher was extremely cautious in what he was willing to say, or in what he believed could be said, about personal immortality, for he feared the influence of speculative, mythical, and self-serving claims about the status of personal identity and consciousness after death. In order to battle against such alien intrusions into dogmatics, Schleiermacher emphasized the primacy of God and community in any conception of life and afterlife as he had in his understanding of the redemptive and reconciling work of God in Christ. Thus, his basic limiting claim is that "faith in the Redeemer as it is here [within the *Glaubenslehre*] described may develop out of a sense of sin calling for redemption, and . . . from it we might infer the communication of Christ's blessedness flows to every moment of life, including the last moment of all, even though we have no conception whatever of a life after death."[140] Unlike Drey, then, Schleiermacher did not believe Christ's prophecies about the afterlife provided us with new knowledge about the future, but conceived them as offering a figurative formulation of what is already presented in faith: "the persistent

---

[139]*Christian Faith*, §§ 157, 159. Schleiermacher was insistent that the consummated Church (previously called the Church triumphant) is not strictly speaking analogous to the Church militant, but believed they should not be viewed as totally unrelated either (697, 704).

[140]*Christian Faith*, § 158, p. 698; see also §§ 101, 108. In his brief dissertation, D. F. Strauss half-heartedly commended Schleiermacher for beginning the work of de-eschatologizing the *apokatastasis ton panton* originally espoused by Origen as an event of the distant future, now transformed into something eternally present. See Strauss, *Die Lehre von der Wiederbringung aller Dinge* (1831), in Gotthold Meller, *Identität und Immanenz: Zur Genese der Theologie von David Friedrich Strauss* (Zurich: EVA-Verlag, 1968) Baser Studien zur historischen und systematischen Theologie, 10:50-82.

union of believers with the Redeemer."[141] The Christian affirmation of "the union of the Divine Essence with human nature in the Person of Christ" indicates the basis for the Redeemer's eternal personal survival, and the basis for Christian hope in the survival of personal identity after death through a perfect union with God.[142]

What Schleiermacher claims about the consummation of the Church and the survival of personality is put forth with the confidence of faith. What more can be expressed about the last things is unclear and less important for the Christian. In accordance with his rejection of the doctrine of double predestination, Schleiermacher's eschatology stresses the saving activity of God in Christ working to bring about the restoration of all things in Christ more than the significance of God's judgment.[143] He restates the Reformers' rejection of the concept of purgatory and challenges the notion of eternal damnation.[144] As he puts it, "there are great difficulties in thinking that the finite issue of redemption is such that some thereby obtain to the highest bliss, while others (on the ordinary view, indeed, the majority of the human race) are lost in irrevocable misery. . . . Hence we ought at least to admit the equal rights of the milder view, of which likewise there are traces in Scripture; the view, namely, that through the power of redemption there will one day be a universal restoration of all souls."[145]

---

[141]*Christian Faith*, § 158, p. 702. see also § 159, p. 705.

[142]*Christian Faith*, § 158. The reconciliation of God and humanity "only very accidentally takes the form of enjoyment and possession; in essence it can never be set forth as more than hope." § 101, p. 434.

[143]*Christian Faith*, § 159, pp. 704-705, § 163, p. 722.

[144]On purgatory, see *Christian Faith*, § 161, p. 711 and on eternal damnation, see § 163, pp. 720-722.

[145]*Christian Faith*, § 163, p. 722. For Schleiermacher's eschatology in relation to nineteenth century Reformed theology, see B. A. Gerrish, *Tradition and the Modern World* (Chicago: University of Chicago Press, 1978), 151-180.

With the rediscovery of apocalyptic eschatologies at the beginning of the twentieth century, there occurred a dramatic shift in the course of modern theology that is still reverberating today.[146] It is not that the rediscovery of apocalyptic currents of thought requires a repudiation of all the contested claims of eschatology within the modern world,[147] but this development has placed the previous accent on continuity and growth in tension with the sense of crisis and tragedy relearned through apocalypticism. Instead of seeing grace mediated through creation and Christ as simply fulfilling that creation, creation and grace are only perceived from the future, and Christ is the proleptic sign of a future fulfillment that is in the present nowhere certainly indicated. The mediating roles of creation, Christ, and the Church reflecting the supernatural within the natural world and suprasensible realities through human and natural vehicles, which characterizes the theologies of Schleiermacher and Drey, are often minimized or

---

[146]See Johannes Weiss, *Die Predigt Jesu vom Reiche Gottes* (Göttingen: Vandenhoeck & Ruprecht, 1900) and Albert Schweitzer, *The Quest of the Historical Jesus* (New York: Macmillan Publishing Co., Inc., 1968 [1st edition, 1906]). Apocalpytic traditions have been selectively deployed in political and liberation theologies, see, for example, Jürgen Moltmann, *A Theology of Hope* (New York: Harper & Row, 1976), Johann Baptist Metz, *Faith in History and Society* (New York: Seabury Press, 1980), Gustavo Gutierrez, *A Theology of Liberation* (Maryknoll, NY: Orbis Books, 1973). More recently there has been a reassessment of the twentieth century preoccupation with apocalyptic literature and traditions from the perspective of new research into Jewish wisdom traditions. In one sense, the theological reception of this rediscovery of wisdom traditions has only begun; in another sense, this rediscovery of wisdom traditions implies the reaffirmation (and undoubtedly reconfiguration) of that tradition of historical interpretation we have called sacramental, of which Schleiermacher and Drey are a part. See Marcus Borg, "A Temperate Case for a Non-eschatological Jesus," *Forum* 2/3 (1986): 81-102; and John Dominic Crossan, *The Historical Jesus: The Life of a Mediterranean Jewish Peasant* (New York: Harper Collins, 1991), Part III.

[147]John Hick makes this point when he examines Moltmann's work in *Death and Eternal Life* (San Francisco: Harper & Row, 1976), 213-215.

displaced by an emphasis on the categories and concerns of apocalyptic and prophetic views of history. From the vantage point of apocalyptic categories, these two German theologians may appear to reflect a simple modern progressive view of history, which claims that the Church has developed and will continue to develop toward its consummation. We have sought to show, however, that Schleiermacher's and Drey's theologies of history, while certainly not as attuned to the themes of crisis, tragedy, and suffering as are present-day apocalyptic-inspired theologians, are not progressivist. Acknowledgement of continuity and discontinuity are both present in Schleiermacher's and Drey's theologies of history, and if the theme of continuity takes precedence because of their interests in ecclesial mediation, it is not at the expense of discontinuity, God's judgment, and the need for moral, spiritual, and intellectual conversion and transformation.

Conclusion

In this brief assessment of Schleiermacher's and Drey's treatment of specific issues we find confirmed what we have witnessed in previous chapters: Schleiermacher's and Drey's theologies of history authorize an openness to doctrinal development.

For Schleiermacher this meant not only the possibility of radically reformulating doctrines but also of critically challenging the doctrinal heritage of the ancient Catholic councils and of more recent Protestant official decrees. The possibility of disease, and hence, the need for criticism always exists. Official ecclesial doctrines continue to be a part of the tradition that informs the communal identity of the Church and therefore they remain historically and dogmatically significant. However, the binding character of specific formulae can and ought to be challenged on the bases of theological arguments that employ warrants taken from the specific criteria: coherency with the primary language of faith, ecclesial piety, the historical rootedness of the Christian faith, and adequacy to modern thought and discourse.

Drey, on the other hand, remained faithful to his own theology of history by emphasizing the continuity of the plan of God. No dogmas, once defined, are open for criticism. There may be further development, but not rejection of those dogmas. Were there aspects of the dogmatic heritage that he remained silent about, because he was dubious? Were there questions which he decided he could not broach? An argument from silence is impossible to reconstruct, and when he speaks, Drey never seems to waver from his faithful adherence to the expressed dogmas. However, it must be recalled that Drey's construal of history not only lends credence to dogmatic development, but it also faces the prospects of error and decay. Just as alien teachings can lead to error, so inertia and hyperorthodoxy can stifle growth; both kinds of errors need to be criticized. To thus fail to recognize the mobility of doctrines is to stifle the Spirit at work in history and in the Church.

In the end, Schleiermacher and Drey fashion a modern approach to doctrines that seeks to be faithful to the heritage of Christian discourse, praxis, and experience, while promoting a conscious dialogue with a variety of voices in the cultural world around them. Both thinkers are reform-minded and forward-looking in their approach to doctrines, yet clearly Schleiermacher is more critical of received doctrines and more creative in his own formulations than is Drey. These differences are rooted partially in their Catholic or Protestant sensibilities about the status and weight of officially pronounced doctrines, and partially in the different weight they gave to the various criteria when assessing doctrines. In both cases, however, their approaches to doctrinal criticism, reform, and development, specifically their recognition of the need for ecclesial continuity, development, and reform, are significantly informed and theologically justified by their theologies of history.

Schleiermacher and Drey ushered in a new epoch in Protestant and Catholic theology. They offered a new attempt to give a credible response to contemporaries who were critical of Christianity. They provided a truly new and fertile understanding of historical theology: the interpretation of the history of Christian life and discourse is the proper context out of which dogmatic theology can emerge. The freshness of their contribution likewise resides in the critical and mediating character of their theologies. Being faithful to the traditions which inform ecclesial identity does not mean for them that simply repeating past traditions. On the contrary, their theologies contend that a hermeneutics of retrieval must include a critical posture toward revered traditions, and that retrieval cannot replace the demands for creative new formulations.

The reception of Schleiermacher's and Drey's understanding of history and doctrinal development has, as can be expected, been mixed. At one end of the spectrum are critics who argue that the paradigm of mediating theology forged by Schleiermacher and Drey is suspect. Schleiermacher and Drey, it is feared, have breathed in too deeply the air of the Enlightenment. Their theologies have incorporated the anthropocentric, historicist, and critical spirit of their age. They have jettisoned the transcendent subject matter of Christian faith and more trustworthy classical theological methods. Accordingly, some Protestants, following Barth, seek to recover what they claim is the classic Reformation understanding of the Word of God in its literal and narrative dimensions and defend the primary language of faith under the Anselmian masthead: faith seeking understanding. Certain Catholic theologians share with Edmund Vermeil the suspicion that the road from Drey to the alleged Modernism of Alfred Loisy and George Tyrrell is short, straight, and smooth. Although the Catholic critics of the modern German tradition from Drey to Rahner are indebted to different theological traditions (Thomas Aquinas and Jacques Maritain, Augustine and Bonaventure, Origen and Pseudo-Dionysius, or the so-called "Denzinger theology"), they all unite in resisting modern mediating brands of theology.

Those theologians who are skeptical of the trajectory of modern theology that proceeds from Schleiermacher and Drey, draw from rich traditional resources and rightly plead for some distance on the modern movement of thought and action. Their alternative theological narratives usually accentuate the supernatural and gratuitous character of revelation and doctrinal development and the correlative humility and obedience required of the theologian. However, sometimes they minimize the human and social dynamics of historical change and discount any critical and creative assessment of previous and emerging positions. While many of those who are critical of modern, liberal, and revisionist trajectories in theology correctly insist upon the unity, integrity, and the continuity of the Christian tradition and its ecclesial identity, there can follow an unwillingness to acknowledge within this traditioning process stagnation, corruption, the plurality of traditions and tension between those traditions, or the discontinuties within the Church's historical experience.

Recurring questions about the legacy of Schleiermacher and Drey concern their criteria for assessing development. Does the attempt to judge whether doctrines are adequate according to modern discourse and practice not violate the integrity of the Bible and conciliar pronouncements? Does such an attempt not put critical reason and alien methods of inquiry before Christian faith? Are we not left with secular experience as the touchstone for doctrinal truth? Finally, is not the attempt to determine the essence of Christianity as a critical norm for the life and practice of faith the clearest indication of the hubris of modern theologians? Schleiermacher and Drey would clearly resist the implications suggested by these questions, yet the subsequent history of theology has returned again and again to these criteriological issues. For many of Schleiermacher's and Drey's adversaries the attempt to mediate Christian faith with modern culture is an ill-advised and bankrupt agenda; modernity is the problem, and they complain that for too many modern theologians it is the solution. Schleiermacher and Drey would demur, and insist that mediating theology takes the historical character of Christian faith seriously and does not baptize any epoch or philosophy.

Besides those who resist or reject the mediating model of theology bequeathed by Schleiermacher and Drey, there has been a wide range of theologians who have assessed their accomplishments positively, even as they have criticized and revised them. As we have suggested in chapter three, there is a winding path that leads from Schleiermacher and Drey to Tillich, Rahner and their heirs. The underlying premise which unites these very different thinkers is that theology is a critical enterprise which seeks to interpret and reformulate the traditions and doctrines of faith in light of current modes of thought, discourse, and practice. Although theology interprets and appropriates past traditions, it is not reduced to retrieval and retelling; theology also entails critical assessment and creative construction, responsive to the contemporary situation.

Understandings of history and doctrinal development have shifted significantly since the time of Schleiermacher and Drey. The sacramental model of history, dominant throughout the history of Christianity, is being reevaluated in light of the rediscovery of apocalypticism initiated in earnest at the turn of the century. The ramifications of apocalyptic modes of discourse for Christian views of history and doctrine have not been thoroughly explored, partially because the phenomenon of apocalyptic discourse and its reception is so varied. Thus we discover that for some the sense of spiritual, political, economic or cultural crisis central to the apocalyptic vision of history has served as a call to strict adherence to the biblical or creedal faith, a faith obedient to a heavenly and cosmic plan and pattern. But for others apocalyptic discourse has provided an impetus for acknowledging upheavals and ruptures within the flow of historical consciousness and a source of motivation for committed action to bring about fundamental change.

The recognition of historical crisis and discontinuity can be detected not only in newly appreciated apocalyptic modes of discourse: witness the purposive negativity in Hegel's dialectical idealism and Marx's dialectical materialism, as well as the role of revolutionary changes in Thomas Kuhn's theory of scientific paradigm shifts, and the importance of discontinuities in Michel Foucault's archaeology of knowledge.[148] Besides apocalyptic

---

[148]See G. W. F. Hegel, *Phenomenology of Spirit*, trans. A. V. Miller, (Oxford: Clarendon Press, 1977), 124 and *Reason In History: Hegel*, trans. by R. S. Hartman (Indianapolis: The Bobbs-Merrill Company, Inc., 1953), 68-71;

currents in theology and crisis-oriented philosophies, historical research into the monuments and traces from the past has raised new questions about the presence of conflict, the use of power, and the reality of historical discontinuities as they bear on the interpretation of doctrinal development.[149] We have observed that often organic models of history have accentuated doctrinal continuity and stability in a process of growth while not acknowledging crises in the Church and discontinuities in development. Though the sacramental and organic model of history embraced by Schleiermacher and Drey can not easily assimilate these apocalyptic and disruptive schemas, we have taken great pains to show that their understanding of history and doctrinal development need not be viewed as antithetical to these currents of thought. Schleiermacher and Drey honestly attend to the experiences of disease and decay in their use of the organic model and acknowledge the presence of discontinuities in Christian discourse and practice. On the other hand, it must be clearly stated that although these contrary schemas provide, in my judgment, important insights into historical experience and a necessary corrective to certain deficiencies in the sacramental model of history, the sacramental model with its emphasis on the Church's

---

Karl Marx, *The Marx-Engels Reader*, ed. R. C. Tucker, (New York: W. W. Norton & Company, Inc., 2nd edition, 1978), 70-81, 160-163; Thomas Kuhn, *The Structure of Scientific Revolutions* (Chicago: University of Chicago Press, 1970); Michel Foucault, *The Archaeology of Knowledge & The Discourse on Language*, trans. A. M. Sheridan Smith, (New York: Pantheon Books, 1972).

[149]Some discussion of these issues can be found in Nicholas Lash, *Change in Focus*, Maurice Wiles, *The Making of Christian Doctrine* (Cambridge: University Press, 1967) and *The Remaking of Christian Doctrine* (London: SCM Press, 1974), Robert L. Wilken, *The Myth of Christian Beginnings: History's Impact on Belief*, and Walter Bauer, *Orthodoxy and Heresy in Earliest Christianity*, eds. R. A. Kraft and G. Krodel (Philadelphia: Fortress Press, 1971).

role in the continuous mediating of Christian identity cannot be renounced.[150]

In addition to the heightened awareness of historical crises and discontinuities since the time of Schleiermacher and Drey, there has been, as we noted at the end of Chapter III, a more explicit recognition of the plurality of traditions throughout the history of theology. While it has long been acknowledged that there were different schools of theology and various theological opinions--this Drey and Schleiermacher readily admit--recent research has uncovered in an unprecedented way the plurality of voices within the communal tradition of Christian faith. No longer can we speak simply of "the" theology of the Bible, or of early Christian theology. Instead we must examine the plurality of theologies within the Bible and throughout Christianity. A significant number of theologians now resist any easy homogenization of these plural voices. This heightened recognition of plurality is, of course, historically rooted in the modern plea for tolerance and the romantic appreciation of individuality. But plurality as an explicit theme remains foreign to Schleiermacher's and Drey's working scheme of things, even though they sought in their historical theologies to appreciate individual voices, traditions, and periods, and within their theological encyclopedias to make room for creativity and freedom.

A growing number of thinkers across the disciplines contend that we stand at the threshold of an epochal shift. Within theology we read of "the end of modernity" and the dawn of "postmodern"

---

[150]See Avery Dulles, *Models of Revelation* (Garden City, New York: Doubleday & Company, Inc., 1983), 211-227. In an analogous vein, Paul Ricoeur insists that one must grant the importance of deviations from traditions and the duty of criticizing dead ends within tradition, but this can and should be done from within traditions. What must be resisted is the schism of utopian expectations from experience informed by traditions. This can only be done by striving to discover "forgotten possibilities, aborted potentialities, repressed endeavors in the supposedly closed past." *Time and Narrative* (Chicago: University of Chicago Press, 1984, 1985, 1988), 2:14-28; 3:207-240, esp. 227, 235.

theology or "postliberal" theology.[151] These appellations are fluid and their usage is ideologically pregnant. But, however they are used, they are meant to convey what is distinctive about the contemporary situation as it defines itself in relation to the period of modernity. The heightened sensitivities to cultural and economic crises and discontinuities, and to the diversity of cultural and linguistic traditions, are indices of this postmodern shift away from the modern sense of scientific, technological, and economic progress, and from the Enlightenment confidence in the power of reason to determine the universal nature of the human person and the foundation for every cognitive and moral claim.

For some theologians this situation elicits a further refinement of neo-orthodox theology: a clear commitment to the cultural-linguistic traditions which inform communal identity and a resistance to any commerce with contemporary currents of thought and discourse that might question those traditions.[152] For others it means the negation of theology with its confining quest for reaping the whirlwind of God's action in history.[153] For yet another group, often called revisionists, it means that the hermeneutical, critical, and constructive tasks of theology fashioned

---

[151]See, for example, George A. Lindbeck, *The Nature of Doctrine: Religion and Theology in a Postliberal Age*; Hans Küng, "Karl Barth and the Postmodern Paradigm," *The Princeton Seminary Bulletin* 9 (1988): 8-31; David E. Klemm, "Toward a Rhetoric of Postmodern Theology: Through Barth and Heidegger," *Journal of the American Academy of Religion* 55 (1988): 443-469.

[152]Karl Barth is the representative figure here, but also included in this tradition is the work of Hans Frei and George Lindbeck. Hans Urs von Balthasar and Joseph Ratzinger are representative figures in Catholic theology.

[153]This option is illustrated by the work of death-of-God theologian Thomas Altizer and deconstructionist a/theologian Mark C. Taylor. See Altizer, *The Gospel of Christian Atheism* (Philadelphia: Westminster Press, 1966), idem., "History as Apocalypse," in Altizer et al., *Deconstruction and Theology* (New York: Crossroad, 1982), 147-177; and Taylor, *Erring. A Postmodern A/theology* (Chicago: University of Chicago Press, 1984).

by Schleiermacher and Drey must be recast in keeping with postmodern sensibilities about the disciplined study of cultural traditions.

For this latter revisionist group, a postmodern theology need not be ideologically opposed to everything modern theology accomplished. In this current situation of instability and reassessment, we are able to examine Schleiermacher's and Drey's work anew and to see that they were critical and ambivalent about the directions of modernity, although clearly not to the extent that many are today. Their ambivalence about modernity affects their vision of the task of Christian theology: uniting Christian piety with scientific study in the service of the ecclesial faith that is handed down through history. For them theologians are organic leaders who foster the life of the believing community through discourse and dialogue. By so doing they seek the affirm and clarify the identity of the Christian Church and they seeks to expand the circle of this community by addressing not only the church, but also the cultured despisers be they within or outside of the community of worship, fellowship, and action. Schleiermacher's and Drey's visions of a modern mediating theology have lacunae and weaknesses that are in need of criticism, yet the many positive aspects of their thought assure their enduring value for the further reform and development of doctrine within the Christian Church. The interpretation of Schleiermacher and Drey offered in this study has sought to show the richness of their understandings of history and doctrinal development and their continued relevance.

SELECTED BIBLIOGRAPHY

Primary Sources

Johann Sebastian Drey

Books

Kurze Einleitung in das Studium der Theologie, mit Rücksicht auf den wissenschaftlichen Standpunkt und das katholische System. Tübingen: Heinrich Laupp, 1819; reprint, Frankfurt am Main: Minerva, 1966; reprint with table of contents and introduction by Franz Schupp, Darmstadt: Wissenschaftliche Buchgesellschaft, 1971.

Die Apologetik als wissenschaftliche Nachweisung der Göttlichkeit des Christentums in seiner Erscheinung. Mainz: Fl. Kupferberg, vol. 1, 1838; Vol. 2, 1843; vol. 3, 1847; reprint, Frankfurt am Main: Minerva, 1967; vol 1, second edition, 1844; vol 2, second edition, 1847.

Articles

"Aphorismen über den Ursprung unserer Erkenntnisse von Gott--ein Beitrag zur Entscheidung der neuesten Streitigkeiten über den Begriff der Offenbarung." *Theologsche Quartalschrift* 8 (1826): 237-84.

"Vom Geist und Wesen des Katholizismus," *Theologische Quartalshcrift* 1 (1819): 8-23; 193-210; 369-91; 559-74. Reprinted in *Geist des Christentums und des Katholizismus. Ausgewälte Schriften katholischer Theologie im Zeitalter des deutschen Idealismus und der Romantik.* Edited by Josef Rupert Geiselmann, vol. 5 in series "Deutsche Klassiker der katholischen Theologie aus neuerer Zeit," Mainz: Matthias Grünwald, 1940, pp. 193-234.

"Grundsätze zu einer genaueren Bestimmung des Begriffs der Inspiration," *Theologische Quartalschrift* 2 (1820): 387-411; 3 (1821): 230-61; 615-55.

"Der katholische Lehrsatz von der Gemeinschaft der Heiligen," *Theologische Quartalschrift* 4 (1822): 587-634.

"Revision des gegenwärtigen Zustandes der Theologie," *Archiv für die Pastoralkonferenzen in den Landkapiteln des Bistums Konstanz*, 1812, Erster Band, pp. 3-26. Reprinted in *Geist des Christentums und des Katholizismus. Ausgewälte Schriften katholischer Theologie im Zeitalter des deutschen Idealismus und der Romantik.* Edited by Josef Rupert Geiselmann, vol. 5 in series "Deutsche Klassiker der katholischen Theologie aus neuerer Zeit," edited by H. Getzeny. Mainz: Matthias Grünwald, 1940, pp. 83-97. Reprinted in *Johann Sebastian Drey: Revision von Kirche und Theologie, Drei Aufsätze.* Darmstadt: Wissenschaftliche Buchgesellschaft, 1971. Ed. Franz Schupp, pp. 1-24.

"Über das Verhältnis des Mystizismus zum Katholizismus, mit Nutzanwendungen für unsere Zeit." *Theologische Quartalschrift* 6 (1824): 219-48. Reprinted in *Johann Sebastian Drey: Revision von Kirche, Drei Aufsätze.* Darmstadt: Wissensaftliche Buchgesellschaft, 1971, pp. 25-54.

Manuscripts

"Ideen zur Geschichte des katholischen Dogemensystems." Printed in *Geist des Christenutms und des Katholizismus. Ausgewälte Schriften katholischer Theologie im Zeitalter des deutschen Idealismus und der Romantik*, ed. Josef Rupert Geiselmann, vol. 5 in series "Deutsche Klassiker der katholischen Theologie aus neuerer Zeit," Mainz: Matthias Grünwald, 1940, pp. 235-331.

"Aus den Tagenbüchern über philosophische, theologische und historische Gegenstände." Printed in *Geist des Christentums und des Katholizismus. Ausgewälte Schriften katholischer Theologie im Zeitalter des deutschen Idealismus und der Romantiker*, ed. Josef Rupert Geiselmann, vol. 5 in series "Deutsche Kklassiker der katholischen Theologie aus neuerer Zeit," Mainz: Matthias Grünwald, 1940, pp. 99-192.

Reviews

Marianus Dobmayer, *Theologia dogmatica*, books 1 and 2, in *Theologische Quartalschrift* 1 (1819) 416-440.

Marianus Dobmayer, *Theologia dogmatica*, books 3 and 4, in *Theologische Quartalaschrift* 2 (1820): 38-55, 309-323.

Marianus Dobmayer, *Institiones theologicae*, ed. Emmeram Salomon, in *Theologische Quartalshrift* 7 (1825): 116-133.

Friedrich Schleiermacher

Books

Der christliche Glaube nach den Grundsätzen der evagelischen Kirche im Zusammenhange dargestellt. 2nd edition of the 1st edition of 1821-22, edited by Hermann Peiter. 2 vols. Berlin: Walter de Gruyter, 1984. 7th ed., based on the 2nd ed. of 1830-31, edited by Martin Redeker. 2 vols. Berlin: Walter de Gruyter, 1960. *The Christian Faith*. English translation of the 2nd edition. Edited by H. R. Mackintosh and J. S. Stewart. Edingburgh: T. and T. Clark, 1928. Since 1976, pulbished in America by Fortress Press, Philadelphia.

Die christliche Sitte. Edited from Schleiermacher's lecture manuscripts by L. Jonas. *Sämmtliche Werke*, division 1, vol. 12. Berlin: G. Reimer, 1834, 2nd edition, 1884.

Dialektik (1811). Introduction by Andreas Arndt. Hamburg: Felix Meiner Verlag, 1986.

Geschichte der christlichen Kirche. Edited from Schleiermacher's lecture manuscripts by E. Bonnell. *Sämmtliche Werke*, divison 1, vol. 11. Berlin: G. Reimer, 1840.

On the Glaubenslehre: Two Letters to Dr. Lücke. English translation of *Schleiermachers Sendschreiben über seine Glaubenslehre an Lücke* by James Duke and Francis Fiorenza. Appeared originally in *Theologische Studien und Kritiken* 2 (1829): 255-84; 481-532. New edition edited by Hermann Mulert. Studien zur Geschichte des neueren Protestantismus, Quellenheft 2. Giessen: Alfred Töpelmann (J. Ricker), 1908.

Hermemeutics: The Handwritten Manuscripts. Edited and Introduction by Heinz Kimmerle. Translated by J. Duke and J. Forstman. Missoula, Montana: Scholars Press, 1977. English translation of *Hermeneutik und Kritik mit besonderer beziehung auf das Neue Testament*. Edited by Friedrich Lücke. *Sämmtliche Werke*, division 1, vol. 7. Berlin: G. Reimer, 1838.

Kurze Darstellung des theologischen Studiums zum Behuf einleitender Vorlesungen. 3rd critical ed. Edited by Heinrich Scholz, 1920, reprint, Darmstadt: Wissenschaftliche Buchgesellschaft, 1961. Scholz notes variations from the first edition (1811) but follows the second (1830). *Brief Outline on the Study of Theology*. English translation of the second edition by Terrence N. Tice. Richmond, Va.: John Knox Press, 1966.

Das Leben Jesu. Edited from Schleiermacher's lecture notes and Students' Notes by K. A. Rütenik. *Sämmtliche Werke* division 1, vol. 6. Berlin: G. Reimer, 1864. English translation by S. Maclean Gilmour. Edited and

Introduction by Jack C. Verheyden. Philadelphia: Fortress Press, 1975. Lives of Jesus Series. General Editor, Leander E. Keck.

On Religion: Speeches to Its Cultured Despisers. English translation of the third edition of *Reden über die Religion* of 1821 by John Oman, 1894, reprint, New York: Harper & Row, 1958. English translation of the first edition by Richard Crouter with introduction. Cambridge: Cambridge University Press, 1988.

Gelegentliche Gedanken über Universität in deutschen Sinn, nebst einem Anhang über eine neu zu errichtende, Schleiermachers Werke. Vol. 4. Leipzig: Felix Meiner Verlag, 1911.

Articles

"Über den Begriff des höchsten Gutes, (Zweite Abhandlung)." *Sämmtliche Werke*, division 2, vol. 3. Berlin: G. Reimer, 1834-1864.

"Über den Begriff des grossen Mannes," in *Schleiermachers Werke, Auswahl*. Leipzig, 1910, vol. 1, pp. 520-531.

"Über die Gegensatz zwischen der Sabellianischen und der Athanasianischen Vorstellung von Trinität." In *Friedrich Schleiermacher und die Trinitaetslehre*. Ed., Martin Tetz *Texte zur Kirchen und Theologiegeschichte*. Gütersloh: Gütersloher Verlaghaus, Gerd Mohn, 1968. Also in *Kritische Gesamtausgabe*, vol. 10. *Theologische-dogmatische Abhandlungen*. Ed. Hans-Friedrich Traulsen (Berlin: Walter de Gruyter, 1988); Transated into English by Moses Stuart in *Biblical Repository and Quarterly Observer* 5 (1835): 265-353 and 6 (1835): 1-116.

"Über die Lehre von der Erwählung," *Sämmtliche Werke*, division 1, vol. 2. Berlin: G. Reimer, 1834-1864.

Review

Friedrich Schelling, *Vorlesungen über die Methode des akademischen Studiums* in *Schleiermachers Leben in Briefen*. Eds., Ludwig Jonas and Wilhelm Dilthey. Berlin: Georg Reimer, 1863. Pages 579-593.

Secondary Sources

Abrams, M. H. *The Mirror and the Lamp*. New York: Oxford University Press, 1953.

_____. *Natural Supernaturalism*. New York: W. W. Norton & Company, Inc., 1971.

Allison, Henry E. *Lessing and the Enlightenment*. Ann Arbor: University of Michigan Press, 1966.

Augustine, *The City of God*. Edited by David Knowles. Translated by H. Bettenson. New York: Pelican Books, 1972.

Barth, Karl. *The Theology of Schleiermacher*. Edited by D. Ritschl. Translated by G. W. Bromiley. Grand Rapids, Michigan: Eerdmans Publishing Company, 1982.

Bauer, Walter. *Orthodoxy and Heresy in Earliest Christianity*. Edited by R. A. Kraft and G. Krodel. Philadelphia: Fortress Press, 1971.

Baur, F. C. "Primae Rationalismi et Supranaturalismi historiae capita potiora. Pars. I. De Gnosticorum Christianismo ideali. Pars II. Comparatur Gnosticismus cum Schleiermacherianae theologiae indole. Tubingen, 1827." *Tübinger Zeitschrift für Theologie* 1 (1828): 220-264.

Bernstein, Richard. *Beyond Objectivism and Relativism*. Philadelphia: University of Pennsylvania Press, 1983.

Birkner, Hans-Joachim. *Theologie und Philosophie. Einführung in Probleme der Schleiermacher-Interpretation*. München: Chr. Kaiser Verlag, 1974.

_____. "Beobachtungen zu Schleiermachers Programm der Dogmatik." *Neue Zeitschrift für Systematische Theologie und Religionsphilosophie*. 5 (1963):119-131.

_____. *Schleieramchers christliche Sittenlehre*. Berlin: Verlag Alfred Töpelmann, 1964.

Blackwell, Albert L. *Schleiermacher's Early Philosophy of Life: Determinism, Freedom, and Phantasy*. Harvard Theological Studies 33. Chico, California: Scholars Press, 1982.

Blumenberg, Hans. *The Legitimacy of the Modern Age*. Cambridge: The MIT Press, 1983.

Boff, Leonardo. *Church: Charism and Power*. Translated by J. W. Diercksmeier. New York: Crossroad Publishing Company, 1985.

Brandt, Richard. *The Philosophy of Schleiermacher*. New York: Harper and Brothers, 1941.

Bretschneider, Karl Gottlieb. "Nebst einer Abhandlung über die Grundansichten der Herren Prof. Dr. Schleiermacher and Marheinecke, sowie über die des Herrn Dr. Hase." In *Handbuch der Dogmatik*. 3rd Edition, 1828. Excerpts in translation. *Sacra* 10 (1853): 598-616.

Brosch, Hermann Joseph. *Das Übernatürliche in der Katholischen Tübinger Schule*. Essen: Ludgerus-Verlag, 1962.

Calvin, John. *The Institutes of the Christian Religion*. Philadelphia: The Westminster Press, 1960. 2 Vols.

Chadwick, Owen. *From Bossuet to Newman: The Idea of Doctrinal Development*. Cambridge: University Press, 1957.

Chesnut, Glenn F. *The First Christian Historians*. Paris: Editions Beauchesne, 1977.

Clayton, John. "Was ist falsch über Korrelationstheorie?" *Neue Zeitschrift für Systematische Theologie* 16 (1974): 93-111.

Collins, John J. *The Apocalyptic Imagination: An Introduction to the Jewish Matrix of Christianity*. New York: Crossroad, 1984.

_____. Ed. *Apocalypse: The Morphology of a Genre*. *Semeia* 14 (1979). The Society of Biblical Literature.

Congar, Yves. *Tradition and Traditions*. London: Burns & Oates, 1966.

Crouter, Richard. "Schleiermacher and the Theology of Bourgeois Society: A Critique of the Critics," *Journal of Religion* 66 (1986): 302-323.

Crossan, John Dominic. *The Historical Jesus. The Life of a Mediterranean Jewish Peasant*. New York: HarperCollins Publisher, 1991.

De Lubac, Henri. *The Mystery of the Supernatural*. Montreal: Palm Publishers, 1967.

Dilthey, Wilhelm. *Dilthey: Selected Writings*. Ed. H. P. Richman. Cambridge: Cambridge University Press, 1976.

Dulles, Avery. *Models of Revelation*. Garden City, New York: Doubleday & Company, Inc., 1983.

_____. *The Catholicity of the Church*. Oxford: Oxford University Press, 1985.

Farley, Edward. *Ecclesial Reflection: An Anatomy of Theological Method*. Philadelphia: Fortress Press, 1982.

_____. *Theologia: The Fragmentation and Unity of Theological Education*. Philadelphia: Fortress Press, 1983.

Fehr, Wayne. *The Birth of the Catholic Tübingen School: The Dogmatics of Johann Sebastian Drey*. Chico, CA: Scholars Press, 1981.

Fiorenza, Elizabeth Schüssler. "To Reject or to Choose?" *Feminist Interpretation of the Bible*. Edited by L. M. Russel. Philadelphia: Fortress Press, 1985.

Fiorenza, Francis Schüssler. *Foundational Theology*. New York: Crossroad Publishing Co., 1984.

Foucault, Michel. *The Archeology of Knowledge & The Discourse on Language*. Translated by A. M. Sheridan Smith. New York: Pantheon Books, 1972.

Frank, Manfred. *Das individuelle Allgemeine. Textstrukturierung und Textinterpretation nach Schleiermacher*. Frankfurt am Main: Suhrkamp, 1985.

Frei, Hans. *The Eclipse of Biblical Narrative*. New Haven: Yale University Press, 1974.

Gadamer, Hans Georg. *Truth and Method*. Second revised edition. Translation of the fifth German edition, revised by J. Weinsheimer and D. G. Marshall. New York: Continuum, 1991.

_____. "The Problem of Language in Schleiermacher's Hermeneutics." Trans. D. Linge. *Journal for Theology and the Church*, vol. 6. *Schleiermacher as Contemporary*. Ed. Robert W. Funk. New York: Herder and Herder, 1970.

Geiselmann, Josef. "Die Glaubenswissenschaft der Katholischen Tübinger Schule in ihre Grundlegung durch Johann Sebastian v. Drey." *Theologische Quartalschrift*. 111 (1930): 49-117.

_____. *Die Katholische Tübinger Schule*. Freiburg: Herder, 1964.

_____. *Lebendinger Glaube aus geheiligter Ueberlieferung*. Freiburg: Herder, 1966.

Gerhardt, Mary and Russel, Allan. *Metaphorical Process: The Creation of Scientific and Religious Understanding*. Fort Worth, Texas: Texas Christian University Press, 1984

Gerrish, B. A. *The Old Protestantism and the New*. Chicago: University of Chicago Press, 1982.

_____. *A Prince of the Church: Schleiermacher and the Beginnings of Modern Theology*. Philadelphia: Fortress Press, 1984.

_____. *Tradition and the Modern World*. Chicago: University of Chicago Press, 1978.

Gottfried, Paul. *Conservative Millenialism*. New York: Fordham University Press, 1979.

Gouldner, Alvin W. "Romanticism and Classicism: Deep Structures in Social Science." *For Sociology: Renewal and Critique in Sociology Today*. New York: Basic Books, 1973.

Gräb, Wilhelm. *Humanität und Christentumsgeschichte. Eine Untersuchung zum Geschichtsbegriff im Spätwerk Schleiermachers*. Göttingen: Vandenhoeck & Ruprecht, 1980.

Gramsci, Antonio. *Selections from the Prison Notebooks*. Edited and Translated by Q. Hoare and G. N. Smith. New York: International Publishers, 1971.

Gustafson, James M. "The Relevance of Historical Understanding." *Theology and Christian Ethics*. Philadelphia: United Church Press, 1977.

Gutierrez, Gustavo. *A Theology of Liberation*. Maryknoll, New York: Orbis Books, 1973.

Habichler, Alfred. *Reich Gottes als Thema des Denkens bei Kant*. Mainz: Matthias-Grünewald-Verlag, 1991.

Harvey, Van A. "On the New Edition of Schleiermacher's *Addresses on Religion*," *Journal of the American Academy of Religion* 52 (1972): 488-512.

Hegel, G. W. F. *Phenomenology of Spirit*. Translated by A. V. Miller. Oxford: Oxford University Press, 1977.

_____. *Reason in History*. Translated by R. S. Hartman. Indianapolis: The Bobbs-Merrill Company, Inc., 1953.

Herder, J. G. *Auch eine Philosophie der Geschichte zur Bildung der Menschheit*. Vol. 5. *Sämmtliche Werke*. Ed. B. Suphan. Gerlin, 1877-1913.

_____. *Ideen zur Philosophie der Geschichte der Meschheit*. Vol. 4. *Herders Werke*. Berlin and Weimar: Aufbau-Verlag, 1982. Abridged trans. *Reflections on the Philosophy of the HIstory of Mankind*. Trans. F. E. Manuel. Chicago: University of Chicago Press, 1968.

_____. "Vom Erkennen und Empfinden der menschlichen Seele," Vol 3. *Herders Werke*. Berlin and Weimar: Aufbau-Verlag, 1982. pp. 431-405.

Hick, John. *Evil and the God of Love*. San Francisco: Harper and Row, 2nd revised edition, 1978.

Hill, William. *The Three-Personed God*. Washington, D.C.: Catholic University of America Press, 1982.

Hinze, Bradford E. "The End of Salvation History," *Horizons* 18 (1991): 227-245.

_____. "Narrative Contexts, Doctrinal Reform," *Theological Studies* 51 (1990): 417-433.

Hirsch, Emmanuel. *Geschichte der neuern evagelischen Theologie*, Vol. 5. Münster: Antiquariat Th. Stenderhoff, 1984.

Hirsch, Emmanuel. *Die Reich-Gottes-Begriffe des neueren europäischen Denkens. Ein Versuch zur Geschichte der Staats- und Gesellschaftsphilosophie*. Göttingen: Vandenhoeck & Ruprecht, 1921.

Hodgson, Peter C. and Robert H. King. *Christian Theology: An Introduction to Its Traditions and Tasks*. Philadelphia: Fortress Press, 2nd enlarged edition, 1985.

Holte, Ragner, *Vermittlungstheologie*. Uppsala: Almqvist & Wiksell, 1965.

Junker, Maureen. *Das Urbild des Gottesbewußtseins. Zur Entwicklung der Religionstheorie und Christologie Schleiermachers von der ersten zur zweiten Auflage der Glaubenslehre*. Berlin: Walter de Gruyter, 1990.

Jursch, Hanna. *Schleiermacher als Kirchenhistoriker*. Buch I, *Die Problemlage und die geschichtstheoretischen Grundlagen der Schleiermacherschen Kirchengeschichte*. Jena: Verlag der Frommannschen Buchhandlung [Walter Biedermann], 1933.

Kant, Immanuel. *The Critique of Judgement*. Translated by J. C. Meredith.Oxford: Oxford University Press, 1952.

_____. *Groundwork of the Metaphysic of Morals*. Translated by H. J. Paton. New York: Harpert Torchbooks, 1964.

_____. *Kant: On History*. Ed., L. W. Beck. Indianapolis: Bobbs-Merrill Company, 1957.

_____. *Religion Within the Limits of Reason Alone*. New York: Harper Torchbooks, 1960.

Kasper, Walter. "Verständnis der Theologie damals und Heute," In *Glaube und Geschichte*. Mainz: Matthias-Grünewald-Verlag, 1970.

Klemm, David E. "Toward A Rhetoric of Postmodern Theology: Through Barth and Heidegger." *Journal of the American Academy of Religion* 55 (1988): 443-469.

Klinger, Elmar. *Offenbarung im Horizont der Heilsgeschichte. Historisch-Systematische Untersuchung der Heilsgeschichtlichen Stellung des Alten Bundes in der Offenbarungphilosophie der Katholischen Tübinger Schule*. Zürich: Benzinger Verlag, 1969.

Koch, Klaus. *The Rediscovery of Apocalyptic*. Trans. M. Kohl. London: SCM Press LTD, 1972.

Kuhn, Thomas. *The Structure of Scientific Revolutions*. Chicago: University of Chicago Press, 1970.

Küng, Hans. "Karl Barth and the Postmodern Paradigm." *The Princeton Seminary Bulletin*. 9 (1988): 3-31.

Kustermann, Abraham. *Die Apologetik Johann Sebastian Dreys (1777-1853)*. Tübingen: J.C.B. Mohr (Paul Siebeck), 1988.

Lachner, Raimund. *Das ekklesiologische Denken Johann Sebastian Dreys*. Frankfurt am Main: Peter Lang, 1986.

Lash, Nicholas. *Change in Focus: A Study of Doctrinal Change and Discontinuity*. London: Sheed and Ward, 1973.

_____. *Newman on Development: The Search for an Explanation in History*. Shepherdstown, West Virginia: Patmos Press, 1975.

Lessing, Gotthold. *Lessing's Theological Writings*. Translated by H. Chadwick. Stanford, California: Stanford University Press, 1956.

_____. "Die Erzeihung der Menschengeschlecht." Vol. 3. *Lessings Werke*. Edited by Kurt Wölflel. Frankfurt am Main: Insel Verlag, 1967, pp. 544-563.

Lindbeck, George A. *The Nature of Doctrine: Religion and Theology in a Postliberal Age*. Philadelphia: The Westminster Press, 1984.

Lonergan, Bernard. *Method in Theology*. New York: Herder, 1972.

_____. *Second Collection*. Philadelphia: The Westminster Press, 1974.

McCool, Gerald. *Catholic Theology in the Nineteenth Century: The Quest for a Unitary Method*. New York: Seabury, 1977.

McFague, Sallie. *Metaphorical Theology*. Philadelphia: Fortress Press, 1982.

McGinn, Bernard. *The Calabrian Abbot: Joachim of Fiore in the History of Western Thought*. New York: Macmillan Publishing Company, 1985.

_____. "Early Apocalypticism: The Ongoing Debate." *The Apocalypse in English Renaissance Thought and Literature*. Edited by J. Wittreich and C. A. Patrides, 2-39. Manchester, England: Manchester University Press, 1984.

Mann, Gustav. *Das Verhätnis der Schleiermachermacherschen Dialektik zur Schellings Philosophie*. Stuttgart, 1914.

Marx, Karl. *The Marx-Engels Reader*. Edited by R. C. Tucker. New York: W. W. Norton & Company, Inc., 2nd Edition, 1978.

Marshall, Bruce D. "Hermeneutics and Dogmatics in Schleiermacher's Theology." *The Journal of Religion*. 67 (1987): 14-32.

Maurer, Wilhelm. "Der Organismusgedanke bei Schelling und in der Theologie der Katholischen Tübinger Schule." *Kerygma und Dogma*. 8 (1962): 202-216.

Menke, Karl-Heinz. "Definition und speculative Grundlegung des Begriffes 'Dogma' im Werke Johann Sebastian von Dreys (1777-1853)." *Theologie und Philosophie* 52 (1977): 23-56.

Metz, Johann Baptist. *Faith in History and Society*. New York: Seabury Press, 1980.

Michalson, Gordan E. *Lessing's Ugly Ditch*. University Park: Pennsylvania State University Press, 1985.

Miller, Marlin E. *Der Übergang: Schleiermachers Theologie des Reiche Gottes im Zusammenhang seines Gesamtsdenkens*. Gerd Mohn: Gütersloher Verlaghaus, 1970.

Möhler, Johann Adam. *Die Einheit in der Kirche oder das Prinzip des Katholizismus, dargestellt im Geiste der Kirchenväter der drei ersten Jahrhunderte*. Tübingen, 1825.

Moltmann, Jürgen. *A Theology of Hope*. New York: Harper & Row, 1976.

Mulert, Hermann. *Schleiermachers geschichtsphilosophische Ansichten in ihrer Bedeutung für seine Theologie*. Geißen: Alfred Töpelmann, 1907.

Newman, John Henry. *Essay on the Development of Doctrine*. Westminister, Md.: Christian Classics Inc., 1968.

Niebuhr, H. R. *Christ and Culture*. New York: Harper and Bros., 1951.

Nowak, Kurt. "Theorie der Geschichte. Schleiermachers Abhandlung 'über den Geschichtsunterricht' von 1793," in *Schleiermacher und die wissenschaftliche Kultur des Christentums*. Eds. G. Meckenstock and J. Ringleben. Berlin: Walter de Gruyter, 1991, pp. 419-439.

Ogden, Schubert. "What is Christian Theology?" Unpublished Manuscript.

_____. *On Theology*. San Francisco: Harper & Row, 1986.

Olsson, Herbert. "The Church's Visibility and Invisibility According to Luther." In *This is the Church*. Edited by Anders Nygren. Translated by C. C. Rasmussen. Philadelphia: Muhlenberg Press, 1952.

O'Malley, John. "Reform, Historical Consciousness and Vatican II's Aggiornamento." *Theological Studies* 32 (1971): 573-601.

_____. "Developments, Reforms, and Two Great Reformations: Toward a Historical Assessment of Vatican II," *Theological Studies* 44 (1982): 373-406.

O'Meara, Thomas Franklin. *Romantic Idealism and Roman Catholicism: Schelling and the Theologians*. Notre Dame: University of Notre Dame Press, 1982.

Pannenberg, Wolfhart. *Jesus: God and Man*. Philadelphia: The Westminster Press, 2nd Edition, 1977.

_____. *Theology and the Philosophy of Science*. Translated by F. McDonagh. Philadelphia: The Westminister Press, 1976.

Pauck, Wilhelm. "Schleiermacher's Conception of History and Church History" in *Schleiermacher as Contemporary*. Ed. R. W. Funk, *Journal for Theology and Church*. vol. 7. New York: Herder & Herder, 1870, pp. 41-56.

Pelikan, Jaroslav. *The Christian Tradition: A History of the Development of Doctrine*. Vol. 1. *The Emergence of the Catholic Tradition (100-600)*. Chicago: University of Chicago Press, 1971.

_____. *Development of Christian Doctrine: Some Historical Prolegomena*. New Haven: Yale University Press, 1969.

_____. *Historical Theology: Continuity and Change in Christian Doctrine*. London: Hutchinson & Co., Ltd., 1970.

Pröpper, Thomas, "Schleiermachers Bestimmung des Christentums und der Erlösung," *Theologische Quartalschrift* 168 (1988): 193-214.

Rahner, Karl. "Nature and Grace." *Theological Investigations*. 4:165-188. New York: Seabury Press, 1974.

_____. "Some Implications of the Scholastic Concept of Uncreated Grace." *Theological Investigations*. 1:319-346. New York: Seabury Press, 1974.

Redeker, Martin. *Schleiermacher: Life and Thought*. Philadelphia: Fortress Press, 1973.

Reill, Philip. *The German Enlightenment and the Rise of Historicism*. Berkeley: University of California Press, 1975.

Reimarus, Hermann Samuel. *Reimarus: Fragments*. Translated and Introduced by C. H. Talbert. London: SCM Press LTD, 1971.

Reinhardt, Rudolf, Ed. *Tübinger Theologen und ihre Theologie: Quellen und Forschungen zur Geschichte der Katholish-Theologischen Fakultät Tübingen*. Tübingen: J.C.B. Mohr [Paul Siebeck], 1977.

Rendtorf, Trutz. *Theology and Church*. Philadelphia: The Westminster Press, 1971.

Ricoeur, Paul. *The Rule of Metaphor: An Interdisciplinary Study*. Toronto: University of Toronto Press, 1977.

_____. *Time and Narrative*, 3 Vols. Translated by K. McLaughlin and D. Pellauer. Chicago: University of Chicago Press, 1984, 1985, 1988.

_____. "The History of Religions and the Phenomenology of Time Consciousness." *The History of Religions: Retrospect and Prospect*. Edited by J. Kitagawa. New York: Macmillan Publishing Company, 1985.

_____. "Schleiermacher's Hermeneutics." *The Monist* 60 (1970): 181-197.

Rief, Josef. *Reich Gottes und Gesellschaft nach Johann Sebastian Drey und Johann Baptist Hirschner*. Paderborn: Ferdinand Schöningh, 1965.

Riemer Matthias. *Bildung und Christentum. Der Bildungsgedanke Schleiermachers*. Göttingen: Vandenhoeck & Ruprecht, 1989.

Ritschl, Albrecht. *A Critical History of the Christian Doctrine of Justification and Reconciliation*. Vol. 1. Translated by J. S. Black. Edinburgh: Edmonston and Douglas, 1972.

_____. *The Christian Doctrine of Justification and Reconciliation*. Vol. 3. Translated by H. R. Mackintosh and A. B. Macaulay. Clifton, New Jersey: Reference Books Publishers, Inc., 1966.

Rorty, Richard. *Philosophy and the Mirror of Nature*. Princeton: Princeton University Press, 1979.

Rossi, Philip and Wreen, Michael. eds. *Kant's Philosophy of Religion Reconsidered*. Bloomington: Indiana University Press, 1991.

Ruf, Wolfgang. *Johann Sebatian von Dreys System der Theologie als Begründung der Moraltheologie*. Göttingen: Vandenhoeck & Ruprecht, 1974.

Russel, Allan and Gerhardt, Mary. *Metaphorical Process: The Creation of Scientific and Religious Understanding*. Fort Worth, Texas: Texas Christian University Press, 1984

Schelling, F. W. J. *Vorlesungen über die Methode des akademischen Studiums* (1802). Hamburg: Felix Meiner, 1974. Translated by E. S. Morgan. *On University Studies*. Athens, Ohio: Ohio University Press, 1966.

_____. *Ideen zu einer Philosophie der Natur*. In *Schellings Werke*. 1:653-723. München: C. H. Beck and R. Oldenbourg, 1927.

Schelling, F. W. J. *System of Transcendental Idealism*. Translated by P. Heath. Charlottesville: University Press of Virginia, 1978.

Schilson, Arno. "Lessing und die katholische Tübinger Schule." *Theologische Quartalschrift*. 160 (1980): 256-277.

Scholtz, Gunter. *Die Philosophie Schleiermachers*. Darmstadt: Wissenschaftliche Buchgesellschaft, 1984.

Schreurs, Nico "J. S. Drey en F. Schleiermacher aan het Begin van de Fundamentale Theologie. Oorsprongen en Ontwikkelinge." *Bijdragen, Tijdschrift voor filosofie en theologie*. 43 (1982): 251-288.

Schupp, Franz. *Die Evidenz der Geschichte: Theologie als Wissenscaft bei J. S. Drey*. Universität Innsbruck, 1970.

Schupp, Franz. "Die Geschichtsauffassung am Beginn der Tübinger Schule und in der gegenwärtigen Theologie." *Zeitschrift für katholische Theologie* 91 (1969): 150-71.

Schweitzer, Albert. *The Quest of the Historical Jesus: A Critical Study of Its Progress from Reimarus to Wrede*. New York: Macmillan Publishing Co., 1960.

Seckler, Max. "Johann Sebastian Drey und die Theologie," *Theologische Quartalschrift* 158 (1978): 92-109.

_____. "Reich Gottes als Thema des Denkens: Ein philosphisches und theologisches Modell." In *Im Gespräch: der Mensch*, pp. 53-62. Edited by H. Gauly et al. Düsseldorf: Patmos Verlag, 1981.

Stalder, Robert. *Grundlinien der Theologie Schleiermachers I. Zur Fundamentaltheologie*. Wiesbaden: Franz Steiner Verlag, 1969.

Strauss, D. F. *The Christ of Faith and the Jesus of History*. Translated by L. E. Keck. Philadelphia: Fortress Press, 1977.

_____. *Die Lehre von der Wiederbringung aller Dinge* (1831). In Gotthold Meller. *Identität und Immanenz: Zur Genese der Theologie von David Friedrich Strauss*. Zurich: EVA-Verlag, 1968. Baser Studien zur historischen und systematischen Theologie, vol. 10.

Süskind, Hermann. *Der Einfluß Schellings auf die Entwicklung von Schleiermachers System*. Tübingen Dissertation, 1909.

_____. *Christentum und Geschichte bei Schleiermacher*. Tübingen: J.C.B. Mohr [Paul Siebeck], 1911.

Swidler, Leonard. Ed. *Consensus in Theology? A Dialogue with Hans Küng and Edward Schillebeeckx*. Philadelphia: The Westminster Press, 1980.

Sykes, Stephen. *The Identity of Christianity: Theologians and the Essence of Christianity from Schleiermacher to Barth*. Philadelphia: Fortress Press, 1984.

Thiel, John. E. *Imagination and Authority. Theological Authorship in the Modern Tradition*. Minneapolis: Fortress Press, 1991.

_____. "J. S. Drey on Doctrinal Development: The Context of Theological Encyclopedia." *Heythrop Journal* 27 (1986): 290-305.

_____. "Orthodoxy and Heterodoxy in Schleiermacher's Theological Encyclopedia: Doctrinal Development and Theological Creativity." *Heythrop Journal* 25 (1984): 142-157.

_____. "Theological Responsibility: Beyond the Classical Paradigm." *Theological Studies* 47 (1986): 573-598.

Thiemann, Ronald. *Revelation and Theology*. Notre Dame: University of Notre Dame Press, 1985.

Tice, Terrence N. *Schleiermacher Bibliography*. (Princeton: Princeton Theological Seminary, 1966.

_____. *Schleiermacher Bibliography (1784-1984): Updating and Commentary*. Princeton: Princeton Theological Seminary, 1985).

Tiefensee, Eberhard. *Die Religiöse Anlage und ihre Entwicklung. Der Religionsphilosophische Ansatz Johann Sebastian Dreys (1777-1853)*. Erfurter theologische Studien. vol. 56. Leipzig: St. Benno-Verlag, 1988.

Tilley, Terrence W. *Story Theology*. Theology and Life Series. vol. 12. Wilmington, Delaware: Michael Glazier, 1985.

Tillich, Paul. *Systematic Theology*. 3 volumes. Chicago: The University of Chicago Press, 1951, 1957, 1963.

Tracy, David. *The Blessed Rage for Order: The New Pluralism in Theology*. New York: The Seabury Press, 1975.

_____. *Analogical Imagination*. New York: Crossroad, 1981.

_____. *Plurality and Ambiguity*. San Francisco: Harper & Row, 1987.

Troeltsch, Ernst. *Der Historismus und seine Probleme. Gesammelte Schriften*. Vol. 3. Tübingen: J.C.B. Mohr [Paul Siebeck], 1961.

_____. "Schleiermacher und die Kirche." In *Schleiermacher der Philosoph des Glaubens*. Moderne Philosophie. no. 6. Gerlin-Schöneberg: Buchverlag der "Hilfe," 1910.

_____. *Troeltsch: Writings on Theology and Religion*. Translated and Edited by Robert Morgan and Michael Pye. Atlanta: John Knox Press, 1977.

Tshibangu, Tharcisse. *Théologie positive et théologie spéculative*. Louvain: Publications Université de Louvain, 1965.

Vermeil, Edmond. *Jean-Adam Möhler et l'école catholique de Tubingue (1815-1840)*: Etude sur la theologie romantique en Wurtenberg et les origines germaniques du modernisme. Paris: Librarie Armand Colin, 1913.

Wagner, Harald. *Die eine Kirche und die vielen Kirch. Ekklesiologie und Symbolik beim jungen Möhler*. Beiträge zur ökumenischen Theologie. vol. 16. Paderborn: Verlag Ferdinand Schöningh, 1977.

Walgrave, Jan Hendrick. *Unfolding Revelation: The Nature of Doctrinal Development*. Philadelphia: The Westminster Press, 1972.

Wehrung, Georg. *Der geschichtesphilosophische Standpunkt Schleiermachers zur Zeit seiner Freundschaft mit den Romantikern*. Strassburg: C. Müh & Cie, 1907.

Weiss, Johannes. *Die Predigt Jesu vom Reiche Gottes*. Göttingen: Vandenboeck & Ruprecht, 1900.

Welch, Claude. *Protestant Thought in the Nineteenth Century*. Vol. 1. New Haven: Yale University Press, 1972.

Welch, Claude. *The Trinity in Contemporary Theology*. London: SCM Press LTD, 1953.

Welte, Bernhard. "Beobachtungen zum Systemgedanken in der Tübinger Katholischen Schule." *Theologische Quartalschrift* 147 (1967):40-59.

Werner, Martin. *The Formation of Christian Dogma: An Historical Study of Its Probelm*. Translated by S. F. Brandon. London: Adams & Charles Black, 1957.

Wiles, Maurice. *The Making of Christian Doctrine*. Cambridge: Cambridge University Press, 1967.

_____. *The Remaking of Christian Doctrine*. London: SCM Press, 1974.

Wilken, Robert L. *The Myth of Christian Beginnings*. Garden City, New York: Doubleday and Company, Inc., 1971.

Williams, Robert R. *Schleiermacher the Theologian: The Construction of the Doctrine of God*. Philadelphia: Fortress Press, 1978.

Willis, Geoffrey, G. *Saint Augustine and the Donatist Controversy*. London: S.P.C.K., 1950.

Wreen, Michael and Rossi, Philip. eds. *Kant's Philosophy of Religion Reconsidered*. Bloomington: Indiana University Press, 1991.

AUTHOR INDEX

SUBJECT INDEX